THE NEW ORGANIC GROWER

THE NEW ORGANIC GROWER

*A Master's Manual of Tools and Techniques for the
Home and Market Gardener*

REVISED AND EXPANDED EDITION

ELIOT COLEMAN

*Illustrations by
Molly Cook Field and Sheri Amsel*

CHELSEA GREEN PUBLISHING COMPANY
WHITE RIVER JUNCTION, VERMONT

Copyright © 1989, 1995 by Eliot Coleman

Except where noted below, illustrations copyright © 1995 Molly Cook Field

Illustrations on the following pages are copyright © 1989 by Sheri Amsel
8, 11, 17, 30, 35, 37, 51 (both), 52, 56, 59, 60, 61, 62, 63, 64, 66, 70, 74 (both), 75 (both), 80-81, 103, 106, 109, 110, 119, 128, 129, 131, 134, 135, 137, 140, 143, 144, 145, 146 (lower), 148, 151, 160, 161, 164, 169, 172, 175, 176, 180, 187, 194, 197, 210, 212 (lower), 213 (both), 214, 217, 219, 220, 268, 273, 276, 296, 298 (both), 300 (both), 301, 302, 303, 304 (both), 305, 306 (both), 307 (both), 308, 309, 310, 311, 312

Printed in the United States of America
First printing, 1995

23 22 21 20 19   15 16 17 18 19

Designed by Ann Aspell

Library of Congress Cataloging-in-Publication Data
Coleman, Eliot, 1938–
  The new organic grower : a masters manual of tools and techniques for the home and market gardener / Eliot Coleman. — Rev. and expanded ed.
      p. cm.
  Includes bibliographical references (p.326) and index.
  ISBN 978-0-930031-75-6
  1. Vegetable gardening. 2. Organic gardening. 3. Truck farming. 4. Organic farming. I. Title.
  SB324.3.C65 1995
  635.0484—dc23
                                95-24528

Chelsea Green Publishing
85 North Main Street, Suite 120
White River Junction, VT 05001
(802) 295-6300
www.chelseagreen.com

To SN and HKN
with thanks

❧

One of the intangible legacies the Shakers left to the world is their demonstration that it is possible for man to create the environment and the way of life he wants, if he wants it enough. Man can choose.

The Shakers were practical idealists. They did not dream vaguely of conditions they would like to see realized; they went to work to make these conditions an actuality. They wasted no time in raging against competitive society, or in complaining bitterly that they had no power to change it; instead they built a domain of their own, where they could arrange their lives to their liking.

—Marguerite Fellows Melcher
The Shaker Venture

CONTENTS

FOREWORD

As an avid reader of books on gardening and agriculture, I am convinced that virtually everything intelligent that can be said and written about the subject exists already, almost certainly in English. From Fukuoka to Jekyll, from Thoreau to Berry, from Rodale to Jeavons, all aspects of these earthly crafts that coax life from dirt have been thoroughly detailed for new or seasoned practitioners. And yet when asked to write this foreword to Eliot Coleman's book on gardening, I agreed immediately because, in this instance, the world needs and deserves another book.

A teacher once advised me to read the book that saved me from reading ten others. *Farmers of Forty Centuries* is such a book; so is *Nutrition and Physical Degeneration.* There must be dozens of books that are offshoots of these, some without even knowing it. When seeking specific knowledge of soil and plant, it can be fairly said that most of the literature one reads is derivative and borrowed. With Eliot's book, this is not the case. Eliot is committing himself to print after three decades of intensive work in field and garden, work which has produced spectacular results not only in yield and bounty but in thought and insight. Simply stated, I know of no other person (what shall we call him—field gardener, truck farmer?) who can produce better results on the land with an economy of effort and means. He has transformed gardening from a task to a craft, and finally to what Stewart Brand would call "local science."

As I write, the anniversary of Rachel Carson's *Silent Spring* is once again being celebrated in the media. This is a timely subject, to be sure, but also one of perennial concern in these days of factory farming and its attendant poisons. Yet Carson's classic warning is not merely an echo, for every time the awareness of manmade toxins in our food arises, the lines at farm stands and organic food stores get a bit longer. There is, here and abroad, a slow, incremental, but ineluctable movement toward food that nourishes both person and place, that is grown with a far richer knowledge and awareness of biology than can be found in the 5-gallon cans of chlorinated hydrocarbons provided by Shell or Uniroyal. If the problems of modern agriculture are centralization, simplification, and biological reductionism, then the answers include diversity, complexity, and local knowledge. Such intelligence cannot be obtained in most of our land grant universities, and it is a pity this is so. For while we are justifiably confident that, when it comes to anthropology, physics, and biogenetics, our universities uphold the highest standards of inquiry and experimentation, it is in the area of our land and food where they have failed us utterly. Here we must look to the land itself, and in particular to those people who "husband" it to find standards of truth that we can live by and that allow us to live in turn.

It is satisfying and tempting to think that the major problems of our day have major answers, but I doubt it. The problems that we face—eroded lands, vanishing topsoil, genetic loss, toxic food, poisoned wells—were created by the temptation to find simple solutions. The answers reside in intimate knowledge of species, biota, soil, climate, and place, a type of observation that is embodied before it is taught or transmitted. Eliot not only embodies this intimate science of place, but has been throughout his life the untrammeled observer, unfazed by theories of any one school of thought, enamored of experience. It is this seasoned knowing that he shares here.

It was Hans Jenny, a soil scientist, who first pointed out that there is often more life below and within the soil than there is above it, including *Homo sapiens*. This inversion of soil as medium to soil as life itself should be enough to convince any agri-scientist to adopt only those means of agriculture that support and nurture this life. But that has not been the case. Instead it has been (and will continue to be) the gardeners, truck farmers, and small landholders who recognize this fact and act upon it. Just as those who broke the prairie sod were pioneers, the new pioneers are those who restore native land and soil. As biota leaves the soil, so does life vanish from society and civilization as we know it. The act of learning to garden and farm, so sincere and simple on its face, is in the hands of Eliot an act of restoration that has implications far beyond one lifetime. It is a practice. And like any practice, it can only be learned through repetition, dedication, and good teaching. This is the good teaching.

—Paul Hawken

PREFACE

SMALL FARMS ARE WHERE AGRICULTURAL ADVANCES ARE NURTURED. New ideas are conceived every day by the folks who are solving Nature's puzzles. Since I turned in the original manuscript for this book six years ago, I have traveled to Europe once again to see what was new there, spent a month with organic growers in Australia, and continued to develop and refine my thinking. I have benefited from the suggestions of those who read the book and wanted more information on certain subjects or wanted data on areas I did not cover. New equipment options are now being imported or manufactured here in the U.S. And in some cases I have finally made up my mind, by acquiring more information, on points where I was ambivalent.

The revisions run the gamut from small changes in detail, to adding a lot of new material to some chapters, to adding whole new chapters where appropriate. I have added scientific references in footnotes for readers who wish to pursue a particular subject in greater depth. I have greatly expanded the material in the chapters on plant-pest balance because the subject is of particular interest to me and of great significance in understanding how the vegetable grower fits into the natural world.

I have a rule that I write only about those things I know how to do. Consequently, there are a number of topics that this book doesn't cover. When I think there are techniques outside my own experience that readers might find useful, I refer them to someone who practices those techniques.

Throughout this book's creation and revision my principal desire has been that it prove helpful to growers and gardeners. To that end I am pleased to have found nothing to change because it was wrong, but rather just areas that I could make clearer or upon which I needed to expand. When I first finished writing this book I said to myself, "I wish I'd had a copy 25 years ago." I still feel that way. It is rewarding to be able to pass along the dependable information I have learned from other farmers around the world, dug out of obscure sources in many libraries, and devised on my own. There are coherent patterns in natural biological systems that can be adapted to producing the highest quality vegetables. I hope this book helps make those patterns more accessible.

PREFACE TO THE FIRST EDITION

I strongly believe in the values and rewards of the small farm. I wish to encourage them. And so this book is written for those with a small-farm dream. But it also has a wealth of ideas to offer the serious home gardener. The efficient, professional techniques described here are basically scale-neutral and can be used to make everyone's vegetable-growing efforts more productive and enjoyable. And who knows? The best home gardeners often move up to become small farmers.

Organic growing is not complicated. Nor is it difficult. It is the most straightforward way of raising plants. Difficulties usually arise from a misunderstanding of how it works. Once the principles are clear, gardeners from backyard to back forty can tune into the existing balances of the natural system and grow the crops they have always dreamed of.

I have been fortunate to learn from a number of excellent teachers over the years. I owe a debt to all of them. As in any learning situation, my teachers were books, people, models, and most important of all, my own curiosity. The lessons I was fortunate to learn from them influenced the form and function of my approach to farming and helped create this book.

I 🌾 AGRICULTURAL CRAFTSMANSHIP

WHY AND HOW DO PLANTS GROW? WHY AND HOW DO THEY FAIL? WHY do plants seem to grow successfully for some people and in some places and not others? The answers lie in those factors that affect the growth of plants: they include light, moisture, temperature, soil fertility, mineral balance, biotic life, weeds, pests, seeds, labor, planning, and skill. The grower can influence some of these factors more than others. The more they can be arranged to the crop's liking, however, the more successful the grower's operation will be.

The Biology of Agriculture

Working with living creatures, both plant and animal, is what makes agriculture different from any other production enterprise. Even though a product is produced, in farming the process is anything but industrial. It is biological. We are dealing with a vital, living system rather than an inert manufacturing process. The skills required to manage a biological system are similar to those of the conductor of an orchestra. The musicians are all very good at what they do individually. The role of the conductor is not to play each instrument, but rather to nurture the union of the disparate parts. The conductor coordinates each musician's effort with those of all the others and combines them in a harmonious whole.

Agriculture cannot be an industrial process any more than music can be. It must be understood differently from stamping this metal into that shape or mixing these chemicals and reagents to create that compound. The major workers—the soil microorganisms, the fungi, the mineral particles, the sun, the air, the water—are all parts of a system, and it is not just the employment of any one of them, but the coordination of the whole that achieves success.

I remember a conversation I had a few years ago with a Kansas farmer in his sixties who farmed some 700 acres. His methods were considered unconventional because he had always farmed without purchasing herbicides or pesticides and bought only small quantities of lime and phosphorus. I asked him on what theory he based his farming. He said there really wasn't any theory that he knew of. It was simply the same now as it had ever been. He mentioned a favorite book of his, a 1930s agricultural textbook that stressed the value of biological techniques such as crop rotation, animal manures, green manures, cover crops, mixed cropping, mixed stocking, legumes, crop residues, and more. He said he used those practices on his farm simply because they worked so well. The book never mentioned any "theory" and probably never knew one. The book referred to these biological techniques as "good farming practices."

My Kansas friend assured me that by basing his crop production on those good farming practices his yields were equal to and often far better than his neighbors'. He saw no yield increase from soluble fertilizer when he had tried it. His crop rotation and mixed-farming system made weeds, pests, and diseases negligible problems. When fertilizer prices rose he felt as secure as ever because his production techniques were so fundamentally independent of purchased materials. And as long as those good farming practices worked and continued to make his farm profitable, he would continue to use them. He concluded by saying that, if there were any theory involved, he would simply call it "successful farming."

I have long followed similar good farming practices—biological techniques—in my system. The secret to success in agriculture is to remove the limiting factors to plant growth. These practices do that efficiently and economically by generating a balanced soil fertility from *within* the farm rather than importing it from without. They power the system through nurturing the natural processes of soil fertility, plant growth, and pest management, enabling them to work even better. In the words of the song, they "accentuate the positive." When chosen carefully and managed perceptively so as to take full advantage of specific aspects of the natural world, these good farming practices are all the farmer needs. As a further bonus they eliminate such negatives as soil erosion, fertilizer runoff, and pesticide pollution at the same time.

Creating a System

I have been compiling and evaluating information on biologically based food-production techniques ever since I started farming. At first I collected this material as a commercial vegetable grower because I needed the information to ensure the success of my own operation. In the process I became aware of the enormous untapped potential of this way of farming and enthralled by the discovery and practice of the simple techniques of an agriculture that is in harmony with the natural world.

In order to develop a dependable vegetable production model, I concentrated on collecting information in four subject areas:

- How to simplify production techniques
- How to locate the most efficient machinery and tools
- How to reduce expenditures on purchased supplies
- How to market produce in the most remunerative manner

From my experience, these four areas represent the basic information needed for small-scale, economically successful, biologically based food production.

The first category explains just how straightforward and rational a successful vegetable production system can be. Although growing commercial crops is often considered for "experts" only, it most emphatically is not. The world of plants is vital, vigorous, and self-starting. Drop a seed in the ground and it wants to grow. The common wisdom possessed by successful farmers is that they understand how to help the seed do what it is already determined to do. The more successful the farmer, the better the understanding of how to enhance the natural processes without overwhelming them. That simply stated idea is the key to successful organic food production.

Next is the importance of efficient and dependable machinery and tools that match the needs of small-scale production. Small farmers can and do compete and succeed economically and practically when they have access to equipment scaled and priced within their means and designed for their specific tasks. The fact that such useful and appropriate equipment has not become readily available has been a contributing factor in the demise of the small farm and the concurrent belief that it cannot succeed. All too often, unwarranted and problematic growth in farm size has been dictated by the need to justify expensive and oversized equipment because nothing else was available.

In order to find, try out, and modify the right equipment, I have looked all over the world. The equipment ideas included in this book originated in many different countries. The recommended tools do their jobs admirably. New models will no doubt appear in the future and should be even better. But I expect the basic relationship of the tasks to the system to remain fairly constant.

Third, the economic success of any operation must be ensured. In order to keep costs down, I emphasize the importance of "low-input production practices." By that I mean practices such as crop rotation, green manures, animal manure management, efficient labor, season extension, and so forth. Production benefits are gained from careful management rather than expensive purchases. Not only will these practices save money in the short run, but they will also increase the stability and independence of the farm in the long run. The more production needs are farm-generated or labor-saving, the more independent and secure the operation becomes. The farm and its economy cannot then be held hostage by the unavailability or high prices of commodities from outside suppliers. The most stable farm economy is one that is built upon the greatest use of farm-generated production aids.

Finally, no matter how successful I might be in the first three areas, it would be of little use to me if I did not have a successful marketing program. Marketing has always been the make-or-break area for small-scale producers. Much depends on highly developed marketing skills that probably would not have led someone to farming in the first place. The recent growth of "farmers' markets" has in many instances helped the marketing of local produce. But there are other solutions. I have noticed on both sides of the Atlantic that farmers who enjoy the greatest economic success have found competitive niches in the larger marketing system. The extent of this market for small-scale growers and ways to reach it are described in the chapter on marketing.

Learning How

There are a number of ways to learn any new skill. You can jump in boldly right from the start and count on the "sink-or-swim" reaction to carry you through. You can work as an apprentice to someone else who knows how to do it. Or you can go to college for a course of study. I followed the first method and I recommend it to anyone who enjoys that type of challenge. You learn quickly because you have to. But be forewarned that it can be an occasionally stressful and exhausting adventure. Especially if you start with minimal resources, as we did, and have to practically create your world before you can inhabit it.

For many people the second option is preferable. The management pressure is on the employer and you can concentrate on details. I think it has a much higher success rate than the third. You will have a better chance to succeed if you have learned well by working for a good grower than if you have studied agriculture in college. The apprentice systems of past centuries turned out very competent practitioners of their crafts. When you want to learn how to do something, go straight to those who are doing it well. In addition to the invaluable hands-on experience you'll gain, you'll also become more motivated for any supplementary reading and book-learning (remember how unmotivated many of us were in school?) because you will have had some solid background and your questions will arise directly from your own experience and interest.

In one of my favorite books, *The Farming Ladder*, the author George Henderson relates both his experience as an apprentice working for other farmers as well as his later role as a master farmer taking pupils of his own.* During his learning period Henderson worked on four different farms, chosen to give him as broad a background as possible. Most impressive to me is the way he threw himself fully into the job. He never missed an opportunity to work harder or longer whenever it appeared there might be something new to learn. He tells a story of when he was battling a fire in a haystack—coughing from the smoke, covered with the soot, soaked by the water—and a neighboring farmer who happened by told him he was a fortunate lad because he was getting all this experience at someone else's expense.

*George Henderson, The Farming Ladder (London: Faber & Faber, 1944).

Later, when he himself was a successful farmer, Henderson treated his pupils as he had treated himself. He provided good training and expected hard work in return. He speaks about compensation systems that were common in those days. The student received room and board but was expected to pay the farmer a monthly fee for the first three months. After three months, if the student was a competent worker, the farmer returned that same fee every month as salary for the second three months. That way, if the student was shiftless and soon departed, the farmer would be paid for his trouble. However, the student who persevered and worked hard would receive six months of thorough training at no cost. Given the price of a college education, the system sounds pretty good. An eager student who wants to work with an exceptionally gifted farmer might want to make a similar proposal in order to be taken on.

After discussing his experience working on other farms, Henderson distills the wisdom he learned into a couple of sentences. It matches closely with my own experience as a self-taught beginner. "Good farming is the cumulative effect of making the best possible use of land, labor, and capital. It is not the acreage you farm, but the intensity of production you maintain, which determines the financial success of the venture."

But It Can't Be Done, Can It?

Most sections of the United States were once fed by small local farms. Today that is considered an impossible dream. Even where professional farmers are involved, the idea of the economically viable small farm is criticized as visionary. Many agricultural experts state that it just cannot work. Their opinion is based primarily on economic and production conclusions drawn from large-scale agricultural operations. Unfortunately, little consideration has been given to the advantages inherent to the small end of the spectrum.

If you understand how the economic and practical realities change when low-cost production methods are allied with the right machinery and marketing practices, then the case does not seem hopeless at all. In fact, the negative opinion of the "experts" is contradicted by the number of successful examples of small-scale food production operations both here and abroad. Those numbers are increasing daily as improved low-cost technologies become more widely available and consumer demand grows for high-quality local produce.

From my experience, one-half to five acres is a highly productive scale of vegetable growing. The management skills needed for an operation this size are enjoyable rather than onerous. It is a comprehensible size for commercial food production—large enough to make a living, yet small enough to retain the emphasis on quality; diverse enough so that the work is never dull, yet compact enough so it is never out of control.

There is a distance, to be sure, between the isolated example and the consistent success. Consistent success can only result if the system makes practical sense, has been well tested and proven over a number of years, and is followed with diligence and understanding. The experts have been mistaken before and they will certainly be mistaken again. What they have failed to realize in the case of the small farm is that, with careful planning, organization, and desire, there is nothing that "can't be done."

2

LAND

EVERYONE SHARES A KINSHIP WITH THE LAND. NO MATTER WHERE WE are in time or distance, the desire for an ideal country spot is very real. Whether the image comes from books, childhood experiences, or the depths of our souls, it has an indelible quality. The dream farm has fields here, an orchard there, a brook, and large trees near the perfect house, with the barns and outbuildings set off just so. The dream is effortless. The difficulty comes in trying to find such a place when you decide to buy one.

I suggest not trying to find that perfect place. Rather than the finished painting, look for the bare canvas. Every ideal farm at one time began as field and woodland. Its transformation was the result of some predecessor's planning, organization, building, and management. This is a satisfying process in itself, and the end result may be far more successful if it springs from the changes the farmer makes himself. This is not a hard and fast rule, merely a suggestion from experience. If you already own or can obtain a productive farm that is well established, then by all means do so. But if that is not possible, then do not hesitate to buy the raw land and create the farm.

A few suggestions follow on things to take into account when looking at a piece of land with an eye toward turning it into a successful small-scale farm.

Soil Type

Almost any soil can be made productive for growing crops. The difference lies in the amount of effort needed to make it so. The less ideal a soil is to begin with, the more attention must be paid to modifying its characteristics. Extreme soil types require an inordinate amount of work. Pure clay or pure sand and gravel are obviously less desirable than a rich loam. On the other hand, while the transformation of imperfect soils requires time and energy, the result can be as productive as initially more promising soils. I have grown magnificent produce on a very sandy-gravelly soil that began with a pH of 4.3. It took a few years of manuring and liming, adding phosphorus, potassium, and trace elements, growing green manures, and establishing a rotation, but it became, and has remained, a highly productive piece of ground.

The dream soil for vegetable production is sandy loam. This is a general term describing the proportions of three ingredients: clay, silt, and sand. Clay consists of fine particles that help the soil hold water and provide a potentially rich store-house of plant nutrients. Sand consists of larger particles, mostly silicates, which keep the soil open for air and water penetration and aid early warming in the spring. Silt falls somewhere between these two. A fourth soil ingredient—humus or organic matter—is the key to productivity. It opens up heavy clay soils for better air and water movement and easier working. Humus also helps hold together and give structure to light sandy soils, creating more stable conditions for the provision of water and nutrients to plants.

My advice is to look for the best soil possible, but not to be put off if it is not perfect. The cultural practices recommended in this book will help put in the organic matter and nutrient supply to make a productive success from a wide range of initial soil types.

Soil Depth

Old adages apply to soils as well as to people. Don't be fooled by a pretty face. What is underneath the surface of the soil will be important in the future, so investigate it from the start. Investigations with a spade or shovel can be augmented by requests to the local Soil Conservation Service office for information on that particular soil or others like it in the area.

Soil depth should be considered in three ways because some soil problems are more easily modified than others. First consider the depth to bedrock. This can't be changed to any degree. So ask hard questions about it and take cores with a soil sampling auger if you are not satisfied. Rock outcrops in the surrounding topography are warning signs of a shallow soil. Secondly, there is the depth to the water table. Land that otherwise appears acceptable may have a seasonally high water table during wet times of the year. This could make early spring planting difficult or impossible. A too-high water table also limits the depth of usable soil by hindering root penetration. In most cases the condition can be cured through surface or subsurface drainage, but these modifications are expensive.

The third consideration is the depth of the topsoil. There are layers in the soil that make up the soil profile. The uppermost layer, the topsoil, is commonly from 4 to 12 inches deep. If you dig a hole, it is relatively easy to determine where the darker topsoil ends and the lighter subsoil begins. Normally, the deeper the topsoil the better, since topsoil depth is closely related to soil productivity. This is the one of the three soil-depth factors that can be most easily modified over time. Subsoil tillage, manuring, deep-rotary tillage, and the growing of deep-rooted, soil-improving crops will all help to deepen the topsoil. These techniques will be described in a later chapter.

Aspect and Slope

The lay of the land in most of the northern half of the United States is a very important factor. Land with a southern aspect has a number of advantages. A southern exposure warms up sooner in the spring. (Of course, the reverse is true in the Southern Hemisphere.) The more perpendicular a slope is to the angle of the sun, the faster it warms up. The grower who plans to compete for the early vegetable market needs this advantage. Land in the Northern Hemisphere at about 43° latitude (the northern border of Massachusetts, Illinois, or California) that slopes 5° to the south is actually in the same solar climate as level land 300 miles to the south.

See Microclimate, The Biological Environment, by Norman Rosenberg, Blaine Blad and Shashi Verma (New York: John Wiley & Sons, 1983).

The logical application is to choose land with a southern slope for early crops.* A southwestern slope is preferable to a southern or southeastern slope. On a southwestern slope, less direct radiation is required to evaporate dew or frost in the early morning, and more is available for absorption once the initial daily warming has occurred. However, in this as in other areas, a compromise may have to be made.

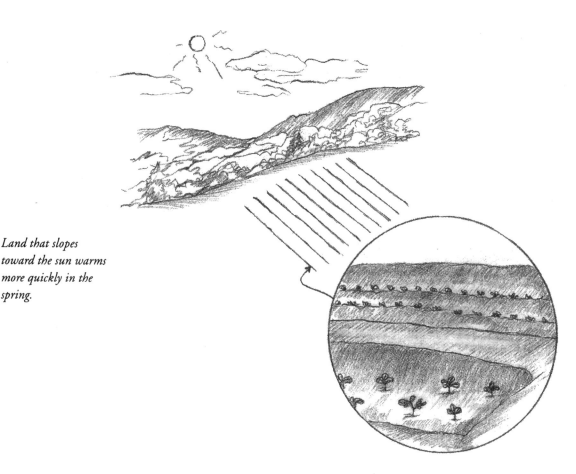

Land that slopes toward the sun warms more quickly in the spring.

Air Drainage

Plants and gardens need to breathe fresh air. A low area with no air movement is undesirable for a number of reasons. Stagnant air encourages fungus diseases, holds air pollutants around plants, and stays colder on frosty nights. The last is an important consideration, because cold air, which is heavier than warm air, "flows" downslope and collects in hollows and valleys. A farm in such a location is at a great disadvantage. Conversely, one on a hillside or near the top of a slope is better protected from frosts because the cold air of late spring and early fall flows down the hillside and settles in the valley. In many cases this cold-air drainage can result in a longer frost-free growing season of two and even three weeks at *both* ends of the season.

Of course the land does not want to be so sloped that it is either difficult to farm or is subject to erosion. Actually, a flat area on the edge of a slope enjoys as much air drainage as the top of the slope does and is probably the ideal situation.

Wind Protection and Sunshine

Although some air motion is good, more is not always better. An excessively windy site can cause physical damage to plants, cause windborne soil erosion, and provide less than ideal growing conditions due to the cooling action of the moving air. A windbreak, which can be anything from trees and tall hedges, to low stone or board walls, to strips of wheat or rye, can minimize the damaging effects of strong winds and optimize the benefits of solar warmth. The temperature of the soil is raised in shelter because, as more surface warming takes place, the accumulated heat is conducted downward into the soil. Windbreaks also help to create more ideal growing conditions by preventing the loss of transpired moisture. Reduction in evaporation means a consequent reduction in heat loss.

A windbreak can improve growing conditions for a distance of up to 20 times the height of the fence.

In many ways a wind shelter does more than just lower wind speeds. It creates a beneficial microclimate far different from that in nearby ground.

Unfortunately, too much of a good thing always causes a loss somewhere else. Too much wind shelter can mean inadequate sunshine. A balance must be struck somewhere between adequate wind protection and excessive shade. In order to achieve that ideal in the right place and at the right time, you must pay close attention to the path of the sun. It is not enough merely to say that the sun is higher in the sky in summer than in winter. It also traces a different path in the sky, rising and setting farther to the north in summer and to the south in winter. The ideal May windbreak should be planned so as not to shade the January greenhouse.

Sunlight is the motive power for photosynthesis. Every effort must be made to take full advantage of it, especially during the early and late months of the growing season. Sometimes that means cutting down a tree to reduce shade. When faced with this situation, I think long and hard about whether the shade cast is serious enough to warrant removal of the tree. If the decision goes against the tree, I don't hesitate to cut it down, but I always replace it with another one that is more suitable for the location. Sunshine is one of the most dependable free inputs in a food-production system, and the grower should make every effort to maximize its contribution.

Water

Excess water is a flood and too little water is a drought. The farmer must make provision for both. River-bottom land is usually fertile and easy to work, but the grower must have access to higher land for dependable early crops in wet years. If the flood-prone land can be planned for a summer rotation or later crops, it will be less likely to cause a failure. Droughts are the other side of the coin. Water supply for irrigation is a major concern in some areas of the country. On average, provision should be made for applying one inch of water per week during the growing season if it is not supplied by natural rainfall. When looking for a good piece of land for vegetable growing, water is a key factor.

The ideal solution is a year-round spring or stream that can be tapped into and that is sufficiently higher than the cultivated fields to allow for gravity feed. The piping for such a system can be laid inexpensively on top of the ground in spring and drained in fall, thus avoiding the expense of burying a long water line. Second best to a gravity system is a dependable pond from which water can be pumped. A well is a good third choice, but it is difficult to be sure of an adequate supply to meet the needs of production at the height of the season. The choice of whether irrigation water will be applied to the fields by surface flow, subirrigation, overhead sprinkling, or trickle systems will depend on topography, climate, and quantity of water available.* Your best source of advice is the experience of other local growers.

Two useful books for background on irrigation methods are Melvyn Kay's Sprinkler Irrigation: Equipment and Practice *(London: Batsford, 1984) and Robert Kourik's* Drip Irrigation for Every Landscape and All Climates *(Santa Rosa, CA: Metamorphic Press, 1992).*

Geographic Location

This is too broad a subject to cover in detail. North, South, East, or West; hot or cold; wet or dry; urban, suburban, rural, or remote: crops can be grown in any and all of these places. The main consideration regarding location is proximity to market. Obviously, a suburban location close to many customers, stores, and restaurants is appealing, but the cost of the land in such areas is high. Land is less expensive in rural areas, but a greater effort must be made to develop and reach an adequate market. One compromise is to locate your farm in a rural area that attracts summer visitors. That market will not be available year-round, but it will appear during your most productive cropping season.

Access

Both you and your customers need to be able to get to and about your land. Access in both instances is often not taken into account. A market location on a busy highway must provide plenty of space for safe parking. If it doesn't, few will stop. A long, unpaved, or seasonally impassable road to the farm will also discourage customers and increase the costs of access and operation. Streams on the property may be picturesque, but if they must be crossed often to get from one field to another, they become a liability. Land for a successful food production operation should be easy to enter, work in, and work around. It should be accessible to large equipment required for deep cultivation and manure spreading. Careful consideration should be given to the flow of activities from seeding through harvest, and provision made so that access to one part of the operation is not hindered by activities in another.

Security

The depredations of both two- and four-legged invaders can prove costly to a small farm. Dirt bikes and other off-road vehicles can destroy a whole spring's work in a thoughtless moment. Fields of raspberries, strawberries, and other fruit are tempting targets for midnight thievery unless they are protected by a fence or are located near inhabited dwellings.

Crows, pigeons, and other winged invaders of newly seeded crops can be stopped in a couple of ways: either by beating them or joining them. To beat them the grower might use the floating crop covers described in Chapter 21. These covers protect seedlings from the birds. But joining the birds can also work. An old-timer once gave me the obvious answer to hungry crows: feed them. His method was to place small piles of corn in easily accessible places around the field, figuring that crows with full bellies won't pull up newly sprouted corn. The feeding continues until the corn is past the susceptible stage. I have followed his suggestion for many years and am very fond of this ingenious and benign solution.

Four-footed marauders also need to be considered. In my part of the world deer can graze off a whole field of newly transplanted seedlings in a few hours. Raccoons are notoriously fond of sweet corn crops. The mere mention of wood-chucks, pigeons, gophers, etc. can put an evil gleam in the eyes of many growers. I know the same situation exists with rabbits, kangaroos, llamas, and elephants in other regions of the world. Although there are a number of temporary measures (chemical repellents, organic repellents, radios tuned to all-night talk shows, and scarecrows, to name a few), the most consistently successful barrier is a good fence.

One effective fencing material is the lightweight plastic mesh with ¾-inch squares which was originally sold as bird netting. Now it is also advertised as deer fence because it can be wrapped around shrubs to prevent deer from browsing in winter. I purchase it in 100-foot lengths that are 7 ½ feet wide. In trials where I merely draped the material around the edge rows of stands of sweet corn it proved to be 100 percent effective against raccoons. I have also kept deer out of a large area by attaching the mesh to posts (I used 2 x 2s) driven in at a 12-foot spacing. This material doesn't deter the critters by strength but by trickery. It feels like a large and frightening spider's web. I can understand how the wild invaders must react by comparing my discomfort when it has caught in the buttons of my shirt while I was installing it. If the material is rolled up and put away when not in use, it will last a long time.

A heavier weight black plastic mesh of the same height but with larger openings is sold as an "invisible" deer fence. The installation instructions suggest running it through the woods just back from the edge of the cleared area. It is supported by attaching to tree trunks with fence staples. The black color cannot be easily seen in the shady woods and it is almost invisible. It is also very effective. I erected it through the woods on one side of a field to shut off a very active deer access route. It forced the deer to either end of the fence, where they were further deterred by bramble hedges and human habitation. I have also used this material successfully (supported by temporary 1-inch PVC electrical conduit posts woven through the mesh) as the only animal protection around temporary trial plots. No varmints got in.

Another "invisible" deer deterrent concept which involves dogs was researched by the Missouri Department of Conservation.* They used the same electronic containment fence and shock collar that suburbanites use to keep pets in their yards. The containment "fence" in these systems is a single wire that can be buried, attached to existing fences, or laid on top of the ground. The dog wears a receiving collar and is trained to the shock it will administer if the dog tries to cross the fence. This idea ingeniously solves two problems of using dogs for deer protection. If the dog is tethered it loses its effectiveness after a short while because the deer become habituated to the barking. Untethered dogs will run deer past the boundaries of the field, thus breaking game laws. The containment fence and collar allow the control advantage of an untethered dog while limiting it to the area you need protected.

The Missouri study suggests that breeds like Australian shepherds, blue heelers, and border collies will be most effective because they have a patrolling and chasing instinct. Two dogs are better than one so they have company; neutering and spaying are recommended. The dogs should live in the field and not alternate between field and farmhouse. The researchers also found the system works best if a 30-foot-wide, mowed buffer strip is left between the fence and the edge of the crop so the dogs can make a perimeter trail and mark scent. Further, placing doghouses, feeders, and waterers where traditional animal trails enter the field increases the chances of the dogs interacting with invaders.

If you want a purely technological solution with more hardware, a traditional electric fence is the answer. The new, lightweight, electro-plastic fencing units that have become so popular in the sheep industry are reasonably priced, simple to erect, easy to move, and are available as both battery and plug-in models. For permanent situations there are high-tensile models with strong wooden posts. They can be designed to keep out everything from raccoons to deer, including even kangaroos and elephants, I suspect. Names of suppliers are given in the tools and suppliers appendix.

Pollutants

Pollutants are a fact of life in most areas. It makes sense to give some thought to this problem in order to know what can be done before it surfaces. Both lead from exhaust and cadmium from tire wear have been found in excessive amounts on food grown within 200 to 300 feet of heavily traveled highways. A 6- to 8-foot-high evergreen hedge bordering the highway can block out the bulk of this pollution before it reaches the fields beyond. Lead from old paint and plaster can be a serious soil pollutant in areas where buildings once stood. Under certain conditions lead and other heavy metals in the soil can be taken up by plants in amounts that are highly detrimental to consumers, especially young children.

Residues from toxic waste dumps can travel downstream or downwind at far greater distances than is commonly recognized. Crops irrigated with water from an aquifer contaminated by one of these sites will cause toxic residues to accumulate both in and on the crops. Areas downwind of large industrial smokestacks suffer a continual dusting of questionable substances, including gases such as ozone, which is directly harmful to plant growth.

Land that has grown commercial fruit or vegetable crops for many years may contain undesirable residues. Old-time agricultural poisons containing lead, arsenic, and mercury were used heavily on orchards and some vegetable crops in the first half of the 20th century, and are known to have permanently compromised the future agricultural use of large areas of land. It is common practice nowadays to test the water quality in the well before buying a rural home. Similarly, it would also be wise to test the soil for heavy metals before purchasing old agricultural land.

These problems may exist to a greater or lesser degree. They are mentioned here as one more factor to be considered in selecting land on which to farm. As with anything that may affect the success of a farm operation, it is best to know beforehand. Nothing could be more discouraging than to put a lot of work into establishing a small farm and to then find that, because of unanticipated circumstances, the site will not produce quality food. Forewarned is forearmed.

Acreage

How much land should you purchase? Some people buy twice what is needed and sell half of it to partially cover their costs. Others purchase more than they need initially so they can modify their plans in the future. Perhaps in addition to fields you'll need wooded land for a firewood supply. You might want to purchase an adjacent area to set aside as wildlife or native plant habitats. Maybe what it comes down to is you just want some extra space.

All these decisions are personal ones. The premise of this book is that you can make a good living on 5 acres or less of intensive vegetable production. Thus it is those acres that concern us most. If 5 acres is all the land you can afford, it is more than sufficient for an economically successful farm. If you can afford more, another 5 acres perhaps, then more options open up. The crop rotation

Careful planning and layout help make a small acreage more productive.

could include small livestock on pasture to take advantage of the long-term soil fertility benefits of leaving land in deep-rooting grass and legume pastures for a few years before rotating it back into vegetable crops. Another one or two acres might be used for berry crops. Beyond that, you must watch out for the trap of more, more, and more. It is easy to farm a lot of land with a pencil and paper, but a lot harder to actually do it. The best advice is to buy only as much land as you will use and to buy the best land you can afford.

Soil Tests

In my experience, the utility of soil tests is controversial. Soil tests appear to be part science and part necromancy. A sample of soil is sent to a laboratory where it is supposedly analyzed, investigated, and divided into its component parts. You then receive a report on its good and bad points. Despite the guise of the laboratory, there is more art than science to a good soil "test." The secret of using the results of a soil test lies in their interpretation. Not everyone agrees on how that should be done. Nor do people agree on how many useful conclusions can be drawn from the data. I recommend in all cases that you make an initial basic soil test on the fields you intend to use for vegetable production. Better yet, have two or three tests made on the same soil sample, each by a different laboratory. Have a state university lab make one of the tests and then send the same sample to one or two private labs. The results are often similar to the old saying, "A man with one watch knows what time it is; a man with two watches is never sure." Still, given the lack of certainty inherent in soil testing, it is better to have two or three opinions from which to draw your conclusions than only one.

The interpretation of soil test results is something that I suggest growers do for themselves. It won't be done mystically or according to one particular theory, but rather by common sense. If the test shows the soil is low in a nutrient, then add it. The method and manner of adding these nutrients is explained in Chapter 10. My recommendation is to add nutrients in their most available but least soluble form. By "most available" I mean that they should be finely ground, and by "least soluble" I mean not immediately water-soluble but rather gradually water-soluble through the action of soil bacteria and dilute soil acids—in other words, through the natural soil processes.

In taking a soil test you want to obtain as homogeneous a picture of the field or plot to be cultivated as possible. Instead of taking one sample from a spot in the middle of a field, a number of random samples should be taken over the whole area and then combined and mixed. This way the soil sent to be analyzed will be a more accurate representation of what you have. It is best to do this sampling and mixing with tools whose composition will not affect the results of the test. For example, if you are testing for iron, don't sample with a rusty iron trowel. In general, a stainless steel soil probe for the samples and a hard plastic bucket for mixing them are best.

The Ideal Small Farm

I doubt you will find the ideal small farm (I never have), but the best of luck to you anyhow. The listing below describes what I believe the perfect piece of land would look like. Please remember that none of this is carved in stone. The determined farmer can transform even the most unlikely site into a model farm by applying the basic techniques of soil building.

For Sale: 30 acres. 20 acres mixed hardwood forest, 10 acres pasture. Description: Reasonably flat (about 5 percent slope to south or southwest), set on the brow of a hill with good air drainage to the valley below. Protected on the north by higher land and dense forest. Excellent year-round gravity water supply. Soil on the cleared land is clay loam on one half and sandy loam on the other half. Topsoil is 12 inches deep, well drained, and highly fertile, with very few stones and a naturally neutral pH; presently growing a grass-legume sod.

3

SCALE AND CAPITAL

THE ECONOMISTS ARE ALWAYS TELLING US THAT AMERICAN FARMS HAVE to get bigger to survive. Small vegetable farms have almost entirely disappeared. But the weakness of small farms has not been one of scale. It has been one of *useless information.* Like a traveler with an outdated map, the small farmer has had to rely on outmoded concepts. Since the standard information sources (government Departments of Agriculture, the agricultural colleges, the farm-supply industry) have not thought small farming possible, they have neither been compiling nor dispensing information on how to do it. To understand this situation we need to understand our underlying attitudes toward farming in America.

Bigger Is Not Better

The most common attitude holds that bigger is better, and the admonition to "get big or get out" is frequently heard. There is a basic assumption in agriculture that a farmer with a few acres in mixed production is less successful and less advanced than the farmer who practices industrialized monoculture on a huge scale. In the recent history of American agriculture, to take one example, such an assumption may have been defendable. American farmers with ambition and entrepreneurial ability took advantage of the resources of capital, transportation, and the agricultural technology that all blossomed in the 20th century to expand their operations, buy more land, and become increasingly specialized. This should not, however, be seen as the only or even the best way to farm. The economic and environmental problems of large-scale agriculture now make headlines every day. It seems the warning should be changed to "get big *and* get out."

The major obstacle I had to overcome when I started farming was a lack of models. There were almost no commercially successful organic small farmers from whom I could get inspiration and with whom I could share ideas. My prototype of the economically viable 5-acre farm didn't even exist. But highly productive small vegetable farms used to exist, so I began with the assumption that if it could be done once it could be done again. The know-how had to be available somewhere. At the start, old books and old-timers were my best sources of information and support. They were a good beginning, but they left me in the past. Nevertheless, I made some headway, but in the process I became aware of the reasons why small farming had died out. The product was excellent, but the process was exhausting. It was neither cost-effective nor efficient. But I wasn't ready to give up. I knew there had to be suitable techniques, traditions, and equipment somewhere that would bring this production process up to date.

The European Model

There are sections of the industrial world where the small farm continues to succeed. Western Europe is one such area. There, the small farmer is an institution that didn't die. Whether through tradition or stubbornness, the European small farmer has persevered, and the tool and equipment producers and information resources have kept up with him.

Entrepreneurial farming in Europe led to *better* rather than *bigger*. In part because more land was not readily available, increased income lay in improving production on existing acreage rather than expanding. But a more important influence was the love of good food. The connection between the quality of the produce and the careful attention of the farmer to the land has always been recognized and practiced in Europe. As a consequence, the output from the average European small farm is the type of exquisite produce that always finds a ready market. Europe's small farmers have traditionally produced the bulk of the food eaten in Europe and made a good living for themselves in the process.

The European farmers provided the model that I knew must exist. They inspired my farm. I saw no reason why regionally based small-scale food production could not be just as successful in the U.S. Unlike grains, fully ripened fruits and vegetables are highly perishable. They are particularly well-suited for local markets. As more and more consumers become disenchanted with the products of industrial agriculture, the availability of fresh, carefully husbanded, farm-ripened food is a tradition we will have the incentive and the market to reclaim. It is a tradition that demands small farms.

In the process of finding the models, the philosophy, the tools, and the technologies of the small farmer, I also learned a great deal about scale and the advantages of staying small. I learned right from the start that one must totally reevaluate the basis for size in farming. The best way to do that is to wipe the slate clean and start thinking from scratch. All the when, where, what, why, and how questions need to be asked anew. How much production can one person or family handle? What kinds of equipment and techniques can be efficiently employed on the family farm? What helps the farm family do more with less?

The Five-Acre Answer

The answers are illuminating. Five acres (2 hectares) is the optimum size because it is about as much land as a couple or small family can manage. By manage, I mean both practically and professionally—practically, by using the low-cost equipment and simple techniques that fit the tasks, and professionally, by making sure there are enough *people per acre* to stay on top of things. To effectively manage a farm operation I believe there is a *person:land area* ratio that cannot be exceeded. Producing quality food requires an investment of effort on the part of the grower that naturally limits the amount of land farmed. For diversified vegetable growing, I place that upper limit at somewhere around 2 ½ acres per person. That ratio is small only in numbers. Two and a half acres is more than sufficient land to grow a year's worth of vegetables for 100 people. Anyone feeding that many folks can honestly consider himself to be running a highly productive farm.

In order to fully understand the potential for practical and economic success on the small farm, it must be understood that scale is not necessarily limiting or static. Size is only one of the components of an economic operation, and growth is more than just a change in size. It is generally accepted that a business must grow and respond to change in order to survive. The same applies to the small farm. But there are countless ways in which a farm can expand: quality, variety, and service are a few examples. I feel strongly that growth and change in the direction of *better* will ensure the economic and agronomic survival of the small farm more assuredly than growth and change in the direction of *bigger*.

It also helps if one can learn to ignore the well-meaning advice of economists, because their understanding of scale is industrial rather than agricultural. Their advice does not apply to biological production. The truth is that what can be accomplished on a small scale in agriculture cannot always be duplicated on a larger scale. The small farmer's aim is to produce a quality product for an appreciative clientele. The production of red-, green-, or orange-colored cellulose for a mass market is not the same thing.

The most encouraging aspect of small-scale farming is that the capital requirements to start up are reasonable. In this and many other ways small scale in agriculture should be understood as a very *positive* factor.

Equipment

The basic high-quality equipment needed to manage 5 acres of vegetable production can be purchased new for about $8,000. If used models are available, that cost can obviously be reduced. However, since much of the equipment I recommend has only recently become widely available, that option may not exist. This equipment consists of:

Walking tractor/tiller	$5,500
Wheel hoes	500
One-row seeder	100
Soil-block equipment	800
Hoes and hand tools	400
Carts and wheelbarrows	700
	$8,000

The single most important concept that keeps the capital investment at this very reasonable level (and simplifies the skills needed for operation and maintenance of the equipment) is the size of the equipment. Instead of a four-wheel tractor with costly implements, I recommend a much simpler two-wheel walking tractor/tiller for soil preparation along with hand-powered tools for seeding and cultivating. Reliance on these tools is not a concession to economics. Their outstanding performance and flexibility alone recommend them.

Additional capital investment for equipment other than the above may be required (or at least desired by the farmer) under many growing and marketing conditions. This should not amount to more than another $7,000. In this category I include:

Greenhouses	$4,500
Irrigation	2,000
Undersowing seeder	500
	$7,000

If the whole $15,000 were spent and paid back over five years (the depreciation life of the equipment) at 10 percent interest, the total cost per acre per year on 5 productive acres would be about $800. Allowing a generous figure of $1,200 per acre per year for annual operating costs (seed, fertilizer, fuel, hired equipment, and repairs) brings the total per acre per year cost to approximately $2,000. If you compare that to the $8,000-plus per-acre income an efficient vegetable operation should realize, you can see that the economics of small-scale vegetable farming are promising. If the local market permits a degree of specialization in the higher-priced crops, the income figure can be raised substantially.

The subscription program suggested in Chapter 20 offers an innovative marketing concept that can help achieve those goals.

The small farmer operates in a unique situation. Definitions of the possible, the economic, the realistic, and the practical are completely changed. More than anything else, a lack of understanding of these definitions and a parallel lack of information on downscaled biological and mechanical technologies have added to the belief that human-scale, regionally based agriculture "can't be done." It can.

4 ❧ PART-TIME HELP

"YOU CANNOT GET GOOD HELP NOWADAYS." "PEOPLE DON'T WORK HARD enough." "People don't care." "They want too much money." "They aren't dependable." Labor can be a problem. Many of these comments may be valid, others not, but all are worth noting. It is wise to make some serious choices ahead of time before you find yourself muttering those very sentiments.

Family Labor

My suggestions in this area are consistent with the food-production premise of this book—small, manageable, and efficient. The family is the best source of labor for the small-scale farm. So, the most important recommendation is to set up an operation that is small, manageable, and efficient enough to be run mainly by family labor. Why? Because farming is hard work, and the rewards at the start are measured more in satisfaction and pride than in large salaries. The farm family will do the work because it is their dream. It is their canvas, and they are painting it the way they've always wanted it to look. Hired help who can involve themselves from the start on such an intense level of participation are not easy to find.

My production system is planned to make the most of family labor in the following ways:

- I have chosen equipment for ease and efficiency of use and repair.
- I recommend growing a broad range of crops to spread the work more evenly over a long season.
- I take a management-intensive approach for fertilization and pest control.
- I stress forethought and pre-planning to avoid panic.
- I propose imaginative marketing approaches to save time and energy.

Most important, this system is based upon a philosophy that aims at stability by establishing long-term, self-perpetuating, low-input systems of production as opposed to short-term, high-input systems.

Outside Labor

The best-laid plans don't always run true, and chances are the grower will sometimes need outside labor. When paid helpers are required, I have some suggestions that may prove useful.

If you find good employees, plan to keep them. Pay a fair wage and investigate profit-sharing options and other rewards. One good worker familiar with your operation is worth three inexperienced workers. Be imaginative. What does the farm have to offer that will attract the ideal people? The usual pool of labor available for part-time farm work has never been the best. But think further. For many people farming is exciting. Most everyone has a farming urge hidden behind their urbanized facade. While most are still dreaming about it, your farm is a reality. So offer potential helpers not so much a job but rather a part-time outlet for their dream. It is surprising how many people share this dream but have not yet decided to pursue it. Offer that reward to those people.

Finding Willing Workers

The potential labor pool extends from the young to the old, from students to retirees. Homemakers whose children are now in school or college are often looking for a new challenge. Working on an organic farm can give them meaningful part-time work and a chance to turn their energy and competence into valuable assets. There are many such people who are reliable, intelligent, hardworking, interested, motivated, and would love the chance to share in someone else's dream. For them the rewards are only partially financial. Since work hours are often limited to evenings or early mornings (harvesting for market, say), the possibility of fitting farm work into standard schedules is increased. Where to look for willing workers? Some of the following are good places to start:

- Retirement communities
- Supermarket bulletin boards (put up help-wanted signs and specify the benefits)
- Local colleges
- Food co-ops
- Ethnic groups
- Garden clubs
- Condominium and apartment complexes

Be Efficient and Flexible

Be efficient. Maximize skills, minimize deficiencies. Labor should be hired to do what the boss does not do best or what he does not need to do. Ideally, the boss is going to be good at growing and marketing. Fine. Then hire help to pick, wash, crate, and distribute. Whoever is best-suited for a certain area of the operation should spend his or her time doing that as well as it can be done. Overall efficiency will be greater. Hire labor to complement rather than replace family skills.

Be flexible. Work out a solution for the particular labor needs of the moment. If the labor arrangement of the farm does not parallel that of modern agriculture, let it be of no concern. Many unique situations are successful. A farm may be next door to a large vegetarian community that will buy everything at a premium and help out to boot. Students from a nearby college may provide all the part-time labor on a work-study program. The farmer may have a dozen brothers and sisters living nearby who eagerly come and help out whenever they are needed. Ignore any claims that a farm only succeeds because of a special arrangement. Success simply means that a farmer is doing something right. Remember, too, that no matter how good a deal is, it should never be assumed to be permanent. Always have an alternative solution or two on hand.

Getting Quality Work

Jobs should be done correctly. The complement to labor is management. That is what the boss must do, and the quality of management determines to a large degree how well labor performs. Horticulture is a skilled profession, and there is a need to work quickly but precisely. Standards must be set. I was impressed in Europe to see how horticulture is respected and understood. The employees are professionals, are proud of their work, and take satisfaction in doing it well. In the past this may have been true elsewhere, but rarely anymore. The boss has to instill that spirit of professionalism.

The repercussions of slipshod garden work are cumulative. Rows planted crookedly in a moment of carelessness cannot be cultivated efficiently and will require hand-weeding for the entire growing season. Weeds that are allowed to go to seed one year will increase the weed problem for the next seven years. The quality of each job will affect the efficiency of the entire operation. Poor work must not be tolerated.

Along with quality production goes excellence of skills. Set work standards and stick to them. Most people have never learned the necessary bodily coordination needed to work well with simple tools. This lack of training and the consequent awkwardness result in making a job much more difficult than it needs to be. Show your helpers how it's done. They should be taught to use garden tools just as carefully as they would be taught to play a musical instrument or speak a foreign language. Remember, any physical work is made easier by planning the job out beforehand, working at an efficient rhythm, and dividing the job up into attainable pieces.

Inspiring the Crew

An important facet of management is attitude. Management must care about labor's satisfaction. Many people will come to work because they are interested, so encourage their involvement. Explain not only what the job is but where it fits into the overall scheme of things and why it is important. If someone is starting in the middle of a process, take a moment to explain it fully so they can see both the beginning and the end. Not only will they be more interested when they understand the rationale for their efforts, but once they see the whole picture they will be able to suggest improvements in the system. Very often a beginner has seen things that I have missed because I was no longer looking at the job from a fresh perspective.

Finally, one last suggestion for dealing with outside labor. As I have said, the farm family is its own best labor force because they are motivated. Think for a moment—why? Because they love what they are doing; because it is creative and satisfies a creative urge; because farming is necessary and fulfilling work; because quality is important, and good growers take pride in producing a quality product. Whatever the reason, the bosses must convey a sense of that to outside workers. Don't hesitate to be inspirational and enthusiastic. If it is the magic of transforming a tiny seed into daily bread, then say so. If it is the joy of providing customers with truly nourishing food that they can trust, talk about it. Not everyone will share the same motivation, but enthusiasm is contagious. Spread it about.

Firing Workers

There are times when it will be necessary to fire someone. Do it nicely, but don't put it off. There is nothing more frustrating than making do with uninterested and unmotivated workers. One determined griper can ruin the experience for everyone else. Nip it in the bud quickly. If there are valid gripes, they should be dealt with fairly and openly. But beyond that, be firm. Some people seem to enjoy complaining. I prefer not to have them around.

A farm can't do without labor. The trick is to do well with it. If outside labor can't be counted on, don't set up a system that relies on it. When outside labor is necessary, use the natural advantages of the farm to attract people who want to be there.

5 ❧ MARKETING STRATEGY

ESTABLISHING A MARKETING STRATEGY IS ONE OF THE FIRST STEPS IN A successful vegetable operation. Which crops? How much to grow? Ready when? Sold to whom? The key to success in marketing is to pay careful attention to one considerable advantage of the small producer—high-quality crops.

The European Lesson

In the early days of my own marketing education, I had the opportunity to visit many small farms in Europe. I learned a great deal there. The farmers I visited were successful first of all because they worked hard. Second, they succeeded because they worked intelligently. They took advantage of their strengths and minimized their weaknesses. For example, they diversified in order to spread their production, income, and family labor over a longer season. They chose agricultural enterprises that fit together spatially or temporally. That is, a particular crop grown in a particular space would fertilize that plot of ground for following crops. The periods of heaviest work did not come all at once. These small farmers succeeded because they had access to modern production technologies scaled to their operations. But most important of all, they were economically successful because they understood how to compete in the marketplace with the most valuable product they had to offer—quality.

Standardization in food does not exist in Europe on the scale it does here. Regional and varietal differences are treasured. Quality in food is demanded as much as is quality in other products. In Europe, small growers are encouraged to produce a more carefully nurtured, high-quality product. What does that quality consist of? Many factors: Truly fresh produce. The tastiest and most tender varieties. The most careful soil and cultural practices needed to grow the crop correctly. The widest selection. The longest season. The personal touch. All are criteria in which a small farmer producing for a local market has a great advantage over bulk-grown, trucked-in foodstuffs. The European farmers' success lies in concentrating on the areas in which the small farm excels.

I think the back-to-the-land movement of the 1960s, which was responsible for increasing the interest in organic growing, missed one important facet of the old rural society—the passion for quality. The old peasant crafters found their joy in doing the job as well as they could do it. And then doing it better the next time. Whatever their field of endeavor, their goal was the creation of an object of beauty.

Quality from Within

I have noted over the years that many people feel uncomfortable about hustling a product, about putting on the hard sell, and so forth. Those people can calm their fears right now. If their product is good, necessary, and really first-class, then they never need worry about finding customers. The negative image many people carry of "salesmen" stems from the association of that profession with unwanted, unneeded, shoddy, poorly made, frivolous products that require fast talking and other unsavory skills to sell. Good growers should understand that they are not in the same category at all. Theirs is a first-class product: it is produced locally without polluting the environment; it saves energy because the food doesn't have to be transported across the country; the production of it stimulates employment and strengthens the local economy. A quality product always benefits the buyer as well as the seller. And that is how transactions between human beings should be, a mutually beneficial two-way exchange.

Ideas need to be sold, too, especially those ideas that are fundamental to good farming. Therefore, this chapter deals with more than just selling a product. It also deals with caring. Quality is the result of the skill of the producer coupled with care. Experience will provide the skills, but caring must come from within. Many customers may not be aware of real quality. The public is not always well informed about agricultural practices and their effect on the quality of food. It's the growers who must care about their agricultural practices and the repercussions, even though there may be no one forcing them to do so. Giving a damn and doing what is right are rewards in themselves. In the long run, producing a poor or deceptive product, or a less-good-than-you-can-do product, is harder on the producer than on the consumer. The consumer may only encounter it once or twice. The producer has to live with it all the time.

Real Carrots

Even though the consumer may be adept at distinguishing quality in manufactured goods, this perceptiveness does not always extend to food crops because he or she often has no standard for comparison. To most people, a carrot is a carrot is a carrot. Well, to tell the truth, it isn't. And the difference is not just looks. Carrots can take up large quantities of pesticide residues when they are grown in soils that contain them. Carrots grown in soil with a low pH take up more lead, cadmium, and aluminum. Unbalanced soluble fertilizers modify plant composition. The lack of minor elements, limited by poor soil conditions, inhibits protein synthesis. There is definitely a "biological value" in food plants that is hampered or lost by inadequate soil fertility and growing conditions.

For the most part, scientific evidence on the subject of food's biological value is contradictory and incomplete.* It remains one of those areas where people are intuitively conscious of differences once they experience them, but tests for those differences are inadequate. There are documented differences in food quality as affected by growing conditions, but not enough to constitute "absolute proof"—as if absolute proof is ever possible with any biological concept. Perhaps we aren't yet wise enough to know what to look for. But the sensible consumer doesn't always wait for science. The consumer has generally led science rather than following it. I remember watching meticulous French customers shopping for vegetables in a rural village. Their standards, which had been honed by generations of awareness, were very high. If "a carrot is a carrot is a carrot," you could not have proved it by them.

Other ideas are spreading as well. Agricultural chemical technologies are under heavy criticism. Consumers are demanding safer food and more control over additives and residues. The idea is dawning that food must be judged not just by its cosmetics but by its composition. The public is aroused because of a sense that the system they have been taught to rely on has betrayed them, and will probably continue to betray them.

That system, which is composed of the regulatory agencies of government—such as those for environmental protection, food and agriculture, and product purity—has compiled a dismal and embarrassing record of failure with regard to

Some books that deal with the ideas of food quality as it is related to the use of fertilizers and pesticides are: Silent Spring *by Rachel Carson (Boston: Houghton Mifflin, 1962);* Nutritional Values in Crops and Plants *by Werner Schuphan (London: Faber, 1961);* Mineral Nutrition and the Balance of Life *by Frank Gilbert (Norman: University of Oklahoma Press, 1957);* Nutrition and the Soil *by Dr. Lionel Picton (New York: Devin Adair, 1949); and* The Living Soil by E.B. Balfour *(London: Faber, 1943).*

safeguarding the public. Stories to that effect appear in the media every day. Pesticides or additives sworn to be absolutely benign one day are banned as hazardous the next. Scientists upon whose knowledge we depend to make those decisions disagree vehemently among themselves over the safety of agricultural practices vis-à-vis the health of the consumer, the pollution of our water supplies, and the long-term productive capacity of the soil. But the consumer is no fool. The disturbing evidence can no longer be ignored. Something is amiss, and whether there is "absolute" scientific proof or not, a groundswell has begun. The emperor has no clothes, and the public, by doubting the adequacy of the regulatory agencies, has begun to make independent decisions to seek safer food.

We may seem to have wandered off the subject of marketing strategy, but not in practical terms. Quality is the lynchpin of a small-scale grower's business. Once consumers realize that certain producers *care*, that they are *sincere* and that their word and their produce are *dependable*, they will patronize them faithfully. I ran a market garden in Maine from 1968 to 1978 in a very unlikely location. The farm was 6 miles from a numbered highway (and the last 3 miles were dirt road). Marketing problems? I had none. Our produce set the quality standard, and we always had more demand than we could meet. Once a reputation for "real" food is established, there is no better advertising or marketing program. The market, as they say, will take care of itself.

The local organic grower has an additional marketing advantage which should be exploited. As the organic food industry expands, large-scale marketers, whose only interest is profit, will soon move in. Despite the existence of a national certification program, deceptive practices will increase, and suspicions about whether the food is truly organic will become commonplace. Consumers will soon realize (and I for one will certainly encourage them to do so) that the best way to be assured of food quality is, in the words of the old quotation, "to know the first name of the grower."

6 ❧ PLANNING AND OBSERVATION

WHEN I BEGAN FARMING FULL-TIME ON MY OWN LAND IN MAINE, I WAS extremely fortunate to have as friends and neighbors Scott and Helen Nearing. The Nearings taught me a wide range of economic survival skills, but the most important were *planning* and *observation*. The Nearings demonstrated those two valuable skills at their best.

They were careful planners and organizers of the work to be done and the crops to be grown, and always sought out the most efficient way to accomplish any task at hand. They were without a doubt the most practically organized country people I have ever met. In fact, I remember marveling that Scott was the one nonagenarian I knew with plans for the future farm project he would be working on ten years hence. Many of Helen and Scott's ideas and experiences as small farmers are described in their book, *Living the Good Life* (Harborside, Maine: Social Science Institute, 1954; reprinted, New York: Schocken, 1970).

Planning on Paper

I soon learned to plan ahead much more efficiently than I ever had—to set out the whole year's work on paper during the winter months and thus have a good grasp well in advance of what resources I would need, where they would come from, how I would acquire them, and how much time I could allot to each task. I organized a notebook into sections for each vegetable crop, for every year in the different rotations I was trying out, for fertilization records on each field, and so forth. There is no way to match the value of organizing and planning beforehand.

The Nearings were masters of observation. They meticulously recorded all the bits and pieces of data gleaned out of day-to-day farm activities—from which variety of lettuce wintered over best to what combination of ingredients made the most effective compost for peas. Some of their observations came from intentional comparative trials, but the majority came by chance—from keeping their eyes open and training themselves to notice subtle differences, where less perceptive observers would pass by unawares. In short, they never stopped learning and were wise enough to record what they noticed so it would be of use to them in the future.

Taking a cue from the Nearings, the first step, therefore, is to plan out your operation in detail. Let's go through this process step by step to figure out which crops to grow, in what quantities, and how to set it all up.

What to Grow

Depending on the market and the climate in your area, the possibility exists to grow anywhere from one to 70 or so reasonably common vegetable crops. Imaginative growers are rediscovering old crops every day. John Evelyn in his 1699 essay *Acetaria: A Discourse of Sallets* listed 77 vegetable crops, and those were just salad ingredients. The 48 vegetables I consider the most promising are listed below and are divided into two categories, major and minor.

Major		Minor
Asparagus	Radish	Arugula
Bean	Rutabaga	Celeriac
Beet	(Swede turnip)	Chinese Cabbage
Broccoli	Spinach	Collards
Brussels sprouts	Squash, summer	Dandelion
Cabbage	Squash, winter	Eggplant
Carrot	Tomato	Endive
Cauliflower		Escarole
Celery		Fennel
Chard		Kohlrabi
Corn		Leek
Cucumber		Mâche
Garlic		Okra
Kale		Radicchio
Lettuce		Salsify
Melon		Scorzonera
Onion, bulb		Shallot
Onion, scallion		Turnip
Parsley		
Parsnip		
Peas		
Pepper		
Potato		
Pumpkin		

One way to begin deciding which vegetables to grow is to write down in chart form any information that will help organize your planning. For example, I might begin by compiling a chart of the months when different vegetables could be available for sale if they were grown in my area. That chart should include the potential for extended availability of these crops if the growing season is supplemented by the protection of walk-in tunnels, the greater protection of a heated greenhouse, or out-of-season sales from a storage building. (For a discussion of the whole range of season extension possibilities, see Chapters 21, 22, and 23.)

A chart of the potential availability of crops for sale in my area, New England, might look like the charts on pages 36 and 37.

Then, depending on whether I wanted to grow just seasonally or for an extended market, I would have an idea which crops could be available and when. The advantage of compiling this kind of information is that it stimulates thinking. It might suggest a specific course of action, such as a degree of specialization, perhaps. A wide variety of crops can be made available year-round. In many markets year-round production can help keep customers or acquire restaurant contracts. A look at the chart shows that many salad crops are capable of year-round production (see Chapter 23). A chart for specialization in salad crops would look like the chart on page 38.

AVAILABILITY OF MAJOR CROPS FOR SALE

AVAILABILITY OF MINOR CROPS FOR SALE

	Outdoor ▮	Protected ▮	Greenhouse ▮

	J	F	M	A	M	J	J	A	S	O	N	D
Arugula												
Celeriac												
Chinese Cabbage												
Collards												
Dandelion												
Eggplant												
Endive												
Escarole												
Fennel												
Kohlrabi												
Leek												
Mâche												
Okra												
Radicchio												
Salsify												
Scorzonera												
Shallot												
Turnip												

SPECIALIZING IN SALAD CROPS

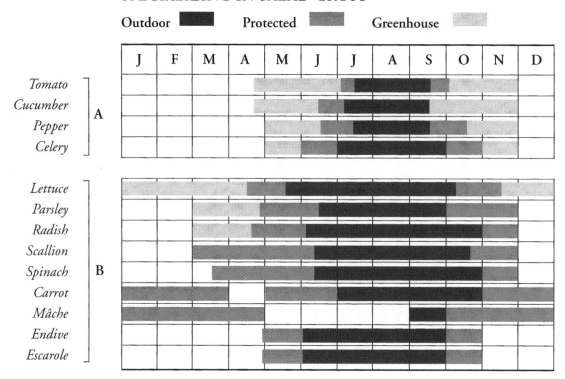

The "A" crops are the most potentially lucrative for the grower, but they are also the most expensive to produce. They need higher temperatures, requiring more heating costs and a more professional greenhouse, one that is taller and stronger for trellising.* They also are not actually year-round crops, although they are long-season. Only the most specialized producers plan on harvesting before April and after November.

The "B" crops can be grown in simpler tunnel greenhouses at lower temperatures. Some, such as mâche, parsley, scallions, spinach, and carrots, can be grown as fall crops with no supplementary heat at all. They can be harvested all at once before real cold sets in, or over a good part of the winter by providing just enough heat to keep them from freezing. (See Chapter 23 for specific information on low-heat and no-heat winter production of these and other salad crops.) The decision depends on your market.

The most basic year-round greenhouse crop is lettuce. It is always in demand. Excellent varieties for winter production are available through the specialty seed catalogs. If the grower uses an adapted variety, lettuce can be grown at

*A good book for those getting started in greenhouse vegetable production is Greenhouse Tomatoes, Lettuce and Cucumbers by S. H. Wittwer and S. Honma (East Lansing: Michigan State University Press, 1979).

low temperatures and winter harvesting can be planned on a regular schedule (see page 260).

Production Size

This is a function of a number of other factors. How much land is available? How fertile is it? How many workers are involved? What kind of equipment is on hand? As I said earlier, I consider 5 acres of intensive production to be the upper limit. The decision about the size of a productive farm cannot be made in a vacuum. The relationship of size to all of the production and marketing factors must never be forgotten.

The market garden layout will obviously be determined by the lay of the land, but in addition there are some general suggestions that are applicable almost everywhere.

Subdivision

No matter what size the field, it should be subdivided. One-hundred-foot-long sections are the ideal size for the scale of machinery to be used. A 5-acre field, sectioned off, might look like this:

Ideally, the field will slope to the south. The rows run across the field. Each row is 100 feet long. The paths in between the sections, which allow for access and turning a walking tractor/tiller at the end of each row, are from 5 to 10 feet wide.

There are some solid reasons for subdividing. Ease of access, of calculating input and production information, and of general organization are just a few. The most important reason is management. Subdivision makes it easy to keep an eye on everything. Care is the key, and nothing must be neglected. Subdivision helps to get the grower and his attention to every part of the operation. The crop that could easily be forgotten in the middle of a large field is more likely to receive care in a smaller space. No matter what the shape of the growing area, it should somehow be divided into workable sections.

Layout and Crop Spacing

The divisions above must now be progressively subdivided again. Just as a country is easier to comprehend when it is divided into states, counties, and towns, a garden is more comprehensible as sections and strips and rows. Each section in the following illustration is 100 feet by 200 feet, or ½ acre. A strip is a part of a

Vegetable fields subdivided for ease of management.

section 100 feet long by either 42 inches or 60 inches wide. That creates 57 (42-inch) or 40 (60-inch) strips side by side in each section.

The choice between 42-inch or 60-inch strips depends upon the equipment available and the crops to be grown. In either case 12 inches of the strip is used as an access path for foot traffic, leaving a 30-inch-wide growing area from a 42-inch strip and a 48-inch-wide growing area from a 60-inch strip. Foot traffic should be confined to the access paths in order to avoid soil compaction in the growing area. Thinking in terms of strips helps to make the production system more flexible. Any strip can be planted after harvest to a succession crop or to a green manure independently of the rest of the section.*

If you have a 26-inch-wide tiller on your walking tractor, or if you have access to a four-wheel tractor, the 60-inch strips will work best. They are also

This is the same layout a tractor-scale grower would refer to as a "bed" system. I haven't used the term "bed" in this discussion because so many organic growers associate that word with double-dug raised beds. Since I consider that extra work unnecessary, I call my beds "strips" to emphasize the difference.

best for those growing a wide range of crops, such as for a subscription market (see Chapter 20), since they are more efficient for the larger, more widely spaced crops. With the 26-inch tiller on a walking tractor, one pass down either side of the 48-inch-wide growing area will prepare the soil. For tractor tillage I recommend setting the wheels on 60-inch centers. A 48-inch or 60-inch tiller can then be used to till the strips. With a 48-inch tiller you will want to add cultivating teeth behind each wheel to control weeds in the wheelings. Or you can cultivate the paths with the 12-inch knife on the wheel hoe (see page 159) as you would if you were not using a tractor. I prefer to use a 60-inch tiller and then the wheelings are also tilled.

One useful hint: when tilling across a sloped field using either a walking or four-wheel tractor, start at the uphill edge of the area to be tilled. Then, as you till the second and subsequent passes, it will be the upper wheels that sink slightly in the softened soil, creating a leveling and slightly terraced effect to the field. If you start at the bottom edge this effect is reversed, and the tilt of the field is increased by the sinking wheels. It becomes harder to keep the tractor on line and to keep the field surface even.

The row spacings used for various crops in the 60-inch strips follow on pages 42 and 43, accompanied by drawings from a worm's-eye view

When growing and marketing specialty salads, I prefer the 42-inch strip width. It is also more comfortable for laying out a home garden, where the more commercially scaled 60-inch dimensions can be awkward. For an operation specializing in salads I recommend a walking tractor with a 30-inch tiller and the wheels set as widely as possible. You can then till the 30-inch-wide growing area in one pass. The 12-inch access paths are cultivated with the 12-inch knife on the wheel hoe.

I began using this spacing years ago for certain greenhouse crops and I soon adapted it to the field. I find it especially suitable when specializing in multicrop, fresh salad production where I am doing a lot of multiple harvest of low-growing crops and need to be able to quickly move across the field. It is easier to step across a 30-inch-wide growing area, and you can straddle it comfortably if you wish while harvesting, a feat that is physically impossible for most people when the growing area is 48 inches wide.

Suggested spacings for all the crops when grown in 42-inch strips are also shown on pages 42 and 43, with sample worm's-eye views.

The space-consuming crops are not as efficient in the 42-inch-wide strips, which is why I suggest this spacing is preferable for a salad cropping system.

STRIP WIDTH	ROW SPACING (on-center)	ROWS PER STRIP	SUGGESTED CROPS	WORM'S EYE VIEW
42"	4"	6	Radish, spinach, mâche, green manure. These can be planted with a multiple-row seeder (see suggestions in Chapter 23).	
60"	4"	10		
42"	10"	3	Carrot, beet (fresh), celery, chard, garlic, lettuce, onion, parsley, spinach, celeriac, chicory, Chinese Cabbage, dandelion, endive, escarole, fennel, kolhrabi, leek, shallot, turnip	
60"	12"	4		
42"	16"	2	Beet (storage), kale, rutabaga, collards, salsify, parsnip	
60"	18"	3		
42"	42"	1	Beans, broccoli, Brussels sprouts, cabbage, cauliflower, corn, cucumber, melon, peas (low), pepper, potato, tomatoes (staked), eggplant, squash (summer)	
60"	30"	2		

STRIP WIDTH	ROW SPACING (on-center)	ROWS PER STRIP	SUGGESTED CROPS	WORM'S EYE VIEW
42"	42"	1	Asparagus, peas (tall), tomatoes (unstaked), melon, squash (summer)	
60"	60"	1		
42"	126"	every third strip	Pumpkin, squash (winter). The unused strips on either side should be planted to a green manure.	
60"	120"	every other strip		

Getting Good Seed

So many factors are important in vegetable growing that there may be disagreement with the values I ascribe to some of them. But I doubt if anyone will dispute the importance of good seed. Without high-quality seed, all the other activities are moot.

The grower will first be concerned with specific named varieties (or *cultivars,* as they are also called). At the start I suggest sticking with tried-and-true, locally adapted varieties from a dependable regional supplier. After the first year or two, the grower should have enough experience about what works and what needs improvement to begin selecting from seed catalogs. With catalogs, it is mostly a case of learning to read between the lines. New seed varieties, no matter how highly praised, are always a risk. This is especially true with the commercial catalogs, which often select new cultivars for their ability to perform under conventional fertilizer/pesticide regimes. Organic growers will find, as I have, that the stable, older varieties often give more dependable results.

Some seed varieties, like some people, thrive best under specific conditions. That is not to say that you should avoid trying newly developed or hybrid varieties. Just never abandon a dependable old variety without being sure about the quality of its replacement. I have always found it rewarding to read specialty and foreign seed catalogs and then conduct trial plantings of promising varieties and even new crops. I have discovered a small but important number of my favorites this way. The number I trial is small because the seed companies are also testing and trialing varieties from many sources with far greater resources than I possess. For the most part their results are thorough and dependable. There always exists, however, the pleasure of a new discovery made on my own, and I heartily recommend the practice of seeking and trying.

Below are some criteria that you may want to consider when selecting varieties:

- *Eating Quality.* This is most important by far and includes the flavor, tenderness, and aroma of the vegetable, both raw and cooked.
- *Appearance.* Color, size, and shape are also important but are secondary to eating quality.
- *Pest and Disease Resistance.* This is useful where a problem exists; otherwise, choose a variety for its flavor and tenderness.
- *Days to Maturity.* This is obviously an important factor in planning early and succession crops.
- *Storage.* Suitability for long or short periods in storage.
- *Vigor.* This includes quick germination and quick growth.
- *Performance.* Does the variety have vigor under a wide variety of conditions?
- *Standability.* This describes noncracking tomatoes, nonsplitting cabbages, and so forth.
- *Ease of Harvest.* Carrots with strong tops are easier to pull, and beans held above the foliage are easier to pick.
- *Time of Harvest.* Various cultivars can extend your growing season.
- *Frost Resistance and Hardiness.* These are spring and fall concerns.
- *Day Length.* There are short-day varieties for winter greenhouse production, and so forth.
- *Ease of Cleaning.* Some leafy greens hold their leaves high to avoid soil splash.
- *Convenience.* This includes self-blanching cauliflower, nonstaking (determinate) tomatoes, and other convenient growers.
- *Ease of Preparation.* This means long as opposed to round beets, round as opposed to flat onions, and so forth.
- *Adaptability.* Many varieties winter over and provide early spring growth.

- *Nutrition.* Some varieties have higher levels of nutrients.
- *Marketability.* This includes specialty, ethnic, and gourmet varieties.

Quantity

Quantity is the next concern. How much seed of each variety should be purchased? Planting techniques will affect this decision. If a majority of crops are transplanted as this book recommends, the grower will be able to get by with far fewer seeds than would be needed if plants were to be sown directly. Information on quantities of seed needed for direct-sown crops is given in most seed catalogs. At the start one might want to purchase extra seed just to be sure. A new seeder or a new setting could easily plant twice the seeds calculated until it is calibrated correctly. Nothing is as discouraging as running out of seed on a perfect spring planting day. The cost of seed for field crops is a small expense in most cases, and buying a little extra is good insurance for the grower.

If there are specific varieties or crops that become important to the farm's production, it is a good practice to purchase an insurance packet of those seeds from a second supplier. This is especially important with succession crops. Along with the first planting of the standard seeds, plant seeds from the insurance packet. If all goes well the extra seedlings won't be needed, but if the standard seeds don't perform well the grower will be covered and know where to order new stock. Be sure to set up credit accounts with favored seed firms so seeds can be ordered by phone quickly if there are any problems during the year.

It is wise to be covered in the same way when you are planning to use last year's seeds. Most of the time and for most varieties, year-old seeds that were stored properly (in cool, dry, and dark conditions) will work just fine. However, the savings are a false economy if a crop or a succession planting is lost because of seed failure. The grower should be sure to obtain each year's seeds as soon as possible. Never wait until the last minute. Early planting dates have a habit of sneaking up on you; before you realize it, spring is here. Whether you purchase seed from a mail-order catalog or from a local supplier will depend upon personal preference. What is necessary in either case is dependability. A grower needs consistent quality and up-to-date information. If the seed stock for a certain variety is poor one year, it is important that the supplier inform its customers of this fact. Smaller growers are often not privy to this information, so it always pays to ask.

I suggest a further precaution. After a few years' experience, a grower should experiment with saving seed from open-pollinated varieties. *Open-pollinated* means that properly grown seeds will grow into plants that are true to type (unlike seeds saved from F_1 hybrids, which typically are either sterile "mules" or revert to one of the hybrid's parent strains). For most crops the vigor and viability of seed grown under the careful cultural practices of this production system will far excel seeds that are purchased.

I make this recommendation for another reason, too. I doubt that the direction of present-day seed breeding, selection, and genetic manipulation is favorable to the producer of high-quality vegetables. Many older varieties are being abandoned or unnecessarily tinkered with. I now save seed from any open-pollinated varieties that I treasure for their eating qualities or excellent growth under my production methods. Seeds are the spark of the farm operation, and the more control the grower can exert, the more dependable the system will be.

When to Plant

The date of harvest depends on the date of planting. The span of time between the two may be longer or shorter depending on the effects of day length, weather, the aspect of the land, the crops grown, and many other growth-related factors. Although control is possible with protected cropping (tunnels and greenhouses), the earliest and latest unprotected outdoor crops are still important. They cost less to produce and they include many crops that are not usually grown with protection.

Early and Late Planting.   The best information on your earliest and latest local planting dates will come from other growers, and not necessarily just the professionals. Good home gardeners are surprisingly astute about planting dates and other matters. More than once I have seen the experienced home gardener beat the pros to the earliest harvest. In truth, this is such a complex subject and one that can be influenced in so many ways that even the best growers are not doing all they could. Without a doubt, the early outdoor production potential of many farms can be improved by paying attention to windbreaks, exposure, soil color, and other microclimate modifications.

As a further refinement there are specific cultural factors to take into account. Sweet corn, for example, is an important crop for most market stands, and earliness is what brings in the customers. But the planting date of corn can be pushed back only so far because of the limits of temperature. Corn won't germinate reliably or at all if the soil temperature is below 55°F. (13°C.). Yet corn seedlings will grow at or below that temperature. That is the factor usually overlooked. Pre-germinating corn seed or transplanting corn seedlings may be worth considering. Remember, we are not talking about the whole corn crop, rather just a few days' worth to catch the earliest market. Corn can be transplanted quite successfully if it is grown in soil blocks (see Chapter 14).

Succession and Greenhouse Planting. If a grower wishes to harvest a crop such as lettuce progressively throughout the year, it may seem logical to plant every week to keep up the continuity of supply. The logic is only partially valid. There may indeed be 52 planting dates during the year, but they will not be at 7-day intervals. The season of the year affects plant growth because of light, temperature, day length, and so on. Planting dates must be adjusted accordingly. Although these dates will vary with the geographical region and lay of the land, certain general patterns can be used as a guide.

Further information on succession planting of greenhouse lettuce can be found in Lettuce Under Glass, Grower Guide No. 21, *published by Grower Books, 50 Doughty Street, London WC1N 2LP.*

The maturity time for lettuce is doubled and tripled for plantings from September through February. The spacing of the planting dates must reflect that reality. In order to harvest lettuce every week from early November through April, Dutch research has determined that the following planting schedule is necessary.* (Growers in the Southern Hemisphere can transpose all these dates by six months and obtain a reasonably close approximation of planting times.)

September 1 to 10	sow every 3½ days
September 10 to 18	sow every 2 days
September 18 to October 10	sow every 3½ days
October 10 to November 15	sow every 7 days
November 15 to December 15	sow every 10 days

Other trials have shown that seed-to-harvest times can be speeded up if lettuce transplants are grown under artificial lighting for the first three weeks.

Outdoor production has similar variables. In my own experience in Maine, lettuce sown in a cool greenhouse on March 1 and transplanted outside April 21 was ready for sale on about May 25, whereas lettuce sown April 1 in the same greenhouse and transplanted outside on May 1 matured on June 2. Remember, specific dates are only guidelines. I wish to stress the understanding of the concept and the general pattern. All growers need to compile information for the climate and conditions of their individual farms. In the long run trial and error will be the best teachers of specific planting dates. This is another area where keeping careful records can be so valuable to the success of your farm.

Despite all the best planning, climate is never consistent. Unusual extremes of heat and cold can make life difficult. One way to offset unpredictable weather

MAJOR CROPS: AN OVERVIEW

	Quantity Consumed: Rank Order (USDA)	Greenhouse Production	Transplanted	Direct Seeded	Row Spacing (inches)	Plant Spacing (inches)
Asparagus	17		*		60	24
Bean				*	30	4
Beet	14			*	18	3
Broccoli	12			*	30	24
Brussels sprouts	12		*		30	24
Cabbage	7		*		30	24
Carrot	9			*	12	1
Cauliflower	12		*		30	24
Celery	10	*	*		18	12
Chard	18	*		*	18	6
Corn	4			*	30	12
Cucumber	6	*		*	30	12
Garlic	20		*		12	4
Kale	7		*		18	12
Lettuce	3	*	*		12	12
Melon			*		60	24
Onion, bulb	5		*		12	3
Onion, scallion	5	*		*	12	1
Parsley		*	*		12	6
Parsnip				*	18	3
Peas	11			*	60	2
Pepper	15		*		30	12
Potato	1			*	30	12
Pumpkin				*	120	24
Radish		*		*	4	2
Rutabaga	19			*	18	4
Spinach	13			*	12	3
Squash, summer	16			*	30	30
Squash, winter	16			*	120	24
Tomato	2	*	*		60	24

is to grow more than one variety of any crop. The varieties would be chosen for their slightly different performance under similar growing conditions, thus allowing the grower to "blanket" the ideal maturity date. The dependability of the harvest is more assured by adding a comfortable flexibility that can absorb some of the shocks of climatic anomalies.

A Final Word

Another lesson I learned from the Nearings is the folly of working seven days a week. There is a strong temptation when starting out in farming, without the benefit of parents and grandparents having done much of the preliminary work years before, to try to do it all right now. Working nonstop day after day is not the best way to achieve that goal. You soon get stale and lose the sense of joy and pleasure that made farming seem so desirable in the first place. Scott and Helen taught me the importance of pursuing something different, at least one day out of the seven, no matter how much work needs to be done on the farm. Even in the midst of the spring rush it always turns out that one day of change allows much more to be accomplished on the other days. Rest and reflection not only heal the body but help provide insight into how to get more accomplished with less work in the future so the same bind won't exist another year.

7 ❧

CROP ROTATION

The most complete bibliography of studies on all aspects of crop rotations up through 1975 is collected in "Bibliografia Sull Avvicendamento delle Colture" by G. Toderi in Rivista di Agronomia, 9 (1975), pp. 434–68.

❧

MOST DEPENDABLE AGRICULTURAL PRACTICES ARE AGES OLD. CROP ROTATION is a good example. Descriptions of the benefits of rotating crops can be found in the earliest Roman agricultural writings. The Greeks and, before them, the Chinese were also well acquainted with the principles of crop rotation. From his experience as a researcher at Rutgers, Firmin Bear stated that well-thought-out crop rotation is worth 75 percent of everything else that might be done, including fertilization, tillage, and pest control. In fact, I think this is a conservative estimate. Rarely are the principles of crop rotation applied as thoroughly as they might be in order to garner all of their potential benefits. To my mind, crop rotation is the single most important practice in a multiple-cropping program.*

In a word, crop rotation means variety, and variety gives stability to biological systems. By definition, crop rotation is the practice of changing the crop each year on the same piece of ground. Ideally, these different crops are not related botanically. Ideally, two successive crops do not make the same demands on the soil for nutrients, nor do they share diseases or insect pests. Legumes will be alternated with non-legumes. A longer rotation before the same crop is grown again is better than a shorter rotation. And, ideally, as many factors as possible will be taken into account in setting up the sequence.

Space and Time

The key to visualizing crop rotations is to understand that two things are going on at once. Rotations are both spatial (crops move) and temporal (time moves). With both crop sequence and time to consider, there may be some initial confusion when considering complicated rotations. Hang in there.

A graphic representation of an eight-year crop rotation would look like the following. There are eight sections with a different crop growing in each section. Now, let's say we want to rotate these eight crops so that A follows B, B follows C, and so on. Adding arrows to the picture indicates the direction of rotation. In each case the letters represent where the crop grows this year. The picture for the next year would follow the arrows one space over and have A growing where B

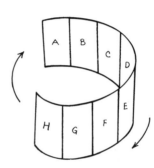

*Graphic representation of an
eight-year crop rotation.*

grows this year, with H growing in A's old place. The following year would have A growing where C grows this year, and so on.

When planning rotations I use 3" x 5" index cards with the crop names written on them. Some of you may wish to use a computer to display your planning options. I move the cards around as I try to determine the ideal sequence for the number of crops involved. Let's see how that works. With two crops, there is no problem. Take corn and beans. Corn is growing this year where beans will be next year and beans are growing this year where corn will be next year.

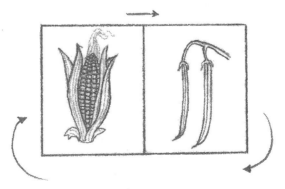

A three-year rotation expands that concept. Once there are more than two crops, a new factor is involved: order. There are now two possible sequences. The index cards can be placed: corn/beans/squash or corn/squash/beans.

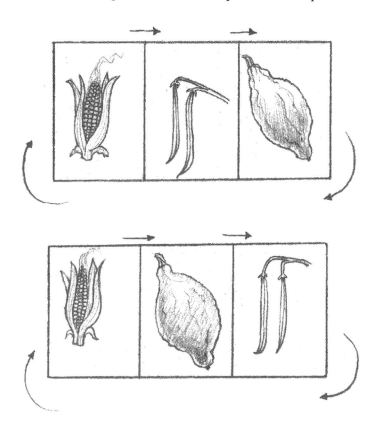

Notice that we are not concerned with the number of ways in which three items can be ordered (of which there are six), but rather with the possible sequences. If we go to a four-year rotation, there are six possible sequences. An eight-year rotation offers 5,040 sequences.

Why Bother?

Decisions, decisions. Why bother with crop rotation? Because there are so many benefits to the grower from setting up a rotational sequence that exploits every possible advantage. Corn, beans, squash, and other crops all take different nutrients out of the soil. All respond to diverse fertilization patterns. All are amenable to specific cultivation practices. All may affect or be affected by the preceding or succeeding crop. Whenever the crop or cultural practices of the current year can be chosen to benefit a future crop, there is reason for bothering. In fact, whenever there is a choice between one or more ways of doing a job, one of them is usually the best way. The determined grower will take the time to think things through to optimize every aspect of his production.

Time spent planning a rotation is never wasted. Not only will you learn a great deal about important biological balances on the farm, but the results will be so effective in halting problems before they occur that you may sometimes have to remind yourself that a lot is happening. Very often farmers fail to take full advantage of a well-planned rotation, because rotations don't have any computable costs and because they work so well at preventing problems that farmers are not aware of all the benefits. Those benefits are, in a sense, invisible.

Insect, Disease, and Weed Control

Rotations improve insect and disease control by managing the system to benefit the crop. Monoculture encourages many pest problems, because the pest organisms specific to a crop can multiply out of all proportion when that crop is grown in the same place year after year. Pests are most easily kept in balance when the soil grows different crops over a number of years. A good rotation spaces susceptible crops at intervals sufficient to hinder the buildup of their specific pest organisms.

Rotations affect weed control in a similar way. The characteristics of a crop and the cultivation methods used to grow it may inadvertently allow certain weeds to find a favorable niche. A smart crop rotation will incorporate a successor crop that eradicates those weeds. Furthermore, some crops can work as "cleaning crops" because of the style of cultivation used on them. Potatoes and winter squash fit into this category because of the hilling practiced on the former and the long period of cultivation that is possible prior to vining for the latter.

Plant Nutrition

Rotations can make nutrients more available in a biological farming system. Some plants are more effective than others in using the less soluble forms of plant nutrients. The residues of these nutrient-extracting plants will make the minerals more available to later, less effective plants in the next sequence of the rotation.

In general, plants of a lower order of evolution have been shown to be better feeders on less soluble nutrient sources than those of a higher order of development. Lowly plants—evolutionarily speaking—such as alfalfa, clovers, and cabbages, are more aggressive at extracting nutrients than more highly developed plants such as lettuce or cucumbers (see note on page 103). Lettuce and cucumbers, I've found, don't feed well on less soluble mineral nutrients. Thus, in my rotations, the choicest spot and the finest compost is always saved for the lettuce and cucumber crops, and their exceptional quality has always repaid that care.

Manure

Rotations encourage the best use of organic soil amendments. Some crops (squash, corn, peas, and beans, for example) grow best when manure or compost is applied every year. Others (cabbages, tomatoes, root crops, and potatoes) seem to grow better on ground that was manured the previous year. Greens are in the former category, with the caveat that the compost should be well decomposed. Obviously, a rotation that alternates manured crops with nonmanured crops will allow a grower to take these preferences into account.

Soil Structure

Rotations preserve and improve the soil structure. Different crops send roots to various depths, are cultivated with different techniques, and respond to either deeper or shallower soil preparation. By changing crops each year, the grower can make use of the full depth of the soil and slowly deepen the topsoil in the process.

Deeper-rooting plants of both cash crops and green manures extract nutrients from layers of the soil not used by the shallow rooters. In doing so they open up the soil depths, leaving paths for the roots of other, less vigorous crops. Deep rooters also incorporate mineral nutrients from the lower strata into their structure, and eventually, when the residues of these plants decompose in the soil, those nutrients become available to the shallow rooters.

Yields

The results of the University of Rhode Island crop-rotation experiments are reported in the following two studies: "A Half-Century of Crop-Rotation Experiments" by R. S. Bell, T. E. Odland, and A. L. Owens in Bulletin No. 303, *and "The Influence of Crop Plants on Those Which Follow: V" by T. E. Odland, R. S. Bell, and J. B. Smith in* Bulletin No. 309 *(Kingston: Rhode Island Agricultural Experiment Station).*

❧

Rotations improve yields not only in the many ways discussed above but also in subtler ways. Some crops are helped and some hindered by the preceding crop. The University of Rhode Island conducted over 50 years of studies on the influence of the preceding crop on the yields of the following crop.* The possible reasons for this are numerous and even after extensive study there is no general agreement on what exactly are the processes involved. Some causes for the beneficial influence of preceding crops on subsequent crops are:

- Increase in soil nitrogen
- Improvement in the physical condition of the soil
- Increased bacterial activity
- Increased release of carbon dioxide
- Excretion of beneficial substances
- Control of weeds, insects, and disease

The injurious effects of preceding crops, which I aim to avoid by careful rotation planning, are produced by:

- Depletion of soil nutrients
- Excretion of toxic substances
- Increase in soil acidity
- Production of injurious substances resulting from the decomposition of plant residue
- Unfavorable physical condition of the soil due to a shallow-rooting crop
- Lack of proper soil aeration
- Removal of moisture
- Diseases passed to subsequent crops
- Influences of crops upon the soil flora and fauna

Patterns

Despite a lack of agreement among researchers, certain patterns emerge from the studies I have read on good and bad rotational effects, as well as from my own observations:

- Legumes are generally beneficial preceding crops.
- The onions, lettuces, and squashes are generally beneficial preceding crops.
- Potato yields best after corn.
- For potatoes, some preceding crops (peas, oats, and barley) increase the incidence of scab, whereas others (soybeans) decrease it significantly.
- Corn and beans are not greatly influenced in any detrimental way by the preceding crop.
- Liming and manuring ameliorate, but do not totally overcome, the negative effects of a preceding crop.
- Members of the chicory family (endive, radicchio, etc.) are beneficial to following crops.
- Onions often are not helped when they follow a leguminous green manure.
- Carrots, beets, and cabbages are generally detrimental to subsequent crops.

These are merely patterns, not absolutes. Still, it is necessary to start somewhere. These patterns have been discerned through research on the influence of preceding crops on subsequent crops and from my own and other farmers' experience. Since these patterns may be soil- or climate-specific, they are offered mainly to indicate the kinds of influences to which alert growers should attune their senses. Whether universal or applicable only to a specific farm, these bits of wisdom can be valuable to the farmer who learns to apply them.

One Percenters

Whereas the rotation guidelines presented earlier in this chapter qualify under the category of standard crop rotation "rules," the patterns above belong more in the category of "suggestions, hints, and refinements." The effect of any of them on improved yield, growth, and vigor may only be 1 percent, an amount that may not seem worth considering to some. What must be understood is that a biological system can be constantly adjusted by a lot of small improvements. I call them "one percenters." *The importance of these one percenters is that they are cumulative.* If the grower pays attention to enough of them, the result will be substantial *overall* improvement. And, best of all, these one percenters are free. They are no-cost gains that arise from careful, intuitive management.

One percenters may not always provide measurable results, but they have a definite influence. I have learned to pay attention and try to make use of them. Sir George Stapleton, an English grassland specialist, referred to this approach as "competent ignorance." He was always aware of how much he did not know and how much science always misses, but he did not want that to limit his ability to act. I think that attitude is wise. Rather than not acting because we can't be certain, I suggest we try instead to apply what we hope we know. The grower should try to take as many intelligent actions as possible to incrementally improve his crops and then be attentive to what happens. Given our limited knowledge about all the interrelated causes and effects operating in the biological world, this seems to be the most productive attitude.

I am presently studying ecological succession to find patterns for devising ever better crop rotation sequences. I am curious about the mechanisms of natural succession in disturbed ecosystems. I want to know the guidelines determining what follows what after fires or landslides or clearcuts and so forth. Is this just a case of the availability of sun and shade, or are there progressive changes in the soil that dictate succession and, if so, how do they proceed? Are the pioneer crops merely opportunistic, do they just add organic matter, or are there other biological, chemical, or structural modifications that improve the soil's suitability to the needs of another crop? In other words, are there patterns, and can I replicate them? Because if there are identifiable patterns, I can employ similarities in the effect of vegetable or green manure crops on the soil to create crop rotations that mimic natural laws. I suspect many of the observations made by growers over the centuries have picked up on a lot of this. But I also suspect there are endless incremental improvements to be made through further study.

A Sample Rotation

Before deciding what crops the As, Bs, and Cs of those earlier illustrations stand for, we must first collect a good deal of information. Toward that end, let's set up a sample rotation for our 5-acre vegetable farm. The following factors need to be considered:

Number of Sections.   A crop rotation works best if the rotational sections are all the same size. That goal is not always easy to achieve on the large farm, where whole fields are involved, but it should be manageable with 5 acres of vegetables. For this discussion let us assume that we will be using 5 acres of land divided into 10 half-acre sections.

Number of Years.   Just as two dozen crops don't necessarily mean a 24-year rotation, you should realize that ten sections don't have to mean a ten-year rotation. Each section can be divided into two, three, or more separate and shorter rotational cropping plans. Possibly a legume-grass pasture could be included for a number of years in rotation. Each grower makes these decisions to suit his or her own situation. For now, let's say that the ten sections will be managed as a ten-year rotation.

Number of Crops.   In the example we are working with at the moment, 24 major crops will be grown. To begin to plan where to grow each crop in the rotational sequence, we need to divide the crops, first by botanical classification.

Poaceae
Corn

Liliaceae
Onion

Chenopodiaceae
Beet
Chard
Spinach

Cucurbitaceae
Squash, winter
Squash, summer
Cucumber

Brassicaceae
Rutabaga
Kale
Broccoli
Cauliflower
Cabbage
Brussels sprouts
Radish

Fabaceae
Pea
Bean

Apiaceae
Carrot
Parsley
Celery
Parsnip

Solanaceae
Potato
Tomato
Pepper

Asteraceae
Lettuce

The reason for this division by vegetable families is based on one of the first principles of crop rotation—not growing the same crop or a closely related crop in the same spot in successive years. Our list is a good start, but more information is needed. It might help to divide up the crops according to more general gardening categories:

Root Crops
Beet
Carrot
Onion
Parsnip
Potato
Rutabaga
Radish

Legumes
Pea
Bean

Vine Crops
Squash
Cucumber

Grain Crops
Corn

Fruit Crops
Tomato
Pepper

Brassica Crops
Broccoli
Cauliflower
Cabbage
Brussels sprouts

Greens
Lettuce
Spinach
Chard
Parsley
Celery
Kale

Although this categorization mixes up the botanical divisions, it adds valuable new information. Since more than one crop will be growing in some sections, it helps to decide which crops have similar cultural requirements or which, such as greens, might need to be harvested together for a specific market.

Space for Each Crop.   The fact that 24 crops will be grown in a ten-section rotation indicates that some of the crops do not need as much growing area to meet market demand as others. And that leads to one of the most interesting of the rotation-planning puzzles: how to meet the different needs of the market and still fit all of these disparate crops into a systematic crop rotation. The best place to begin is by deciding how much space or what percentage of the total cultivated area each crop needs in order to produce the right amount for market. We can determine those space requirements by creating six different categories, from the largest space needs to the smallest. From my experience, divisions for our 24 crops would look like this:

More Space ←					→ Less Space
6	5	4	3	2	1
Corn		Potato	Tomato	Lettuce	Onion
		Pea	Cauliflower	Pepper	Beet
		Winter	Broccoli	Carrot	Chard
		squash		Summer	Parsley
				squash	Celery
				Bean	Parsnip
				Cabbage	Rutabaga
				Spinach	Kale
					Radish
					Brussels
					sprouts
					Cucumber

Now the index cards come into play. Each card will represent a section of the rotation. Write each of the names of the left-hand crops (those requiring the most space) on a separate card (or two cards, in the case of larger crops like corn). Take a pair of scissors and cut up proportional sections of other cards to represent the smaller areas needed by the right-hand crops. More than one of the smaller-space crops will occupy the same rotational section. Next, tape a number of them together in the space of one card. Whenever possible, put crops that are in the same family or require similar cultivation conditions together.

The Crop Rotation Game

At this stage, the arrangement and rearrangement of the cards is something like a board game. The rotation principles and patterns discussed earlier are the "rules." New rules are added as the grower becomes aware of them through experience, reading, and suggestions from other growers. The game begins by placing the cards on a flat surface and adjusting their positions to make up one rotational sequence or another. The aim is to determine if it is possible to grow all the crops desired on the land available and in the quantities necessary, while at the same time satisfying all the rules. The winner is the sequence that comes closest to the ideal pattern, one that optimizes as many of the beneficial aspects of a crop rotation as can be achieved with these specific crops.

So let's give it a try. The two corn crops should not be side by side. Put one in the middle of the rotation and one at the end, thus placing the corn crops as far from each other as they can be in a ten-year rotation. We know that potatoes yield best after corn, so put the potatoes in Section 4. That naturally suggests a place for the tomatoes and peppers in order to create distance between them and the related potatoes.

Since grain crops (corn) traditionally do well after legume crops (peas and beans), what if we precede the corn with the two legumes? Granted, there are the cabbage family crops sharing the bean section (and one of our patterns suggests that cabbages are negative preceding crops), but corn has been found to be the least affected by a preceding detrimental crop. Further, the corn field will likely be manured, helping to offset any negative effects.

Since beans are not affected too much by the preceding crop, let's put the often detrimental roots (carrots and beets) in front of them. Now a nuance can be considered. Onions have been shown to be a very beneficial crop before the cabbage family. We aren't growing enough onions to take advantage of that in whole sections, but they can still be effective depending upon where the crops are placed in a section. In this case we can grow the carrots and beets where they will be followed by the beans, and grow the onions, as much as possible, where they will be followed by the cabbage family. What the heck? They have to grow somewhere, so it might as well be where they have a chance of doing some good. And since those cabbage family crops are in the bean section, the other brassicas ought to be set apart from them. Section 7 would seem to be ideal.

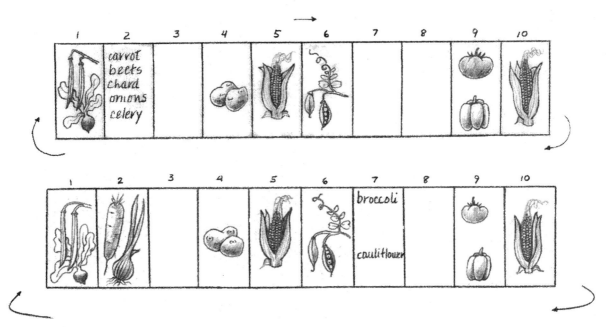

Now for the final two sections. Squash is a generally beneficial preceding crop, and it is well suited to growing with an undersown leguminous green manure (see Chapter 8). Since that green manure would be excellent before the broccoli-cauliflower section, let's put the squash card in section 8. By default, the greens go to Section 3.

Now let's see if this fits in with some of the rules we haven't considered yet. What about the crops that most benefit from manure or compost the same year it is applied? The ideal situation has those crops alternating with the others. Not bad at all.

I would suggest that the manure for the corn in section 5 could be omitted, since the pea crop will be finished early enough, even in my short season (120 frost-free days), to allow a leguminous green manure to be seeded and get well established by the end of the growing season. When tilled under the following spring, the green manure should provide more than adequate nourishment for the corn crop to follow.

If manure and compost are in short supply, some selective decisions will have to be made. It would be nice to aim for a manure application at least one year in three, but even that isn't vital. Instead, the grower has recourse to another management practice, the undersown green manures mentioned earlier. Those techniques will be discussed in the next chapter.

Multi-Year Crops

There is no problem including in the rotation those crops that need to remain in the ground for more than one year. They are assigned as many sections as the number of years they are to grow. A six-year rotation for four crops would look like this in Year 1:

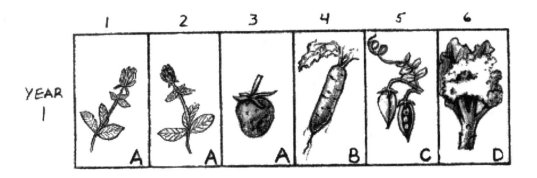

Let's say crop A is strawberries. In Year 1, only Section 3 would be planted to strawberries. The other sections could grow green manure or any other crop unrelated to B, C, or D. In Year 2, Section 4 would be planted to strawberries.

The strawberries in Section 3 are now in their second year and cropping. Section 2 can be treated again as in Year 1. Then, in Year 3, the rotation is off and running.

The strawberries in Section 3 will give a second crop this year before being turned under. The Section 4 berries are in their first year of cropping, and the Section 5 berries have just been planted.

The sequence continues in future years. If the "As" were a pasture or hay crop, the same system would prevail. One new section would be seeded each year and one old section would be tilled up and readied for the following crop. In fact this would be an excellent way to use a perennial deep-rooting legume like alfalfa or a legume-grass mixture (red clover/alsike clover/timothy, for example), to include some serious soil fertility improvement in a rotation. The perennial soil-improving crops have been found to achieve optimum benefit to soil structure and produce increased organic matter if they can be left for three years. The virtues of alfalfa and many other green manure crops are discussed in the next chapter.

Short Rotations

Not surprisingly, the reality is often not as perfect as the ideal. When there is no way to run a long rotation, you have to make the best of things. If a single crop dominates a large part of the production program, it may be necessary to repeat it every other year—or, as in the case of some greenhouse lettuce production, even twice a year. In these short-rotation situations, changes should be introduced at every opportunity. That even includes changing the variety of the crop. Any slight genetic difference should be exploited if it adds diversity to the cropping program. A succession crop sown after the main crop can help. A green manure can follow or be undersown (see Chapter 8). Mustard or rape, traditional cleansing crops for sick soil because they stimulate soil microorganisms, can be very effective so long as the dominant crop is not a fellow brassica.

In other words, aim for as great a variety of unrelated crops as possible in the span between related crops. Some growers advocate growing two consecutive crops (of, say, lettuce) followed by a longer break instead of alternating the crop with shorter breaks. I have not found that to be better, but I encourage a trial if the idea seems appealing. Other growers suggest that the more intensive the cropping, the more care must be taken to optimize all the growing conditions, especially by using extra soil-improving organic amendments like compost. I agree fully with that suggestion.

In some cases, no rotation at all is recommended. Many old-time growers insist that tomatoes do best if planted every year in the same spot. They even recommend fertilizing them with compost made from the decayed remains of their predecessors. I once grew tomatoes that way for eight years in a greenhouse. In truth, they were excellent, and they got better every year. I do not grow field tomatoes that way now and cannot really defend my decision except to say that it is more convenient when they are part of the rotation. It could be that I am just uncomfortable about breaking the rules I have found to work so well with other crops. It could also be that I am unnecessarily limiting my options. I suggest that you try growing tomatoes (or any crop, for that matter) without rotation. Nothing is as stifling to success in agriculture as inflexible adherence to someone else's rules. With a little daring and imagination whole new vistas may open up. Remember, the aim of this farming system is independence, reliability, and sustainability. Any practices and attitudes that contribute to that goal should become part of the rule book.

A Tried-and-True Rotation

The ten-year rotation we just developed was meant as a teaching exercise. It may need refining for your operation. The eight-year rotation presented below is a good one to conclude with because it is one I have followed since 1982. It has been well tested. I have thought about modifying it countless times but never have. Its virtues always seem to outweigh its defects, although that isn't to say it can't be improved. I'm sure it can. But it has been a dependable producer, and I offer it here as a tried-and-true example of a successful rotational sequence that incorporates many crop benefits.

The goal of this particular rotation was to grow 32 vegetable crops in adequate quantities to feed for a year the community of 60-some people who eat daily in the Mountain School dining hall (see page 290). Since we have found that we can feed 40 people per acre, the rotation below represents 1½ acres of land. The salad crops not included here were grown in a separate small salad garden close to the kitchen.

Potatoes follow sweet corn in this rotation because research has shown corn to be one of the preceding crops that most benefit the yield of potatoes.

Sweet Corn follows the cabbage family because, in contrast to many other crops, corn shows no yield decline when following a crop of brassicas. Secondly, the cabbage family can be undersown to a leguminous green manure which, when turned under the following spring, provides the most ideal growing conditions for sweet corn.

The Cabbage Family follows peas because the pea crop is finished and the ground cleared by August 1, allowing a vigorous winter green manure crop to be established.

Peas follow tomatoes because they need an early seedbed, and tomatoes can be undersown to a non-winter-hardy green manure crop that provides soil protection over winter with no decomposition and regrowth problems in the spring.

Tomatoes follow beans in the rotation because this places them four years away from their close cousin, the potato.

Beans follow root crops because they are not known to be subject to the detrimental effect that certain root crops such as carrots and beets may exert in the following year.

Root Crops follow squash (and potatoes) because those two are both good "cleaning" crops (they can be kept weed-free relatively easily); thus there are fewer weeds to contend with in the root crops, which are among the most difficult to keep cleanly cultivated. Also, squash has been shown to be a beneficial preceding crop for roots.

Squash is grown after potatoes in order to have the two "cleaning" crops back to back prior to the root crops, thus reducing weed problems in the root crops.

8 ❧

GREEN MANURES

NOT ALL CROPS ARE FOR SALE. GREEN MANURES ARE GROWN NOT FOR cash but to contribute to the care and feeding of the soil. A green-manure crop incorporated into the soil improves fertility, but the eventual benefits are far greater than that.

Low-Cost Returns

The most comprehensive treatise on green manuring is still the classic Green Manuring by Adrian J. Pieters (New York: John Wiley, 1927). Obviously, good basic information is never out of date.

❧

Green-manure crops help protect against erosion, retain nutrients that might otherwise be leached from the soil, suppress the germination and growth of weeds, cycle nutrients from the lower to the upper layers of the soil, and—in the case of legumes—leave to the following crop a considerable quantity of nitrogen. Other contributions of a green manure are improved soil structure, additional organic matter, enhanced drought tolerance, and increased nutrient availability for plants.*

The value of green manures has been appreciated since the earliest days of agriculture. It should hardly be necessary to extol their virtues here, yet the situation is similar to that of crop rotation. The full potential of green-manure use is still underappreciated and unexploited. Also like crop rotation, green manures represent a management benefit; they are farm-generated production aids that offer an excellent return from little effort or expense. Granted, the seeds for a green-manure crop may have to be purchased, but their inclusion in the crop rotation yields benefits far exceeding their small cost. When green manures are included in the overall soil-management program, the combination of green manures and crop rotation can result in a truly unbeatable vegetable production system.

Growing green manures has traditionally been viewed as an either/or situation. You grew either a paying crop or a green manure. If the use of green manures means replacing a cash crop, then the lack of interest in them is understandable. There are other options. But first, let's review the general benefits of green manures.

Inexpensive Nitrogen

Leguminous green manures are a most economical and inexpensive source of nitrogen. The nitrogen is produced right where it is needed—in the soil. In fact, when leguminous green manures are used effectively and levels of organic matter are maintained, any additional application of nitrogen is often unnecessary. The symbiotic process by which leguminous plants fix nitrogen from the air depends upon a number of factors for its success. First, the soil pH should ideally be between 6.5 and 6.8. Second, the proper rhyzobium bacteria for the specific legume must be present in the soil. A bacterial inoculant should be applied if there is any doubt. Inoculants for specific legumes come in both powdered and granular form and can be purchased from farm stores or seed catalogs along with seeds. Finally, a soil test for the trace elements molybdenum (Mo) and cobalt (Co), both known to be important catalysts for symbiotic nitrogen fixation, is often a worthwhile investment.

Humus

For a complete discussion of the decomposition of green manures in the soil, see Soil Microbiology *by Selman A. Waksman (New York: John Wiley, 1952).* Soil Micro-Organisms and Higher Plants *by N. A. Krasilnikov (1958), which is available from the U.S. Department of Commerce, 5285 Port Royal Road, Springfield, VA 22161, provides an amazing wealth of information about the effects of different crops on soil properties.*

Every little bit of organic matter added to the soil helps add to the all-important store of humus. Humus, the end product of organic-matter decay in the soil, is the key to good soil structure, nutrient availability, moisture supply, and the biological vitality of the soil. Some forms of residues are more long-lasting than others. Very young, sappy, green growth will stimulate a lot of activity in the soil but will not contribute much, if anything, in the way of lasting humus. Old, dry residues take longer for the soil processes to digest but are more valuable in building humus reserves. A 2- or 3-inch growth of recently sown oats or clover is an example of the former. Brown, frosted, and dried-out corn stalks would be at the other end of the scale. A lush green manure is probably better mowed and left to wilt for a day before being incorporated into the soil, to help slow down what could be a too-rapid decomposition. The tough, mature crops will decompose faster if they are chopped or shredded before they are incorporated in the soil. Most of the green-manure crops that we will be concerned with fall somewhere between these two extremes.*

Stable Nutrients

Plant nutrients can be lost from unprotected soil. During fall, winter, and early spring, when commercial crops are not in the field, the growing green-manure crops will not only hold the soil against erosion, but their roots will capture and use available plant nutrients that might otherwise be leached away. Prevention of this waste is considered to be so important on most of the small European farms I have visited that the farmers think of the harvesting operation as having two inseparable parts: first, the harvesting of the crop, and, second, the seeding of the land to a winter green manure. Seeding is done as soon as possible after harvesting.

In addition to the nitrogen nodules on the roots of legumes, green manures provide further contributions to the mineral nutrition of subsequent crops. The green-manure plants themselves, once decomposed by soil organisms, provide the most direct contribution. An indirect contribution results when the process of decomposition aids in making further nutrients available. Decaying organic matter can make available otherwise insoluble plant nutrients in the soil through the action of decomposition products such as carbon dioxide and acetic, butyric, lactic, and other organic acids. Carbon dioxide is the end product of energy used by soil microorganisms. Increasing the carbon dioxide content of the soil air as a result of the decomposition of plant residues increases the carbonic acid activity, thus speeding up the process of bringing soil minerals into solution.

Soil microorganisms are also stimulated by the readily available carbon contained in the fresh plant material, and their activity results in speeding up the production of ammonium and nitrate. Even soils naturally high in organic matter, such as peats or mucks, are improved by the incorporation of a green-manure crop, which makes them more biologically active.

Biological Subsoilers

The deep-rooting ability of many leguminous green-manure crops also makes them valuable as "biological subsoilers." Where soil compaction exists, deep-rooting green manures can bring a startling improvement in subsequent crops, solely by penetrating and shattering the subsoil with their roots. This opens up the soil, permitting the crop roots to more easily reach lower soil levels, where they find greater supplies of water and nutrients. Studies have shown a considerable improvement in drought resistance and crop yields following lupines, sweet clover, alfalfa, and other tap-rooted green manures.

Overwintered Green Manures

There are three ways in which green-manure crops can be managed: as overwinter crops, main crops, and undersown crops. Green manures can be sown for overwintering after a market crop has been harvested. For example, in the crop rotation at the end of Chapter 7, a leguminous green manure could be sown after the pea harvest which would occupy the ground until it was tilled in the following spring prior to planting cabbages. The other option would be to plant a second market crop after the peas. In many cases that might be desirable, but the benefit from a wintered-over legume that provides ideal growing conditions for next year's crop is a strong incentive for growing it.

Main-Crop Green Manures

In this case the green manure occupies ground in place of a market crop during the growing season or, even better, for up to three years. If extra land is available, this is a highly recommended practice, and, when the green-manure crop can be grazed by livestock, it serves a double purpose. If a grower prefers to put all the land into market crops, however, a choice must be made between the future benefits of the green-manure crop and the potential income from a market crop. Since this is a choice that usually goes against green manures, often at the expense of the soil, I recommend a third management option, one that allows the grower to have a leguminous green-manure crop and the cash, too: that option is known as undersowing.

Undersown Green Manures

Undersowing, also known as overseeding or companion seeding, is the practice of growing a green manure along with the market crop. When done correctly, undersowing provides the best of both worlds. It is established practice in small-grain growing. The clovers or other legumes are sown with or shortly after the wheat or oats, for example, and grow slowly in the understory until the grain crop is harvested. In vegetable growing this practice was not common, to the best of my knowledge, but since the 1980s has begun to be seriously considered.

The advantage of undersowing is that the green-manure crop is already established at harvest time. In my northern New England climate, winter rye is the only green manure that can be seeded after fall harvest. A legume cannot be established that late in the season. Since in my experience legumes are the most beneficial green manures, I try to use them whenever possible. The only way I can do that without taking land out of cash-crop production is to undersow them.

Timing Crops and Green Manures. The practice of undersowing is something like planting desirable weeds between the crop rows. In a way that is very similar to the relationship between weed competition and crop growth, the effect of the undersown plant—the deliberate weed—upon the crop plant depends upon the age of the crop. Weeds can overwhelm young crops if they both start at the same time. Weed research has shown that crops will do fine if they have an adequate head start. If most crops are kept weed-free for the first four to five weeks after establishment, later competition from low-growing weeds will have little effect on them. If we interpret that correctly, then the best crops for undersowing would be low-growing, and the best sowing date for green manures would be four to five weeks after the establishment of the crop plants, whether direct-sown or transplanted. My experience bears that out.

Where timing is important, there is a tendency to err on the safe side. Why not wait six weeks or more before undersowing the green manure just to be sure? The problem is that the balance is tipped too far in the other direction. Since the undersown "weed" is deliberate, I want to be sure it grows. If I wait too long before undersowing, the crop plants will be large enough to overwhelm the green manure. The trick is to undersow when the crop plants are well enough along not to be adversely affected by the undersowing, but not so well established as to hinder growth of the undersown green manure.

How does this timing work out in actual practice? In my cool climate, where crops such as corn, beans, squash, and late brassicas are often not planted or set out until June 1, I find the Fourth of July to be just about perfect, year in and year out, as the date for undersowing those crops. Obviously, later crops or succession crops will have their own dates. In those cases the four- to five-week delay before planting the undersown crop may be shortened if the growth rate of the crop is more rapid due to the warmer soil. Once you acquire experience you can also judge timing by the size of the crop plants. The only crop for which I can give reliable size data is corn (maize). Undersowing once the corn reaches a height of 10 to 12 inches has proven most successful for me.

Before Undersowing.   Successful undersowing requires a clean, weed-free seedbed. Sowing the green manure is no different from sowing the crop: when seeds are planted into a weedy mess they become the seeds for failure. I have often thought that another side benefit of undersowing is that it motivates the grower to pay attention to clean cultivation right from the start simply because there is one more reason to do so. Like any problem "nipped in the bud," weeds are easiest to control early in the season. The clean seedbed prepared for undersowing is a by-product of early weed control. At least three cultivations should be made prior to undersowing, the last one just a day or two beforehand.

The goal of the grower is to provide every opportunity for the undersowing to get well established without weed competition. Unless the garden has a lot of weed pressure, the canopy of the undersowing will join with the crop canopy to keep later weeds from germinating. The few that do pop through should be pulled before they go to seed. Occasional forays down the rows will keep these competitors from becoming a problem.

Seeding the Undersown Crop.   I have seeded undersown crops both by broadcasting and drilling, and I emphatically recommend drilling. If the undersown crop is broadcast in the standing market crop, there is no way to cover all the seeds to ensure their establishment and germination. In a hot, dry spell the green manure can be a total failure. When I use a cultural practice I want to be able to depend on its performance. If the undersown crop is drilled between the crop rows with either a single- or multi-row drill, the seeds are planted at the proper depth, in contact with moist soil, where they are much more certain to germinate.

The single-row drill is the same garden seeder I use for corn, carrots, and peas. It is equipped with an appropriate plate for whichever green-manure seed I am planting. The multi-row drill consists of five of these single-row seeders bolted together side-by-side, with common axles and a common push bar. That gives the tool a total width of 20 inches, which fits nicely within the 30-inch row spacings at which corn, beans, and brassicas are planted.

When using the multi-row model, all five hoppers can be filled with either the same seed or different seeds. Each hopper can be fitted with its own seed plate. Under some conditions, the grower might want to alternate rows of different legumes or legumes and grasses.

A Few Examples.   The garden is most easily visualized as a series of strips 100 feet long (let's use the 60-inch-wide strips from Chapter 6). Forty-eight inches of that width is given over to the crops and 12 inches is used as an access path. For crops such as carrots, onions, and lettuce planted in 12-inch rows, there are four rows side by side with a 12-inch spacing.

The one-row seeder can be used to drill three rows in the path. A single undersown row can be drilled between each crop row. In this case I usually sow dwarf white clover in the paths. White clover or biennial sweet clover can be used between rows of onions or carrots. The rows spaced at 18 inches are similarly undersown, with three rows in the path and one row between the crops.

For the 30-inch spacing at which corn, beans, brassicas, and so on are planted, the five-row drill is used. One pass is made down the center between each crop row. Depending on the vegetable crop, dwarf white clover, sweet clover, red clover, hairy vetch, and soybeans all work well as green manures.

In the crops spaced at 60 inches (tomatoes and melons, for example) two passes are made with the five-row drill. Dwarf white, red, and sweet clover are all good choices here.

At the widest spacing, 120 inches for pumpkins and winter squash, everything except a strip about 2 feet wide on either side of the row is drilled (four passes with the five-row drill). My favorite undersown crop for squash and pumpkins is biennial sweet clover.

Thinking It Through

Sowing dates and equipment for undersown green manures should be as well thought out as those for the cash crops. Sowing dates should be marked on the calendar. The seeds should be ordered ahead. The equipment should be quick, simple to use, and in good working order.

At the end of this chapter is an illustrated flow chart that shows what my crop rotation and undersown green manure recommendations look like when they are combined. Obviously, green manures are most effective when they are considered as an important component part of the crop-rotation planning.

There is another parallel between green manures and crop rotation that should be noted. Variety in green manures is as important as variety in the market crops. Because green-manure plants also have different faults and virtues that affect the soil and following crops in different ways, green manures should be "rotated" to include as many different varieties as possible.

In studying the undersown green-manure chart on pages 80–81, you will note that six of the eight rotational plots are undersown, a seventh is sown to legumes after early harvest, and only one—potatoes—is seeded to rye after fall harvest. The ground is never bare. The soil is always growing either a market crop or next year's fertility. For much of the summer it is growing both!

Which Green Manures?

My choices of green-manure crops for different uses are:

- With tall crops—sweet clover, vetch, red clover, or alsike clover
- For sodlike cover—dwarf white clover
- For resistance to foot traffic in picking—dwarf white clover or vetch
- Before potatoes—soybeans or sweet clover
- Under corn—soybeans, sweet clover, or red clover
- Between rows of root crops—sweet clover or dwarf white clover
- Soil protection that will winter-kill—spring oats, spring barley, or, in warmer climates, a winter legume that will complete its growth in spring and can then be mowed off
- For the latest fall planting in cold climates—rye or winter wheat

In the milder European climate, mixtures of green-manure seeds are sown after harvest to provide late fall grazing. In parts of Germany these mixes of species for a green manure are known as *Landesberger Gemenge*. A Landesberger mix commonly consists of two legumes, a grass, and a cabbage family crop. When a field of Landesberger is ready for fall grazing it looks like a tossed salad for livestock.

Sample mixtures might include:

- Oats, red clover, field peas, and mustard
- Wheat, white clover, purple vetch, and rape
- Rye, ladino clover, winter vetch, and oil radish

In order to become well established they should be sown at least six weeks before the first fall frost.

Green-Manure Review

Green-manure varieties and combinations are endless and are not limited to the ones listed here. The varieties mentioned here worked for me as I developed the biological production technologies for my particular soil and climate. Instead of talking about specifics that are so often regional, I want to emphasize principles that are more nearly universal—not only because different parts of the globe require different green manures but because there are no hard and fast rules. Although it is possible to present the broad outline of a biological system inside a book, the fine-tuning that goes on within that outline is the province of the grower. The best innovations and improvements usually come from the grower and not from any chart or list, no matter how complete it supposedly is. Whatever an expert does or does not say should not limit your options. The more involved a grower becomes in taking charge and perfecting the system proposed here, the more independent, reliable, and sustainable the system will become.

Below is a list of considerations when choosing green-manure crops:

- *Time of Seeding.* Early, late, intercrop, undersown, overwinter, year-round?
- *Establishment.* The ideal crop is easy to establish and grows rapidly.
- *Time of Incorporation into the Soil.* How mature is the green manure? I often refer to full-maturity, soil-improving crops as "brown manures" because they are higher in celluloses and lignins, which are resistant to quick decomposition and thus result in longer-lasting soil organic matter. What is the following crop—seed or transplant? Legumes turned under in the fall lose 70 percent of added nitrogen, but only 38 percent when turned under in spring. With a winter-killed green manure it may be possible to transplant the spring crop directly without incorporating the green-manure residues into the soil. The same can be done with overwintered green manures if you wait until they have matured sufficiently in the spring so they will no longer regrow after cutting.
- *Rotational Fit.* The green manure should not share susceptibility to diseases or insect damage in common with the crop plants.
- *Feed Value.* When a green manure serves as animal feed, manure is deposited on the soil, and fertility is enhanced even more.
- *Soil Microorganisms.* Rape, for example, stimulates the biological activity of the soil.* Soybeans improve scab control in potatoes.**
- *Beneficial Insects.* Some green manures can serve as nurse crops for useful insects. This is an emerging field of knowledge with much to be learned!
- *Cost.* Is the seed expensive? Can it be easily produced on the farm? Will the crop yield both seed and feed? Will a less costly seed be as effective if it is managed properly?

*Selman A. Waksman, Soil Microbiology, (New York: John Wiley 1952), p. 256.

❧

**A.R. Weinhold, et al, "Influence of green manures and crop rotation on common scab of potato." American Potato Journal 41:9 (1964), pp. 265–73.

Undersowing Legumes

Considerations when choosing an undersown legume include:

- Shade tolerance
- Ability to grow with the crop
- Effects, including competition, on this year's crop
- Beneficial effects on next year's crop
- Erosion control
- Winter hardiness (In some situations a legume that winter-kills is preferable, to avoid having a vigorous residue in the way of an early spring sowing.)
- Weed control (Rapid growth and broad leaves are a plus.)

Green Manures in Rotation

Undersown green manures can be used extensively within the eight-year crop rotation discussed at the end of the previous chapter. The following sequence has worked out very well in practice. The illustrated flow chart on pages 80–81 shows how all the pieces can fit together.

Potatoes cannot be undersown easily if the cultivation method used is hilling. I have grown potatoes without hilling by planting at a depth of 6 inches and filling the furrow partly at first, then completely after the potatoes emerge. Vetch can then be planted as an undersown legume. If the green manure is to be established following the potato harvest, winter rye is probably the best choice as a green manure.

Sweet Corn is undersown to soybeans because research shows a soybean crop almost totally inhibits potato-scab organisms in the soil. The soybeans also grow well in the understory of the corn and provide excellent weed suppression.

The Cabbage Family is undersown to sweet clover, which is one of the best leguminous green manures to turn under for next year's corn crop. It grows well under the cabbage family because it is a tap-rooted crop that does not seem to interfere with the more shallowly rooted brassicas.

Peas are not undersown but are followed by a mix of clovers as soon as the peas can be cleared. This combination of legumes grows until it is turned under the following spring, by which time enough nitrogen has been fixed to ensure a splendid crop of brassicas.

Tomatoes are undersown to oats or some other non–winter-hardy grass crop. Certain grasses have been found to be excellent preceding crops for legumes such as peas, since they produce an allopathic effect that suppresses grasses and other weeds, but not legumes. It is important to choose a non–winter-hardy cultivar so there will not be a mass of fresh green growth in the spring to impede early soil preparation and planting of the pea crop.

Beans are undersown to winter vetch. It is a dependable preceding green-manure crop for tomatoes.

Root Crops are undersown to dwarf white clover (both in the paths and between the rows) because it will grow in the crop understory and because it provides good erosion protection for the soil over winter.

Squash is undersown to sweet clover in the empty strips between the squash rows. Beets, carrots, and other root crops grow very well following sweet clover. The onion crop, on the other hand, grows best with no preceding green manure, so plant onions in the strips that were occupied by the squash plants themselves.

The flow chart is an attempt to show visually the combination of crop rotation and undersown green manures in an eight-plot rotation over three years. The rotational sequence has the crops in Plot 1 moving to Plot 2, the Plot 2 crops to Plot 3, the Plot 8 crops to Plot 1, and so forth. If you look across the top half of the Plot 1 strip you can see over the three years how the beans are followed by tomatoes and the tomatoes by peas. If you look across the bottom half of the Plot 1 strip you will see the undersown legumes that are tilled under prior to the seeding or transplanting of the crop and then undersown in the crop at the appropriate time. They remain through the winter until they are turned in the following year before the next crop.

Continuing to use Plot 1 as an example, notice that, in addition to producing three crops (one crop per year over 36 months) here in my cool climate, that plot has also spent 26½ of those months covered with an undersown green manure. In milder climates two factors will change. The plot may be double-cropped (two crops in one season) and/or the list of potential green manure crops will be greatly expanded, as will the winter period during which the weather is mild enough for continued green manure growth.

A discussion of the possibilities of basing the entire soil fertility program on farm-generated inputs such as composts, crop rotations, and green manures—no matter what your climate—is presented in Chapter 11.

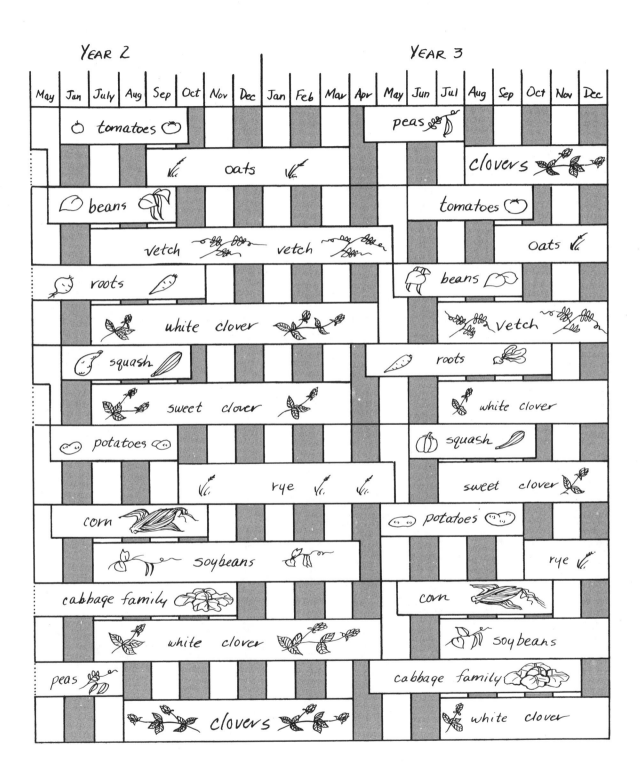

9 🜨 TILLAGE

Tillage is the general term for soil preparation in agriculture. It includes working the soil; incorporating lime, fertilizers, and manures; turning under green manures and crop residues; and any other mechanical processes involved in preparing the land for raising crops. The traditional implements are the plow, the disc, the harrow, and occasionally the subsoiler. Plowing with a moldboard plow is the method popularly associated with farming. In the process of plowing, the soil layers are turned over, either wholly or partially, depending on the adjustment of the plow. Since this operation alone does not produce a suitable planting surface or sufficient mixing action to fully incorporate fertilizers or organic materials, supplementary operations are necessary.

A tractor pulling a 5-shank chisel plow.

In order to come closer to the ideal of tillage, plowing is commonly followed by discing and harrowing. The idea is to loosen the soil; incorporate air, organic matter, and fertilizers; and remove weeds in order to prepare a clean seedbed. As a result of tillage, the air, moisture, temperature, chemical, and biological levels of the soil are modified. The intent is to optimize their effects on the growth and development of the crops.

Tillage operations are divided into those that work the soil deeply and those that work it shallowly. Deep tillage can go down as much as 2 feet. Shallow tillage disturbs no more than the top 6 inches of the soil, and preferably only the top 3 to 4 inches.

Deep Tillage

More and more scientific studies are pointing to subsurface soil compaction from plow pans and wheel traffic as a serious problem in crop production. The subsoiler is the original tool for deep-soil tillage, which ideally loosens the lower soil layers and breaks up hardpans and compaction layers without inverting the soil or mixing the subsoil with the topsoil. In addition, deep tillage can aerate the soil to a considerable depth—improving drainage, increasing rooting depth, making soil nutrients more accessible for the roots, and initiating a process of topsoil deepening, which greatly increases the fertility of the soil.

The Chisel Plow

For our purposes the chisel plow is more effective than the subsoiler. The chisel plow dates from the 1930s, when it was conceived as a soil-conserving alternative to the moldboard plow. The chisel plow consists of a strong metal frame bearing a series of curved, soil-penetrating shanks (chisels) about 2 inches wide and 24 inches long that can be fitted with different tips. When pulled through the ground, the chisels penetrate to depths of up to 16 inches, but they do not turn over the layers like a moldboard plow. Rather, they simply lift and loosen the soil and break up hardpan and compacted soil.

This is not a small-scale implement. Using it once a year for deep tillage involves renting a tractor or hiring an operator. The latter is the simplest and most economical way to go if you live in an area where the services and equipment are available. If not, the solution might be for a group of growers to collectively purchase a small chisel plow and hire a tractor to pull it. If rocky land is involved, the tractor should have a front-end loader to help in collecting and removing rocks.

Many growers believe a chisel plow is suitable only for rock-free soil. In my experience that is not the case. I have used a chisel plow on both stone-free land in Texas and fairly rocky land in Maine, Massachusetts, and Vermont. It performed well in both cases. In fact as a tool for preparing New England soil for vegetable growing it is invaluable. The chisel plow finds rocks and brings them to the surface. You can then remove the rocks by rolling them into the tractor bucket on the next pass.

There is no need to despair if you find it isn't possible to get a chisel plow. There are other options. The hand tool (broadfork) suggested below and certain biological techniques will also do the job. The more attention you pay to improving pH, drainage, and organic matter while minimizing compaction, the less you'll need mechanical deep tillage. I do, however, recommend the chisel plow as an extremely valuable tool in the *initial years of creating a fertile soil* for vegetable growing.

After the first few years, though, you should be able to gain the same tillage effect with the roots of green manures. Deep-rooting green manure crops (alfalfa, sweet clover, lupines, soybeans, and red clover) are very effective at improving conditions in the subsoil. The deep rooting not only improves the soil physically by loosening it but also increases its fertility by bringing up more nutrients from the lower strata. The root channels remain long after the green manure has decomposed. They measurably help improve the soil's porosity and water-holding properties as well as preventing future hardpan formation.

The Broadfork

This two-handled deep tillage tool is known by different names, but *broadfork* comes as close to describing it as any other. Like most agricultural tools its genesis surely dates far back in agricultural history. It consists of a 2-foot-wide spading fork with a 5-foot-long handle at either side of the fork. The teeth on the fork are spaced 4 inches apart and are about 12 inches long.

I first encountered this tool in the 1960s as the "Grelinette," after a farmer from France named Grelin. During the 1970s copies of the Grelinette began to appear in altered designs. As is often the case when a farmer builds a tool that is then redesigned by an engineer, Grelin's original design is far superior to the copies. Certain important nuances of Grelin's design are missing from the modern knockoffs, because they can be appreciated only through constant use and are not apparent on the drawing board. The copies, which are often fabricated entirely of metal to make them stronger, have a number of flaws.

First, the all-metal construction makes the tool too heavy. Granted, one can occasionally break a wooden handle; however, I much prefer working with a pleasant tool and being inconvenienced occasionally by a broken handle rather than working with a cumbersome tool all the time. A second mistake in the copies is the use of straight tines attached to the bottom of the cross bar. In the original Grelinette the tines are designed with a parabolic shape and curve down from an attachment point at the back of the crossbar. This difference is the key. The parabolic curve of Grelin's original design works with an easy, rolling motion. As the handles are pulled down, the tines curve under and lift the soil easily. With straight tines, a prying rather than a rolling motion is used, and you must muscle the soil upward using brute force.

Using the Broadfork

The broadfork is held with the handles tilted slightly forward of vertical. It is pressed into the soil as far as possible by stepping on the crossbar, then the two handles are pulled back toward the operator in an easy rocking motion. The broadfork is then lifted from the loosened soil, the operator steps backwards 6 inches, and the maneuver is repeated (see illustration). The tool is comfortable to use and makes the work pleasant.

How large an area can be managed with a broadfork? It is certainly scaled for use in commercial greenhouse vegetable production. I have used it outdoors on areas up to 1 acre without feeling too much strain. The work can also be divided into sections and done only as needed prior to planting different crops. Anyway, there is no need to do every square foot. Just going down the row for widely spaced crops such as winter squash is sufficient. If the broadfork is used selectively during the planting season, even a 2-acre garden is not unreasonably large for this tool. Some crops respond more than others. Sweet corn, root vegetables, and crops with extensive root systems such as tomatoes are greatly benefited by deep tilling.

The broadfork should be used prior to surface tillage, and preferably during the previous fall for sections of the rotation where the earliest crops will be planted. As with any tool it should be used with the eyes open: if there appears to be no difference in crop response, or a difference is apparent only on certain crops, then adjust when, how much, or how often you use the broadfork.

Deep Tillage

The advantages of deep tillage are:

An excellent bibliography is the "Annotated Bibliography on Soil Compaction" available from the American Society of Agricultural Engineers, 2950 Niles Road, Saint Joseph, MI 49085–9659.

- Breaks up soil compaction.*
- Provides soil aeration.
- Aids the soil structure.
- Improves drainage.
- Extends crop-rooting depth.
- Increases the range of soil nutrients available to plant roots.
- Helps deepen the topsoil, which greatly increases soil fertility.

The disadvantages of deep tillage are:

- Custom operators with chisel plow equipment may be hard to locate.
- A group of local growers may not exist to purchase a chisel plow collectively.
- In some soils the broadfork may be impractical on far less than 2 acres.

Solutions:

- The rotary tiller can be used as deeply as possible as long as not too much subsoil is brought to the surface.
- When deep rotary tilling, you must be sure to mix extra organic matter with the soil to encourage an improved soil structure.
- Establishing the ideal biological soil conditions that favor bacteria and earthworms will improve soil structure and depth over time. Important practices include crop rotations, green manures, addition of organic matter, pH between 6 and 7, and adequate mineral nutrients.

Shallow Tillage

Shallow tillage is the preparation of the top few inches of soil. For many years I have used a rotary tiller for shallow tillage. It has many advantages over the traditional plow, disc, and harrow. First, it does the work of all three conventional implements in one operation. Second, it does the work at a speed that makes it considerably more efficient overall. And third, it does the job better.

The Rotary Tiller

In rotary tillage the soil is prepared by means of specially shaped soil-working blades (tines) which are rotated by a powered axle. A rotary tiller mixes and incorporates fertilizers, plant residues, and organic amendments (manures and composts) uniformly throughout the tillage depth and leaves them in contact with the greatest number of soil particles. This thorough mixing distributes organic materials and assures the availability of minimally processed fertilizers.

The low-solubility mineral fertilizers I recommend in this book work best when they are mixed well throughout the soil rather than banded or layered. They then have the greatest contact with the soil acids and microbiological processes that make the soil nutrients available for use by plants.

The rotary tiller most easily incorporates manures, composts, and other soil amendments when they are spread on the surface of the soil before tilling. The relative density between the soil and the amendments affects how thoroughly the mixing can be accomplished. Mineral fertilizers, which tend to have the same density as soil particles, can be mixed in most uniformly. When organic materials are mixed in, the lighter stuff tends to remain higher in the soil profile while the heavier material goes in more deeply. The ability of the rotary tiller to mix both organic and mineral amendments uniformly throughout the soil profile is an important feature of this tool. It increases the fertility and biological activity of the soil that is so necessary to the establishment of a viable biological system.

There is evidence that the rotary tiller—or, for that matter, any soil-tillage equipment—can be detrimental if it is overused. The effect of rotary tilling on the soil is like using a bellows on a fire: it speeds up the combustion process. Extra aeration of the soil hastens the decomposition of organic matter, which can be good or bad depending on when it is done.

Spring tilling can have a beneficial effect. Early in the season the soil is cool and may well profit from tilling to help warm it up. Later in the season, most of the soil will be undersown to green manures. When there is an early green manure, or when there are residues of a preceding crop to till under before a late crop, the extra air and thorough mixing will help decompose the residues faster and make the soil ready for planting of the following crop sooner.

Alternatives

The Europeans have used alternatives to rotary tillers for a number of years. My commercial-vegetable–growing colleagues across Europe have universally replaced their rotary tillers with spaders—either rotary spaders or reciprocating spaders. These machines share the rotary tiller's ability to mix material throughout the soil profile while avoiding its often criticized tendency to beat up and overwork the soil.

The *rotary spader* looks something like a large diameter rotary tiller but with spade-shaped blades on the end of long, curved arms. The spades move in a circumference three to four times greater than that of a rotary tiller. The spades also move more slowly through the soil than tiller tines and duplicate reasonably the soil mixing action of a gardener using a spade.

Even more similar to hand-spading is the action of a *reciprocating spader*. The spades move up and down and then push backwards by virtue of a camlike action which transfers the power of the engine to the spades. This action stirs and mixes the soil about as gently as can be done with a mechanical device. Both the rotary and reciprocating spaders move forward over the ground at a slower operating speed than rotary tillers. Consequently the area that can be covered per hour of work is not as great. Nevertheless, all the growers I have contacted who use spaders agree the quality of soil preparation is sufficiently superior to more than make up for the increased time required.

The main difference between rotary and reciprocating spaders is that the former is superior for turning under a heavy green manure directly, or when you wish to work the soil deeply. Some of the larger tractor-mounted rotary spader models advertise their ability to work the soil to a depth of 16 inches. Whether such deep-soil working is less detrimental with this tool or under certain cropping conditions, I cannot say. But my instincts lead me to be cautious. On a shallow soil, such as the one with which I started, any soil turning that went below 6 inches would likely bring up subsoil.

On the other hand, the reciprocating spader is acknowledged to be more gentle to the soil because its action more closely copies that of a gardener using a spade. It is the tool of choice in greenhouses and in cultures where heavy green manures are mowed before being incorporated into the soil. It might be at a disadvantage where large quantities of semi-decomposed crop residues are a major part of the soil fertility program. The power sources for the greenhouse models are often modified so the engine runs on propane, since this fuel creates less air pollution in the greenhouse than gasoline or diesel.

Because of its method of action the reciprocating spader does not create a "plow pan," nor does it compact the soil underneath the wheels. It also deals with a stony soil, even the occasional large stone, much better than does the rotary spader. Most of the articles I have read from European sources agree that the reciprocating spader is the all-around better choice. Growers like its beneficial effect on the soil; it increases root growth as well as improving water infiltration. The reciprocating spader also works organic matter into the top layers of the soil most effectively.

Another tool which incorporates organic matter even more gently and shallowly, by working horizontally rather than vertically, is the *rotary power harrow*. It is similar to having a number of small spiketooth harrows that rotate on a vertical axis. The power harrow mixes the surface soil like your hand would if you put your fingers in a circular pattern, stuck the tips of them shallowly into the soil, and turned your forearm. Although not suitable for primary cultivation (turning under sod or green manures) the rotary harrow incorporates any crumbly amendment like compost to a shallow depth very effectively. A power harrow is usually paired with a crumbler roller to maintain working depth and give a finished surface.

When the time comes to replace my present rotary tiller I expect I will choose a reciprocating spader. Although I have not used a spader or a rotary harrow on my land, I have seen their effect on the soil on other farms, and my farmer's eye approves. Companies in the U.S. sell spaders and power harrows for both walking tractors and four-wheel tractors. They are a more expensive option, averaging over twice the price of a rotary tiller. Addresses are given in the appendix.

The Walking Tractor

A walking tractor is a two-wheeled power source. The rotary tiller in this system is powered by a 12-horsepower walking tractor. The tiller width should be 26 inches if you intend to use it for inter-row cultivation of the crops planted on 30-inch rows in the 60-inch strip system (see page 41). A tool width of 30 inches is preferable for preparing the 30-inch-wide growing area in the 42-inch strip system (see page 41). This equipment will give you enough power to do an excellent tilling job under almost all conditions. The walking tractor also has the flexibility to be equipped with a wide range of other implements such as seeders, rollers, mowers, hillers, pumps, and harvesters if the farm operation requires them. All of these attachments are available from the walking tractor manufacturer, but very often a grower can adapt the necessary implements from other sources. A walking tractor is my choice for the power unit in this small-scale operation for a few reasons: It is less expensive than a four-wheel tractor; it is smaller and easier to work with when modifications or repairs are needed; and it is much easier to learn to operate. The walking tractor has long been the small farmer's best power source.

Of course life might seem easier sitting on top of a powerful four-wheel tractor equipped with large equipment. But the economics would not be the same. A well-built 12-horsepower walking tractor with a 26- to 32-inch-wide tiller can be purchased for a price that would purchase little more than the tiller for a large tractor. This same walking tractor/tiller also serves as the cultivator for the crops planted on 30-inch row spacing.

Obviously, if the farm already owns a four-wheel tractor and tiller, then by all means use it. The walking tractor is not *better* than a riding tractor, but it is perfectly adequate for the tasks you'll need it for. It is also more affordable, nicely scaled, and less expensive to maintain.

Advantages of a Walking Tractor/Tiller

Economics: The initial cost is less than a four-wheel tractor, as are the operating costs.

Performance: Top-of-the-line models till as well as or better than many tractor-mounted tillers (except in old sod).

Flexibility: A walking tractor is basically a power source on wheels and it is adaptable to many needs. It does the wide-row cultivation and hilling. Implements such as a water pump or a rotary mower can be run off the same unit, but I leave my machine set up just for tilling.

Simplicity: It is much easier to operate than a full-sized tractor, which means inexperienced helpers can quickly learn to use it, too.

Maintenance: It is less overwhelming and complicated than a full-sized tractor when repairs are needed. With its approachable scale, you will soon feel confident about making home repairs.

Lighter Weight: It creates minimal soil compaction and leaves no deep wheel ruts.

Smaller Size: It is far more maneuverable and less headland is required to turn it at the ends of the rows.

Tillage: The Future

Now that I've presented my best options for deep and shallow tillage, what about the possibility of reducing tillage, or eliminating it altogether? I think the idea is worth serious consideration. But it has to be done in a way that is more efficient rather than more complicated for the grower or it won't happen. I am not necessarily opposed to tillage. Where the results favor it, I continue to use it. But I am always on the lookout for any crop-specific benefits (yield, plant health) that might result from other techniques. Since 1984 I have used a non-tillage (or, more accurately, a *surface cultivation**) system in my permanent greenhouses, and I believe it produces superior results. Instead of digging, tilling, or using other conventional soil preparation methods, we shallowly hoe the soil clear of weeds and crop residues and add a new layer of compost to the surface prior to planting the next crop. The encouraging result is that the soil structure continues to improve.

The book that first inspired me to think in terms of surface cultivation was Intensive Gardening *by Dalziel O'Brien (London: Faber, 1956). It is also a first-class work on the subjects of small-scale growing, compost, soil fertility, and labor management.*

I am obviously interested in whether non-tillage can work in the field on the scale of a commercial market garden where, as in this system, extensive use is being made of green manures. I continue to experiment. While the general concept is workable, it's the specifics that need refining. Whether the answer lies in mowing the residues and leaving them as mulch, using specially designed culti-vators to clean the surface, or in growing winter-killed green manures that are easily brushed aside in the spring, will depend on soil type, climate, and crops to be grown.

I am always impressed when I remove a straw mulch that has been down for a few months. The improved soil structure from the extra earthworm activity emphasizes how effective nature can be when I don't interfere.

A 1945 issue of *The Land*, a journal published by the Friends of the Land in the 1940s and '50s, reports on research in progress at the South Carolina Agri-cultural Experiment Station involving no-till green manures.* Corn was planted into narrow furrows in clover sod. When the corn was 12 inches high, the clover was killed by cutting it just below the surface with special sweep cultivators. The clover was then left in place as a mulch.

*J. N. Collins, "Hoeman's Folly," The Land, vol. 4, no. 4 (1945), p. 445.

**Aref Abdul-Baki and John Teasdale, Sustain-able Production of Fresh-Market Tomatoes with Organic Mulches, USDA Agricultural Research Service Farmers Bulletin FB–2279 (1994).

***Anonymous, "Good Crops and an End to Soil Damage," Ecos, 69 (Spring 1991), pp. 1–6.

Many related investigations have been done recently. USDA research in the northeastern U.S. uses overwintered hairy vetch as both a cover crop and a mulch. The vetch is mowed with a flail mower late enough in the spring so it won't regrow. The residues are left as a surface mulch for transplanted crops.** The eventual improvement in soil fertility from a surface-mulched green ma-nure is the same as if it were tilled into the soil, plus it offers the additional benefit of retaining moisture while it is being used as a mulch.

Two Australian researchers have devised a no-till green-manure fertility pro-gram they call "Clever Clover."*** Using separate fields for summer and winter production, they rotate both the vegetables (summer and winter crops) and the mulch varieties (subterranean clover and alfalfa). On one field the residues of subterranean clover, which grows during winter and dies out in the spring, serve as a summer mulch for transplanted crops. In the fall, depending on the variety, the clover can either be reseeded or will reseed itself to grow next year's mulch. The alfalfa, on another field, is mown every six weeks in summer. In autumn it becomes dormant, and winter vegetable crops are transplanted through the al-falfa residues. Come spring, the alfalfa begins growing again.

It is important to establish a vigorous cover crop so that weeds will be smoth-ered. In all of these trials, plant diseases and pests were significantly reduced by the surface mulch technique.

Just because I have been successful over the years in creating fertile soils with the mechanical tillage systems described in this chapter, I am not complacent. A better technique is always out there waiting to be found. My preference for biology over technology makes me hopeful that the new technique will involve replacing mechanical solutions with biological solutions, in order to mimic the healthy, natural structure of undisturbed soil.

10 ❧

SOIL FERTILITY

The main problem of permanent fertility is simple. It consists, in a word, in making sure that every essential element of plant food is continuously provided to meet the needs of maximum crops; and of course any elements which are not so provided by nature must be provided by man.

—*Cyril Hopkins*

I LEARNED MY FIRST IMPORTANT LESSON IN SOIL FERTILITY FROM THE United States Department of Agriculture, albeit by default on their part. It happened in 1966 when I began growing vegetables on rented land in New Hampshire. Since I had limited farming experience at that time, I eagerly read everything I could find on the subject. The USDA, in an article about fertilizer nutrients in agricultural production, stated unequivocally that nitrogen was nitrogen and phosphorus was phosphorus. They said that it did not make any difference to the plant where the nutrient came from. Nitrogen from manure and nitrogen from a bag of store-bought fertilizer were the same. To me, that was welcome news indeed.

Bring on the Free Manure

I was not aware at the time that the reason for these pronouncements was to discredit the organic farmers who claimed that manure or compost produced superior plants. In my naiveté, what I saw was a chance to save some money. I would not have to buy fertilizers! Just down the road was a horse farm with huge piles of rotted manure that the farmer was *giving* away, even delivering free to anyone who wanted it. Chicken manure, which the article said was high in phosphorus, was available from another neighbor. I figured that if the USDA experts said there was no difference between the elements in manure and those in store-bought fertilizer, that was good enough for me. I went with the manure and started a couple of acres of vegetables with what I assumed was the assurance of the USDA that everything would work out just fine.

And work out fine it did. During the three years I farmed that place, I had the best vegetables anywhere around. Not only that, but they got better every year. In fact, the old-timers were coming and asking the new kid how he did it rather than the other way around. Obviously, soil fertility was a function of a number of factors, and they did not have to be chemically processed or cost a lot of money to work.

When I did need to purchase nutrients, I continued to take the USDA at their word that elements were elements. I purchased unprocessed minerals such as rock phosphate. In the long run they were less expensive. Since they weren't water-soluble and subject to leaching, enough could be applied at one time to last a number of years. The lesson: food for plants does not need to be prearranged in a factory. Nutrient availability is a result of biological and chemical soil processes that are stimulated by the agricultural practices I learned to use and trust—crop rotations, green manures, and animal manures. This biological system comes full circle. Each practice aids another, and the result is synergistic.

Building the Soil

To build a fertile soil, five amendments should be supplied as raw materials.

Organic Matter: Compost or manure applied at the rate of 20 tons per acre every other year.

Rock Phosphate: A finely ground, natural rock powder applied every four years (quadrennially).* There are two forms—hard rock phosphate, containing 33 percent P_2O_5, and colloidal phosphate containing 22 percent P_2O_5. I prefer the colloidal form, but other growers will make an equal case for the hard rock.

Greensand Marl (Glauconite): An ancient seabed deposit containing some potassium, but principally included as a broad-spectrum source of micronutrients. Applied quadrennially. Dried seaweed is another popular (although more expensive) source of potassium and micronutrients. It breaks down more rapidly and has the additional benefit of stimulating biological activity in many soils.

Limestone Rock: A ground rock containing calcium and magnesium that is used to raise the soil pH. Sufficient lime should be applied to keep the pH within the range of 6.2 to 6.8.

Specific Micronutrients: Elements such as zinc, copper, cobalt, boron, and molybdenum are needed in very small quantities but are absolutely essential for a fertile soil. They will usually be adequately supplied if the grower has paid attention to pH and organic matter. The need for supplemental appli-

*Powdered or pelleted soil amendments need to be spread evenly. At one time or another, I have used the following methods: (1) Mix them together with the compost or manure and spread, or (2) spread with a metered spreader, such as the Gandy, which can be adjusted for accurate coverage. I recommend the latter. A 4-foot-wide Gandy spreader is easy to pull or tow with the walking tractor and allows for accurate spreading at almost any rate.

For very light applications of trace elements, use a hand-cranked, chest-mounted seeder filled with the soil amendment rather than seed.

See Appendix 4 for the source of Gandy spreaders.

cation of micronutrients is best gauged through careful soil testing and grower observation. In many cases boron is the one element most likely to need amending. Obviously, if a soil test indicates that one of these micronutrients is already well supplied, that supplement will not be needed.

Two Ways to Fertilize

Although this is a chapter on soil fertility, I am first going to discuss philosophy. That may be unconventional, but it is crucial to an understanding of the supplements recommended above. There are two basic philosophical approaches to fertilization:

- *Feed the Plant Directly.* This involves using soluble fertilizers so the nutrients are "predigested" for plant use without the need for the natural soil processes.
- *Feed the Soil and Let Soil Processes Provide for the Plant.* This involves creating and maintaining the optimal conditions of a fertile soil, under which a healthy soil-plant economy can exist.

In the first case, the farmer provides plant food in a "predigested" form because the soil processes are considered inadequate. A symptom—poor plant growth—is treated by using a temporary solution—soluble plant food. In the second case the farmer makes sure that the soil processes have the raw materials needed, not only to be adequate, but exceptional. The cause of poor plant growth—lack of sufficient plant food in the soil—is corrected by providing the soil with the raw materials needed to produce that plant food.

Natural Processes

Although we are dealing with agricultural techniques, we can't ignore the patterns of thinking that lead toward choosing one agricultural technology over another. These thought patterns stem from different points of view about the "natural system" that governs plant growth. Some questions:

- Are natural processes so inefficient that we can do better by taking over their roles, even though the energy cost of such a choice is high? Or can natural processes provide all that we need if we work to enhance them?
- Is it wise to rely on a crop-production system that is totally dependent on purchased materials involving great cost, supply networks, and safety considerations over which the farmer has no control? Or is it preferable to create a

farm-generated system that relies on minimal quantities of off-farm products and maximum enhancement of the soil's inherent fertility?

- Is it acceptable to add only enough nutrients to "get a crop"? Or is it more worthwhile to try and provide all the known and unknown nutrients and growing conditions to allow the plants to grow at their optimum?

I have encountered many responses to these questions. There are always some growers who say, "Natural processes and growing optimum be damned. I just want to grow the crop with the least possible effort and deal with any problems later." Unfortunately, later problems, when they occur, are not limited to low yields, but involve insects, diseases, and poor crop quality. Other "purchased products" (pesticides, fungicides) are then used to deal with the new problems. Since agricultural systems are interconnected, one action leads to another and one problem begets a subsequent problem.

My own position on these issues is that I simply do not know enough to tamper with the natural system, and I have no desire to do so. I am an admirer of the intricate cyclical systems of the natural world, and I prefer to study them in order to make *less* work for myself, not more. Even if I thought I knew everything, I would rather let it be done for me by the real experts. The real experts in this case are all the processes that take place in a fertile soil—the interrelated activities of bacteria, fungi, dilute soil acids, chemical reactions, rhizosphere effects, and countless others we are unaware of.

My attitude toward the natural world is one of respect for a marvelously efficient system. If I attempt to feed the plant directly, I am in effect deciding that I can do a better job. On an infertile soil, where the system is working poorly, maybe I can. But on a fertile soil the system can do a better job on its own. Therefore, my responsibility as a farmer is to add to the system the ingredients necessary to support a fertile soil. Those basic raw materials are organic matter and minerals in the form of powdered rock. So don't buy finished products. Buy the few raw materials that cannot be farm-produced, and let the soil processes finish the job. Not only does that policy make good sense agronomically, it is also the most successful, most practical, and most economical approach.

How It All Works

Let's say we start with an infertile soil. If we take the off-farm approach and add soluble fertilizers, a good crop can usually be grown. The soil serves merely as an anchor for plant roots, and the majority of the food for plant growth is provided by the fertilizer. The soil remains infertile, however, and the fertilizer application will have to be repeated for every crop. The situation is similar to helping a student by providing the answers to the test. The result may be a good grade, but the help will have to be given every time.

If, on the other hand, the second approach is chosen, we try to create a fertile soil by adding those ingredients that distinguish a fertile from an infertile soil. The fertile soil will then do what fertile soils do naturally—grow exceptional crops. To continue our student-teacher metaphor, this second process is like providing the student with the raw materials of knowledge (good books and study habits) so the student can develop the ability to excel on exams without help. I think most readers will agree that this second approach is the preferable choice in education. It is also the best choice for plant nutrition.

Feeding the Soil

The things that turn an infertile soil into a fertile soil are minerals and organic matter. If these are provided, the soil can excel on its own merits. Instead of a temporary crutch that must be provided time after time, a process is established that becomes self-sustaining. A fertile soil, like an educated mind, is a cumulative process, and with care it is capable of continuous improvement.

There are two sources of nutrients for the soil: the remains of previously living organisms that make up the organic matter, or humus, and the finely ground rock particles that constitute the mineral portion of the soil. Nutrients from both sources are made available through the biological and chemical actions that take place in the soil.

Organic Matter

For best quality and best growth, vegetables require the richest soils of all farm crops. And that richness has to be real. Not stimulants, but what British farmers so aptly call "a soil in good heart." Organic matter is the key to "heart" in a soil. The best book I ever read on farming was not technically about farming. *Soil Microbiology*, Selman Waksman's classic text, dealt with the life in the soil (see the Bibliography). That book influenced my approach to soil fertility more than any other source. Waksman wrote from the point of view of one who had studied all the different life processes in the soil and how they affect nutrient availability and plant growth. His information opened my eyes to the marvelous world of living organisms under our feet and to the importance of organic matter for the well-being of that world. The quantity and quality of organic matter is the foundation for the microbiological life in the soil. This microbiological life grows and decays, solubilizes minerals, and liberates carbon dioxide as part of its life processes.

Organic matter also opens up heavy soils to make them more easily workable and binds a sandy soil so that it holds water better. In short, the organic matter portion of the soil is more than simply a source of plant food and physical stability. It is also the power supply, so to speak. Organic matter is the engine that drives all the biological (and some of the chemical) processes in the soil.

Although raw organic materials such as crop residues can be added directly to the soil, it is often better to compost them in a heap. Sheet composting in the soil involves biological processes that preclude crop growth for a period averaging two to four weeks or more, depending on how resistant to decay the material is. In an intensive vegetable-growing system that "soil time" would be better spent growing the next crop. For example, where early peas are to be followed by a succession planting, I will remove the pea vines to a compost heap rather than turning them under. The next crop can then be planted or transplanted immediately.

Compost

I have the highest regard for composted organic matter as a long-term soil builder. The crumbly, dark, sweet-smelling product from a heap of assorted plant residues mixed with straw is the finest compost of all. Well-made compost has been shown to have plant-growing benefits far in excess of its simple "nutrient analysis" and to be an active factor in suppressing plant diseases and increasing plant resistance to pests. Producing quality compost is the most important job on the organic farm. A lot of the problems I see on farms I visit could be solved by making better compost.

On the small scale I recommend making heaps inside straw-bale enclosures (constructed by laying up straw bales like bricks, two or three bales high, as walls to contain the heap). I make the interior dimensions 5 feet wide and as long as I need to. This insulation keeps the compostables moist and warm right to the edge while still letting in adequate air. For more air, leave spaces between the ends of the bales. The bales usually hold together for two years (if baled with wire or plastic twine), and the straw then becomes an ingredient in future heaps. I alternate 2- to 3-inch layers of straw with 1- to 6-inch layers of green ingredients—thinner for moist ingredients that might mat (e.g., young grass or clover mowings, packing-shed wastes), thicker for loose, open materials, (e.g., pea vines, tomato plants). I sprinkle a thin layer of topsoil over the green layer. If I'm adding montmorillionite clay (see page 115) I sprinkle it on the straw layer. Since the ingredients are enclosed by the bale walls they decompose right up to the edge and no turning is necessary. The heap is ready after a year and a half. This system makes consistently high-quality compost.

Large quantities of organic matter should be formed into windrows for composting. These windrows are 6 to 8 feet wide, 4 feet high, and can be any length. The top should be flat or slightly sloped. A shady spot is best to avoid the drying effect of the sun. For best composting, the ingredients must be moist but not wet. A hose sprinkler can be laid across the top to add moisture in dry weather. These windrows can be turned with the bucket loader on a tractor or loaded into a stationary manure spreader and flung out for a well-aerated turning. I always cover the heaps to keep the sun from drying them and the rain from leaching them. I use landscape fabric as a covering material because it is opaque to light but lets both air and moisture permeate.

Composted animal manure has long been one of the staples for soil improvement in vegetable growing. Manure can either be produced on the farm or purchased in truckloads from neighboring farms or stables. It may be given away or sold. Either way, you will usually pay for the trucking. There is an assumption that organic agriculture and use of manure as fertilizer are synonymous. That is not the case. It is organic matter (and not necessarily manure) that is so vital for soil improvement. Once it has decomposed in the soil or the compost heap, almost any addition of organic matter can be as effective as any other. That includes autumn leaves, straw, plant wastes, spoiled hay, or other locally available materials. Further, the green manures and cover-crop rotations discussed in Chapter 8 are equally viable methods for adding organic matter to the soil in lieu of using off-farm supplies. Composted manure is a wonderful soil improver. By all means use it. But if manure is not available, you can plan your soil-improvement practices around many other sources of organic matter (see Chapter 11).

Minerals

The mineral nutrients we are adding—limestone to keep the pH in the most favorable range for biological activity, colloidal phosphate (or rock phosphate) to supply phosphorus, and greensand for a broad range of micronutrients plus some potassium—are raw materials for the soil. (If greensand is unavailable, a dried seaweed product like kelp meal will fill the same bill.) Colloidal phosphate and greensand are considered to be unavailable sources in a "feed the plant" system because they are not highly water-soluble. But in practice their nutrients are made available for plants as a by-product of the soil's biological processes, which are stimulated by the cultural practices—high levels of organic matter, adequate moisture, soil aeration, green manures, crop rotations—mentioned so often in this production system.

To optimize the growth of crops, a grower must first optimize the workings of the biological "factory" in the soil. That is just what is done by all the cultural practices mentioned above. I can't stress enough the vital interrelations involved in this process; how much the benefits of these cultural practices are cumulative and synergistic; how much one makes another one work better. The cyclical concept is reaffirmed. No matter what the topic, we return again and again to cycles, because a sound biological system is a cyclical system.

Why Do It This Way?

But why do it this way? Why not just use water-soluble chemical fertilizers? Because plant quality is dependent on a balanced availability of nutrients. The advantage of using the basic rock minerals in their natural form is that they are made available by the biological fertilizer factory of the soil at the rate plants need them. The two systems are harmonious. They evolved together. The correlation between availability of nutrients and their use by growing plants is a function of soil temperature, air temperature, moisture levels, and diurnal variation. Both plant and soil processes are affected simultaneously. During warmer, moister periods, plants grow better and nutrients are made available faster.

Thus, with natural rock minerals there are no problems caused by an excess supply of a soluble nutrient that upsets the mineral balance of the plant. Since there are no excesses, there is similarly no leaching of soluble nutrients such as nitrogen and potassium, which can be washed out of the soil to the detriment of both the groundwater and the farmer's pocketbook. Phosphorus doesn't leach out easily like nitrogen and potassium but rather becomes tied up in a soil that hasn't been programmed to release it. Either way, when water-soluble nutrients are used to "feed the plant," they do not contribute to a lasting soil fertility.

Other Rock Powders

Since the major structural component of soils is finely ground rock particles, from which bacterial action and plant roots extract mineral nutrients, some agriculturists have proposed amending the soil with rock powders other than lime, phosphate rock, or greensand. The suggestion makes sense.

Finely ground rock powders (usually waste products from quarrying operations)* add to the soil a material that approximates the composition of highly

*Your State Geologist or Department of Mines can usually provide you with a list of quarries or rock-crushing operations in your area that may have finely ground rock powder wastes (called "trap float" at my local basalt quarry). These are often available free for the hauling. Ask for an analysis to make sure there are no undesirable contaminants.

fertile, unweathered "young" soils. Soil scientists classify soils as young, early maturity, late maturity, and old. Young soils provide large amounts of essential plant nutrients because easily acquired minerals from fresh surfaces (the un-weathered primary mineral particles) are abundantly available. In older soils the weathering has already either partially or totally taken place, and the nutrients are no longer being liberated in such abundance, if at all. According to experimental work that has been done on this subject, a number of factors determine the performance of rock powders as soil amendments.* These include the type of rock, the fineness of grind, the type of soil, and the type of plant.

*A large number of studies have been done. Two are representative: A. S. Cushman, "The Use of Feldspathic Rocks as Fertilizers," USDA Bur. Plant Indus. Bulletin No. 104 (1907); and W. D. Keller, "Native Rocks and Minerals as Fertilizers," The Scientific Monthly, vol. 66 (Feb. 1948), pp. 122–30.

Type of Rock.   The first important variable is the type of rock. Over the years, trials have been conducted with volcanic dusts and pumices, granites, feldspars, and basalts, among others. Certain volcanic products have shown promise. Some granites have proven high in usable potassium, and biotite was the best of the feldspars. But the most researched and recommended have been the basalts.

The basalts are well-balanced rocks from the point of view of supplying soil nutrients. Basalts weather more easily than granites because they contain less silica and more calcium and magnesium. Soils derived from basalts are rich in clay and iron oxides and are usually very fertile. Basalt dusts are produced in large quantities as a result of trap-rock crushing operations, and at present they are a by-product looking for a use. European rock powder research has focused on basalt dusts in recent years, and they are used as an amendment in certain European biological farming systems. I suspect that in the future other rocks may also be appreciated as slow-release carriers of specific nutrients. An ideal product may someday be formulated that consists of a tailored blend of many different rock powders.

Fineness of Grind.   The second most important effect on the ability of rock powders to supply nutrients to plants is the size of the particles. The finer the grind, the greater the surface area of rock particles from which nutrients can be extracted. Other conditions being equal, the larger the surface area, the greater the availability of minerals. You can get an idea of the importance of particle size to mineral availability from the following statistic: a pound of average rock in a solid cube would have a surface area of about 30 square inches. But when ground to a 300-mesh powder (very fine), the surface area is increased to some 16 million square inches.

Feeding Power.   The activities of a plant's root system through contact with the mineral particles of the soil constitutes its "feeding power." This is another

30-square-inch surface area

16-million-square-inch surface area

C.C. Lewis and W. S. Eisenmenger, "Relationship of Plant Development to the Capacity to Utilize Potassium in Orthoclase Feldspar," Soil Science, *vol. 65 (1948), pp. 495–500.*

factor in determining the availability of nutrients from less soluble sources. Studies have shown that plants of the lower order of evolution, botanically speaking, have a better ability to extract less soluble minerals from rock sources than those plants that are more highly developed.* Examples of strong feeders are cotton, okra, apples, peaches, berries, roses, alfalfa, clovers, kale, cabbage, cauliflower, and radishes. Some weaker feeders are cucumbers, lettuce, sunflowers, grasses, and mints.

It would seem logical, then, to use rock powders to fertilize those crops and green manures that have been shown to utilize them most effectively, then turn the crop residues and green manures into the soil to make their nutrients available for subsequent crops. Or, as one last interesting option, rock powders could be made on the spot as a by-product of getting rid of rocks. Tractor-mounted machines are available that will crush rocks right in the soil. The machine could be set to crush progressively finer every few years when it was used again. It is appealing to think about turning the disadvantage of a stone-filled soil into the advantage of a long-term, slow-release source of minerals for plants.

Cool-Weather Cures

There are times of generally unfavorable growing conditions when the grower may want to use a temporary stimulant for plant growth. Let's take one common example. It is usually true that using soluble nitrogen or phosphorus to get plants growing in a cool spring may increase the bulk of the crop. Research has shown, however, that other nutrients (zinc for example) are also immobilized by cool conditions and are unavailable to plants. Hence, the increase in bulk is an increase in quantity without quality, because the composition of the plant is imbalanced. Where a grower wants to stress food quality as a marketing tool, nutrient imbalance is unsatisfactory.

If growing conditions are inadequate, then that is where the improvement should be made. The answer to cool conditions is to cure the problem by providing climatic protection such as walk-in tunnels or low covers for early crops. In the warmer conditions created by this protection, the natural soil-nutrient mobilization processes will be able to function without artificial stimulation.

For field crops such as corn, where climatic protection is not practical, I recommend two valuable human attributes—patience and confidence. Patience because all will turn out well in the end, and confidence because it is often difficult to persevere when at first things look bad. Although the corn in a chemically fertilized field may be taller and greener early in the season, I guarantee that the corn from the biologically fertile soil will equal or surpass it by harvest time.

It is a little bit like getting up in the morning. We can begin the day with some sort of stimulant or drug in order to "get going," but we pay the price later on through fatigue and continued reliance on the stimulant. Or we can accept the normal rate of mobilization of human energy that eventually results in a dependably productive day. There are a number of "natural" products on the market (liquid seaweed or fish emulsion are examples) that claim to offer plant stimulation without producing an imbalance. These products appeal to our human inclination to look for the "magic bullet," a secret potion that will make everything work better. In my opinion these products have mostly a psychological benefit. They make the grower feel more secure because something has been done whether it was necessary or not. Unquestionably, they can be helpful at times when things go wrong despite your best efforts. But I encourage you to use them as an occasional tool, not as a continual crutch. In most cases, a grower would be better off spending that money to build up long-term soil fertility.

Natural Reserves

In many cases the use of mineral amendments may not be necessary. If the soil has adequate trace elements, or if the manure is from animals fed a trace-mineral supplement, the micronutrient concern may be avoided. I do, however, recommend having some soil tests and tissue analyses made initially just to be sure. If the field has been heavily fertilized with superphosphate for many years past, there will usually be sufficient residual phosphorus for many years to come. Although the potassium content of the greensand is useful, it may not be necessary if manure is available. Further, the average agricultural soil has natural potassium reserves of from 20,000 to 40,000 pounds of potassium in the top 6 inches of each acre. Since I consider the usable soil depth for root feeding to be

24 inches, and since the subsoil is equally rich in potassium reserves, the aggregate amounts are considerable.

Sandy soils do not contain as much native potassium, so they should be treated differently. But even these will often have adequate stores of potassium if they are considered to a depth of 24 inches. Sandy soils may need heavier applications of organic amendments both initially and on a maintenance basis, not only to raise their potassium level, but also to improve their structure and water-holding ability. Ways to provide extra livestock manure for the farm at low cost, no cost, or even at a profit are suggested in Chapter 24. Obviously, any outside sources of organic material such as autumn leaves or manure from stables and racetracks should be investigated.

In some cases it might be a good idea to include an extra year or two of a small grain undersown to clover in the rotation, if only to have the straw for a humus-building soil amendment. Or, three years of alfalfa might be included in the rotation and the four cuttings per year fed to livestock, composted, used as a mulch, or added directly to the soil and tilled in. On soils of lower initial fertility or on excessively sandy soils, one or more of these extra steps will be needed. The technique can vary as long as the goal is clear: long-term dependable fertility, not short-term plant stimulation.

Maintaining a Fertile Soil

A most important point to understand when following a "feed the soil" philosophy is that it is not necessary to apply every single year the amount of fertilizer required by the crop. Under a long-term approach, once a fertile soil has been established, it only needs to be maintained for plants to grow well. Obviously, in order to maintain and to improve the fertility of the soil, enough nutrients should be added to at least replace what is lost through erosion, leaching, and the sale of crops. If green manures are employed as assiduously as I recommend, though, there will be minimal losses from erosion and leaching, since the green manure roots will both hold the soil and use nutrients as they become available.

Once a truly fertile and productive soil has started to function, all that is necessary is to replace the equivalent of what leaves the farm in the produce that is sold. For example, if a farmer wishes to grow corn, the entire amount of the nitrogen (N), phosphorus (P), and potassium (K) necessary for the corn crop does not need to be applied each crop year. Adequate levels of these nutrients are available in the soil as a consequence of cultural practices and the quadrennial application of minerals.

How is that possible? Well, once a workable crop rotation has been established (see chart on pages 80–81), not only is there a high level of fertility in the soil ready to assist the corn crop, but the preceding brassica crop has been undersown to a legume—white clover—which will be turned under in preparation for the corn. The crop residues from the brassica crop are also incorporated (they account for over 75 percent of the crop mass that grew), and the quadrennial phosphate, greensand, and lime applications are all up to date. If there is manure or compost available, that will more than complete the package, but it is not absolutely necessary. Using this system, I guarantee a first-class corn crop.

To look at it from another point of view, all that will be removed and sold from the corn crop are the ears. They represent less than 10 percent of the total nutrients in the corn plant. The rest of the plant is returned to the soil. If one calculates the amounts of P and K physically removed from the farm by the sale of corn, it would amount to approximately 17 pounds of P and 19 pounds of K, given an average 4-ton-per-acre yield. The cabbage crop preceding the corn, if it gave an average yield of 20,000 pounds per acre, would have removed about 6 pounds of P and 50 pounds of K.

Taking those two heavy feeders as representative crops, let us assign 12 pounds of P and 35 pounds of K as the average removed from each acre of land each year. That amounts to 48 pounds of P and 140 pounds of K removed every 4 years. Our quadrennial mineral fertilization, which consists of ⅛ ton of colloidal phosphate containing 80 pounds of P and ½ ton of greensand containing 140 pounds of K (in addition to the micronutrients), makes up for those withdrawals. Supplement those figures with the 40 tons of manure or compost that may have been applied over the same four years—manure containing an additional 200 pounds of P and 400 pounds of K—and it is obvious that the soil is gaining both biological and mineral fertility.

The other major nutrient that hasn't been mentioned thus far, nitrogen, I do not consider to be in short supply. Nitrogen is available from the leguminous green manures, from crop residues, from non-symbiotic nitrogen fixation, and as a component of the manures or compost. These sources alone are sufficiently nitrogenous to cover all demands.

Self-Sustaining Soil Fertility

I arrived at these "feed the soil" concepts over many years of observing how best to grow plants and conduct the business of agriculture. But they are not new. Nor am I their only advocate. The ideal of sustainable soil fertility has been understood for ages and has been expressed by many writers. Perhaps the most forceful champion in this century was Cyril G. Hopkins, Chief Agronomist and

BIOLOGICAL AND MINERAL ACTIVITIES OF THE SOIL

1. The majority of plant nutrients are most available between the pH range of 6.2 to 6.8.
2. Soil microbial life is most active within that pH range.
3. The nitrogen fixation by legumes and bacteria is also most effective within that pH range.
4. Most soils contain immense reserves of potassium, which become available if the soil is biologically active.
5. Organic matter is the fuel that makes all soil processes work.
6. Many trace elements are crucial not only to the quality of the crops grown, but also to the optimum functioning of both the symbiotic and non-symbiotic nitrogen-fixation processes.
7. Finely ground rock powders (usually waste products of the rock-crushing industry) can be valuable soil amendments in a biologically active soil. European farmers who have explored these concepts consider basalt rock to be highly effective.
8. The more finely ground the supplemental rock minerals, the greater their surface area and the more effectively their nutrients can be liberated by bacterial action in the soil.
9. The most complex systems are the most stable. For example, the best compost is a broad mixture of ingredients. A compost of varied plants, weeds, garden wastes, and manure is better than one made only of barley straw or pine sawdust.

eventually Director of the Illinois Agricultural Experiment Station from 1911 to 1919. Hopkins had his own "feed the soil" philosophy, which he called "The Illinois System of Permanent Agriculture." He advanced his ideas both in his best-known book, *Soil Fertility and Permanent Agriculture*, and in many experiment station publications. As Hopkins understood it, the fertility of the soil could be maintained with limestone, phosphate rock, and organic matter. I'll let him state the case in his own words:

> *For practically all of the normal soils of the United States . . . there are only three constituents that must be supplied in order to adopt systems of farming that, if continued, will increase, or at least permanently maintain, the productive power of the soil. These are* limestone, phosphorus, *and*

organic matter. *The limestone must be used to correct acidity where it now exists or where it may develop. The phosphorus is needed solely for its plant-food value. The supply of organic matter must be renewed to provide nitrogen from its decomposition and to make available the potassium and other essential elements contained in the soil in abundance, as well as to liberate phosphorus from the raw material phosphate naturally contained in or applied to the soil.*

The real question is, shall the farmer pay ten times as much as he ought to pay for food to enrich his soil? Shall he buy nitrogen at 45 to 50 cents a pound when the air above every acre contains 70 million pounds of free nitrogen? Shall he buy potassium at 5 to 20 cents a pound and apply 4 pounds per acre when his plowed soil already contains 30,000 pounds of potassium per acre, with still larger quantities in the subsoil? Because his soil needs phosphorus, shall he employ the fertilizer factory to make it soluble and then buy it at 12 to 30 cents a pound in an acid phosphate or "complete" fertilizer when he can get it for 3 cents a pound in the fine-ground natural rock phosphate, and when, by growing and plowing under plenty of clover (either directly or in manure), he can get nitrogen with profit from the air, liberate potassium from the inexhaustible supply in the soil, and make soluble the phosphorus in the natural rock phosphate which he can apply in abundance at low cost?*

*Cyril G. Hopkins, "Shall We Use 'Complete' Commercial Fertilizers in the Corn Belt?" Univ. of Illinois AES Circular No. 165 *(1912), pp. 1–20.*

Prices may have changed, but the basic truths about long-term soil fertility and economic independence for the farmer are as clear now as they were then.

The efforts of Cyril Hopkins serve as a metaphor for independent truths set up against an advertising and sales blitz that tries to pretend the truths don't exist. The result of more than a half century of fertilizer salesmanship is that no one today remembers Cyril Hopkins. The soil fertility truths that he championed, although they were understood for generations, have been forgotten so long that they are now regarded as some sort of revolutionary heresy.

Hopkins was well aware of that possibility. He wrote numerous experiment station bulletins encouraging farmers to realize that no salesman was going to tell them about these ideas because there was so little to sell. He warned them that the large fertilizer manufacturers were concerned first and foremost with selling and only secondarily with farming. He predicted that the manufacturers would push their products endlessly, until farmers forgot how well agriculture could work with a bare minimum of purchased materials. Well, Cyril Hopkins may have lost that struggle and been momentarily forgotten, but the truth of "permanent soil fertility" is still right there in the earth for those who care to look.

GENERAL SOIL AMENDMENT RECOMMENDATIONS

Initial application
(applied prior to year 1)

For a soil initially of low fertility:
40 tons/acre manure or compost
2 tons/acre colloidal phosphate
2 tons/acre greensand

For a soil initially of medium fertility:
20 tons/acre manure or compost
1½ tons/acre colloidal phosphate
1½ tons/acre greensand

For an initially fertile soil:
10 tons/acre manure or compost
1 ton/acre colloidal phosphate
1 ton/acre greensand
In all cases add sufficient limestone to maintain a pH of 6.5

Maintenance application
(applied in years 2, 6, 10, and so on)

⅛ ton/acre colloidal phosphate
½ ton/acre greensand
Limestone as required
(Not necessary if a soil test indicates P, K, and trace
   minerals are adequate.)

Maintenance application
(applied every other year)

10–20 tons/acre manure or compost

❧ Note: Follow these general guidelines if you have no more specific recommendations from professional soil tests or based on a known history of previously applied soil amendments.

Where green manures figure prominently in the crop rotation, the quantities of manure or compost can be lowered as conditions indicate.

GROWING AN ACRE OF CORN: TWO APPROACHES

Feed the Soil

Soil fertility is understood as a biological process. Once established, fertility can be maintained and improved by crop rotations that include legumes plus the addition of mineral raw materials.

Only the actual quantity of nutrients that leave the farm in stock or crops sold need to be purchased as inputs to maintain fertility. Nitrogen is not a purchased input because it is supplied by symbiotic and non-symbiotic processes.

Inputs are purchased in their least processed and least expensive form. Nutrient solubility and availability is considered to be a natural function of the biological processes in a properly managed soil.

Any feed brought onto the farm is calculated on the plus side of the input ledger. On average, 75 percent of the nutrient value of feed consumed by animals is returned in the manure as a nutrient input to the farm.

Sustainable

Feed the Plant

Soil fertility is understood to be an imported commodity. It is supplied by fertilizer inputs from off the farm, which are calculated in terms of so many hundred pounds of fertilizer applied to "create" the crop.

All the nutrients (N, P, K, Ca, Mg) known to be required to "create" 1 acre of corn (roots-tops-grain) are purchased as inputs each year. Nitrogen is a very important purchased input.

Inputs are purchased in their most processed and most expensive form. Nutrient solubility and availability is considered to be an industrial function of the chemical processes in a fertilizer factory.

Any feed brought onto the farm is calculated solely as a feed expense and is not credited for its manurial value. Animal manure, in general, is treated as a problem rather than as an asset.

Nonsustainable

FARM-GENERATED FERTILITY

VEGETABLE GROWERS CULTIVATE THE SOIL INTENSIVELY FOR FAST-GROW-ing, annual crops. Unlike the perennial culture of pastures, hayfields, and orchards (in which organic matter levels are maintained because the soil is permanently covered with vegetation) or field crops like corn and soybeans (in which a rotation with small grains and legumes can maintain production levels), the demands of intensive vegetable growing require extra inputs of organic matter. Those inputs have traditionally been acquired by importing animal manures from other farms. However, as those other farms begin to modify their production practices to create more sustainable, low-input systems, they are logically coming to consider the animal manures as valuable resources for their own use. One immediate result is that manure, when available, has risen considerably in price. Another change affecting manure supplies is the demise of so many farms. More often than not the neighboring farm no longer exists.

I encountered that latter reality in 1990 when I returned to my farm in Maine after 12 years running farms and research projects in other parts of the U.S. Farming is not a growth industry in my area, and there was only one dairy farm left in the whole county. Four years later there were none. Fortunately, I had begun exploring the potential of farm-generated systems that didn't import manure many years earlier. I had always been bothered by my dependence on manure from other farms. It seemed to me like the one flaw in my organic vegetable production system. I could understand the use of imported manure in the early years, when it provided almost instant soil improvement; or on a small acreage with all of the land in vegetable production. But if organic vegetable growing continues to succeed only because there are nearby farms from which fertility can be robbed, then it clearly cannot be portrayed as either a universal or a sustainable means of producing food.

Even though I employ all the green manures and ingenious crop rotations I can devise, I still need extra organic matter for my intensive production. If I were located near a supply of municipal leaf compost, fishing industry wastes, or some similar resource, I could investigate that option. But there are none nearby, and I am also concerned about the potential contamination of those products in a world where organic wastes are all too often polluted by toxins. The latest

*D. Fritz and F. Venter, "Heavy Metals in Some Vegetable Crops as Influenced by Municipal Waste Composts," Acta Horticulturae, 222 (1988), pp. 51–62.

❧

evidence on many of the municipal and waste product composts cites high levels of undesirable heavy metals. And, as the authors of one study state bluntly, once heavy metals are introduced into the soil it is hardly possible to get them out.* The obvious solution is to grow my own raw materials and compost them.

My original inspiration came many years ago when I drove past a defunct neighboring farm that had been bought up as a vacation home by out-of-staters. They had hired a local contractor to rotary-mow the fields and pastures to maintain the "farm look." My first thought was why didn't I try to get hired to do that and also convince the owners that they should additionally pay me to collect and haul off all those unsightly grass wastes. Why continue to buy spoiled hay for mulching if I could get it free or at a profit?

As I pondered the delightful scenario of being paid to truck away raw materials for mulching, light bulbs began to appear in the comic strip balloon above my head. Why not compost the chopped grass? What was manure anyway but hay and other forages chewed and digested by livestock? Isn't a rotary mower the equivalent of the cow's teeth? (I now call it the "iron cow.") Aren't the bacteria in soil and in compost heaps as effective at breaking down those raw materials as the digestive bacteria in the cow's stomach? Wouldn't turning the compost heap duplicate the additional mechanical processing of the cow's cud chewing? My answers were positive to all of the above.

The idea is not new. As far back as the middle of the 19th century, and with increasing frequency in the early part of the 20th century as horsepower gave way to internal combustion, many growers who had depended upon manure from the stables to fertilize their vegetable land became concerned about finding new sources of organic matter. They experimented with composting organic wastes and they used the terms "vegetable manure" or "artificial manure" to define composts made directly from plant material without first feeding it to an animal. A few books and pamphlets were published before the interest faded.** All too soon, artificial manure became confused with artificial fertilizer, and chemicals momentarily seemed to be the answer farmers were looking for.

**Arthur B. Beaumont, Artificial Manures (New York: Orange Judd, 1943). George Bommer, New Method Which Teaches How to Make Vegetable Manure (New York: Redfield and Savage, 1845).

❧

Like mine, most farms have potential forage land available. If not, it should be possible to rent land in the vicinity. In addition to old hay fields there is usually land either too steep, too rocky, or too wet for vegetables. It makes sense to establish selected forage crops on all these areas and harvest them for composting. I realize this won't quite approximate the cyclical flow of natural systems, but it does begin to make my organic vegetable farm more honestly sustainable. On the surface this solution seems very straightforward. But, to turn good concept into good practice, a number of specifics must be determined and questions answered.

1. **Which forage sources will be most successful in such a system?** Based on experience and criteria of expense, ease, and yield I have narrowed down my choices. Exotic, high-yielding crops like comfrey and Jerusalem artichokes were tried and rejected because of the extra work required for establishment and management. The easiest option is using old hay fields that presently exist. There are no establishment costs, and the hay field supports a mix of plant species. I also recommend new seedings of alfalfa on well-drained land, reed canary grass on wet land, or other high-yielding forages. Alfalfa is an obvious first choice. It is a perennial, deep-rooted, drought-resistant, leguminous forage crop that can be grown successfully in most parts of the country. Even in my short summer three cuttings are possible.

   An arable rotation can be used on land that will rotate back into vegetables after a few years. One that I like begins with seeding winter rye after clearing vegetables in the fall. The rye is undersown to a biennial sweet clover early the following spring. I mow the rye for compost material in midsummer and let the sweet clover grow on through the second winter. The clover is mowed the second summer and followed by buckwheat. I mow that in fall before sowing a rye-hairy vetch mix which occupies the land over the third winter until it is tilled under for vegetables the next spring. The land is out of vegetable production for two growing seasons, during which time I mow off heavy yields of three different forage crops for composting and end with a green manure.

2. **At what stage of growth should the forage crops be harvested?** My experience and the information from the books I consulted agree that forages used for composting should ideally be harvested at the same stage as they would be for consumption by livestock. The carbon-nitrogen ratio at that stage is within the recommended limits for successful composting. Since the ideal harvest time may also be a busy time for vegetable growers, I have done trials where I harvested the forages whenever it fit into my schedule, even late into the fall when all the hay was stemmy. Some of that material required two years to become finished compost, but it still worked, and I was very pleased with the results.*

   *The following study reinforces my experience: Andrew G. Hashimoto, "Final Report: On Farm Composting of Grass Straw," Oregon State University (1993).

   ❧

3. **What is the most efficient method for harvesting and composting?** I'm sure it might be nice to have a forage chopper and transport wagons and a compost turner. But I have always found that not having access to "ideal" equipment makes me more inventive. When I began these trials I had access to a small tractor with a rotary mower and a hay rake. They worked just fine. My basic method is to mow the field and let the material wilt before raking it into windrows. I collect the windrows by using the loader on the tractor as a buckrake. I

start at one end of a windrow, open the bucket up so the blade is vertical, set the edge about an inch above the soil, and drive forward as quickly as I can, pushing an increasing mound of forage in front of me as I move it across the field. After depositing all the windrows at one side of the field, I push them into a compost windrow with the bucket and let the decomposition process begin.

There is very little friction between dry forage and the stubble beneath it. The buckrake (also called a sweep rake) is a series of 6- to 8-foot-long parallel wooden poles that are spaced 1 foot apart and that can skim over the surface with a backboard behind them to push the hay. The rake takes advantage of that slippery surface to move large amounts of forage. Since the tractor bucket worked fine as is I didn't need to add wooden fingers, but I could have, or I could have made a simple buckrake from sapling poles that could be pushed by any old vehicle.

On the smaller scale I now have a rotary mower for my walking tractor. I borrow an old horsedrawn dump rake from a neighbor and pull it with the walking tractor. I am currently making a small buck rake for the walking tractor, but I have used a jury rig on the front of an old truck with no problem. For those with a bent towards hand work, the scythe is a very efficient mowing tool. In the old days, a good worker with a scythe could mow an acre a day. I prefer the continental European models with a straight snath (handle) and lightweight blade. The first lesson, as with any cutting tool, is to keep it sharp. The second lesson is to keep the blade parallel to the ground through each smooth, circular stroke. You cut obliquely across the face of the uncut grass, not directly at it, taking a small strip with each stroke.* Sources of scythes are listed in the tool appendix.

The best part of mowing and collecting forage for composting is the lack of concern about weather. Anyone who has ever struggled to make hay in an uncooperative climate will appreciate this new, relaxed attitude. Instead of worrying about the hay crop being rained on, I look forward to it. Instead of carefully setting the hayrake to just skim the surface, I intentionally set it too deep so it will kick soil and old thatch into the new mowings. All the practices that would be negatives if I were striving to make hay for feeding four-legged livestock become positives when I want the mowings to compost. My new "livestock" are the microorganisms in the compost heap, and they love wet and dirty hay. This kind of haymaking puts a smile on my face.

I compost in windrows. I pay attention to getting all the material thoroughly moist to prevent fire-fanging. I lay a perforated sprinkler hose on the windrow and run it as needed. I turn the compost by hand or with the tractor bucket at least twice, more often if I have time. I keep the heaps covered, using a landscape

*An excellent instructional manual is The Scythe Book *by David Tresemer (Brattleboro, VT: By Hand & Foot, Ltd., 1981).*

fabric that is permeable to air and moisture but still blocks sunlight and sheds rain. I don't plan on using the compost until it is one and a half to two years old.

In order to enhance the decomposition process and the quality of the resulting compost, I incorporate 1 to 2 percent by weight of a montmorillonite-type clay with the forage crops in the windrow. Montmorillonite is an expanding-lattice clay that has been determined to have both biotic and abiotic effects in aiding the conversion of organic matter into stable humus.* The resulting clay humus fraction that develops is very beneficial to soil fertility and plant growth. Montmorillonite (also sold as Wyoming bentonite) is mined for numerous industrial and agricultural uses. I have obtained my supplies either through the livestock feed industry, where it is used as a binder for pelleted feeds, or directly from wholesalers. Prices in quantity average about $40 per U.S. ton.

Some background on this topic can be found in P.M. Huang and M. Schnitzer, eds., "Interactions of Soil Minerals with Natural Organics and Microbes," SSSA Special Pubn., No. 17 (Madison, WI: Soil Science Society of America, 1986).

4. **How can fertility be maintained on the forage stands?** Since we are growing the forage crops in order to transport their organic matter and nutrients elsewhere, we must plan to supplement the land on which they grow so as to maintain the system. I could treat them as I have treated forage fields in the past, tilling them up every four or more years and incorporating lime and other low-solubility mineral nutrients before reseeding. Or, if I wished to make my system as locally based as possible, I could use the finely ground rock powder waste from local rock-crushing operations.

Many of the popular vegetables are not strong feeders on the less soluble minerals in rock powders. However, many of the vigorous forage crops are strong feeders. Therefore the system, in its simplest form (as I suggested in the previous chapter), would be to select bulk-yielding forage crops with strong feeding power on less soluble nutrient sources, grow them on land fertilized with locally available waste rock minerals, and then harvest and compost them for the vegetable land. Alfalfa, for example, is a very strong feeder on insoluble soil minerals and in addition is very deeply rooted.

5. **What is the ratio of acreage of feeding land (the forages) to that of consuming land (the vegetables)?** This would depend on the quality of the soil, the intensity of the vegetable cropping, and to some extent on the crops themselves. I suspect a 1:1 ratio would be adequate in most conditions, but I can see it going as high as 3:1 or 4:1 to get a low-fertility soil up to speed. In a delightful old book (*Farming with Green Manures* by Dr. C. Harlan, published in 1883), the author describes working to a 3:1 ratio, but in a very efficient manner. He had a 20-acre field of clover which he mowed three times during the summer. Each time he mowed it he raked the clippings from 15 of the acres onto the remaining

5 acres. By the end of the summer he had an enormous quantity of material on the favored 5 acres. He plowed and harrowed that section and grew vegetables there the next summer while he mowed and raked to concentrate the clippings on a second 5-acre parcel. That new section grew vegetables during the third year, while the first piece went back into clover. And so he continued to rotate the 5-acre parcels. If, instead of 20 acres of good land, he had had only 5 acres suitable for vegetables and 15 unsuited, it could have worked just as well, and those otherwise unproductive acres would have made a real contribution.

A comparison with manure use is instructive. If the ratio of feeding land to consuming land is calculated based on the number of livestock that can be fed off the forage of an average acre and the quantity of manure produced, the old-time market gardener's manure application of 50 tons per acre is equivalent to spreading the production of 8 to 10 acres of land onto 1 acre. Obviously, heavy applications of organic matter will raise soil fertility more quickly at the start, but a 1:1 ratio combined with seasonal green manures should be more than adequate to maintain fertility on any intensively cropped soil.

Another option in the search for farm-generated inputs is to work cooperatively with other farms. I visited a large organic vegetable farm in France that followed a 12-year crop rotation. For three years out of the 12 the land was in alfalfa, and one year in wheat undersown to clover. A neighboring dairy farm harvested the alfalfa and gave the vegetable farm their manure in return. Another neighbor harvested the wheat, for which they were paid, but left the chopped straw to till under with the clover. It was a nice system and a very productive farm.

Permanent Soil Fertility

*M.M. Mortland, A.E. Erickson, and J.F. Davis, "Clay Amendments on Sand and Organic Soils," Michigan State University Quarterly Bulletin, 40:1 (1957), pp. 23–30. A more recent study confirms those results: Gerhard Reuter, "Improvement of Sandy Soils by Clay-Substrate Application," Applied Clay Science, vol. 9 (1994), pp. 107–20.

In my pursuit of a permanent soil fertility that can be maintained with fewer inputs, I have added clay (specifically, montmorillonite/bentonite types) directly to the soil in my greenhouses. I spread the clay on top of a layer of peat moss (for long-lasting organic matter) and till them in together. That practice was inspired by Michigan State research,* which indicated impressive improvements in yield, moisture retention, and nutrient availability on sandy soils amended with montmorillonite clay. Montmorillonite has the highest cation exchange capacity (CEC) of all mineral soil components. Investigations of soils that suppress soil-borne plant diseases have found the common thread to be their content of montmorillonite clay. But best of all, I like the idea of making a permanent addition to the soil, one that will effect a long-term improvement rather than a short-term stimulus.

Adding clay to sandy soils was a common practice in Europe and, to a lesser extent, in the U.S. in centuries past. Henry Colman, who investigated the practice thoroughly in his 1846 book, *European Agriculture and Rural Economy*, refers to the soil improvement by claying as being of a "substantial and permanent character." Colman describes his visits to different farmers who were spreading clay at rates between 25 to 100 tons to the acre. Every one of them attested to the benefits of the practice in terms of higher yields and the higher quality of the produce. On one farm belonging to the Duke of Bedford, clay had been spread on a total of 420 acres. The common technique was to distribute the material on grassland or plowed fields in the fall, let it become well pulverized by winter freezes, and then incorporate it with a harrow in spring. Those spreading clay at the lighter rates noticed additional improvements if the application was repeated after 20 years time.

Since I have a preference for correcting causes rather than treating the symptoms of problems, I am very interested in permanently correcting the low initial fertility of my sandy soil by adding clay. I can justify the use of purchased montmorillonite (at 10 tons per acre) on my greenhouse soils because they are cropped intensively over a long season. But the cost would be prohibitive if I wanted to do my outdoor fields. The opportunity to spread clay on the outdoor fields came after we had dug an irrigation pond. When we were planning the pond, I knew I would have uses for the peatlike, muck soil from the top layer. I further assumed, and rightly so, that the gravelly underlayer would be perfect for building farm roads. However, I was pleasantly surprised when huge piles of a rich, blue marine clay appeared from the deeper levels. I emulated the good Duke of Bedford, albeit on a much smaller scale, spreading it on my fields and leaving it over the winter before incorporation. The difference in crop yield and quality was apparent right from the start, especially with the onion family, which had never appreciated our sandy soil, and it looks like a permanent improvement.

The peatlike material from the top of the pond site was put to use improving the soil for a new greenhouse. All organic growers understand the importance of organic matter. But I have long felt that compost or manure can be used to excess in greenhouses. It's entirely possible to get too much of a good thing.

In greenhouses, the best way to improve soil quickly is to get soil structure and plant nutrition from two different sources. I like peat for structure. I think of it as a "low-octane" soil improver as far as plant food is concerned. To extend my fuel metaphor, peat is valuable for helping to fill the tank, without being so powerful as to burn out the valves. When I use peat as the organic ingredient to take care of the structural part of soil improvement, I can subsequently use a much lighter compost application for just the right amount of nutrition.

The peat I used on that greenhouse soil came from this farm. But I have also purchased bales of peat for soil improvement as well as for potting mixes. I do not share the anti–peat-moss sentiment I occasionally hear expressed. The anti-peat movement began in Europe where, because of population density, limited peat deposits, and centuries-long use of the resource, they are at the point where finding substitutes for peat makes sense. But the same is not the case in North America. Of the peat lands in North America, only 0.02 percent (²⁄₁₀₀ of 1 percent) are being used for peat harvesting. On this continent peat is forming some five to ten times faster than the rate at which we are using it. And even if we don't include bogs located so far north that their use would never be economic, peat is still a resource that is forming much faster than we are using it. To my mind that is the definition of a renewable resource.

Obviously, it behooves us to make sure that every natural resource is managed sustainably and that unique areas are protected. My investigations into the peat moss industry don't give me cause to worry. Just out of curiosity, though, I have explored locally available peat alternatives. The crumbly insides of well-rotted maple and birch tree trunks on the forest floor gave reliable results in potting mixtures.

For warmer climates kenaf has shown promise. The kenaf plant, which can grow up to 15 feet tall in four months, is cut and dried in the field. Its fiber is valuable for papermaking, and the remaining stem cores, both composted and uncomposted, have been used as a growing medium. In some trials a kenaf substrate proved more successful than peat moss.*

*Yin-Tung Wang, "Kenaf," Greenhouse Management and Production (Jan. 1995), pp. 53–58.

Someday we may need to find a substitute for peat moss, but I do not believe that day is here. In fact, I do not believe it ever needs to arrive. But if we do need a substitute, some of the present contenders, like coir fiber imported, at great expense and energy, from faraway South Pacific islands, which need that organic matter to maintain their own soil fertility, make very little sense. If I am going to react against using peat to improve agricultural soils, I want to do it with all the facts at hand, both as to whether the problem actually exists and as to whether the supposed solution is logical and environmentally appropriate.

12 🌸

DIRECT SEEDING

THE AIM OF SEEDING IS TO PLACE THE VEGETABLE SEEDS DIRECTLY IN the ground where they are to grow. The key tool for this process is a *precision seeder*. The perfect precision seeder will plant any size seed at any desired spacing and at the proper depth with reliable accuracy.

Since seeds come in so many different sizes and shapes, this is no easy task. Many seeders work well only with round seeds or pelleted seeds which have been made round by coating them with a claylike material. Although pelleted seeds are easier for many seeders to handle, they do not always germinate well. They are also more expensive and are available in only a limited number of varieties. Frequently, the varieties of greatest value to the small-acreage grower (by virtue of flavor, tenderness, texture, storage, specialty market, and so forth) are not the commercial bulk-shipping varieties, and hence are not available as pelleted seed.

The seeders most desirable for my production system are those that will handle naked seed. This is made easier if the seed can be bought "sized"—that is, separated by small increments into lots of identical dimensions. Sized-seed lots also germinate evenly and grow with equal vigor for, with most crops, these qualities correlate with seed size. Thus, crop uniformity and harvest predictability are further returns from a sized-seed lot.

Although many vegetable producers direct-seed the majority of their crops, I recommend direct seeding only those vegetables that are not practically or economically feasible to transplant. These are the tap-rooted crops (carrot, parsnip); the low-return-per-square-foot crops (corn, pumpkin); the easily drilled crops (pea, bean); and the fast-growing crops (radish, spinach). My reasons for broad-scale reliance on transplanting are outlined in the next chapter. One result of this preference is that it simplifies the direct-seeding system to fewer crops. The right choice of precision seeder is then the key to planting those crops as effectively as possible.

Precision Seeders

There are a number of one-row, hand-pushed precision seeders available.

Fluid Seeder. The seeds are pre-germinated and mixed with a carrier gel in which they are squeezed out into the seed furrow with a fair degree of precision. Fluid seeding is principally of value with a slow-germinating crop like carrot, or one, like corn, that won't germinate in cold soil, in order to get the earliest outdoor harvest from a spring seeding. That virtue alone, though, is probably insufficient reason to justify the cost and complications of a fluid seeder.

Vacuum Seeder. Although single-row vacuum seeders are pushed by hand, the vacuum mechanism is powered by a battery. The seeds are picked up individually by a rotating series of vacuum pipes fitted with special tips. As each pipe rotates past the seed-drop tube, the vacuum is removed and the seed falls to the soil. These seeders are reliably accurate with small seeds but are probably too expensive and high-tech for the requirements of a small-scale system.

Belt Seeder. In this design a moving belt with seed-sized holes passes under the seed hopper and carries the seeds over to a seed-drop tube. Spacing is determined by the number of holes in the belt. A special belt is required for each size of seed. These models are very popular with vegetable growers but are highly reliant on pelleted seeds for best results.

Cup Seeder. A disk mounted with a series of small individual cups (different sizes for different seeds) rotates through the seed hopper picking up individual seeds and then dropping them one by one as the cups pass over the seed tube. Spacing is determined by adjusting the speed of rotation of the cup disk. This is the best of the four types of seeders mentioned so far, since cups are available for almost any size seed, and this model works very well with naked seed. Unfortunately, it costs around $1,000 and cannot handle corn or pea seed.

Plate Seeder. At present this is the best design for our needs on the grounds of flexibility and price. A notched plate is mounted to rotate on one side of the seed hopper. The notches, which are either cups, holes, or depressions formed along the edge of the plate, pick up individual seeds as the plate turns. Spacing is determined by the number of notches on the seed plate. The seed carried by the plate passes next to a hole in the wall of the seed hopper and falls through into the seed tube. The seed plates are made of plastic, and a dozen different types are available to handle every size seed. You can also purchase blank plates and drill or cut them to deal with specific seed sizes and spacings.

Desirable Features

A good one-row, hand-pushed precision seeder has certain features:

- *It is easy to push in a straight line.* This is crucial for ease of cultivation. Straight rows can be mechanically cultivated right up to the seedlings, saving a prodigious amount of hand-weeding.
- *It gives precise seed placement.* Good seeds cost money and waste is expensive. Ideally, there should be no thinning required. When seeds are dropped where they are to grow and at the optimum spacing for best growth, the result is higher-quality produce. Overly crowded plants grow poorly and are slower to mature.
- *It allows accurate depth adjustment.* Depth of planting affects germination, emergence, and early growth. The adjustment and maintenance of the necessary depth must be dependable. It is incumbent upon the grower to provide a smooth seedbed without hummocks and hollows if the best results are to be obtained.
- *It is easy to fill and empty.* In a multicrop system many different seeds are involved. The seeder should be designed so that the seed hopper is easy to fill and easy to empty of excess seed. Changing from one size cup, plate, or belt to another should not involve extra tools or complicated procedures.
- *It is flexible and adaptable.* For a wide range of seeds, there needs to be a wide range of adjustments possible for seed size, seed spacing, and depth of planting. There should be no problem in making or obtaining special size cups, plates, or belts for the grower's needs.
- *There is a visible seed level and seed drop.* Nothing is more frustrating than to seed a crop and then find out that the seeder was not functioning correctly, or that the seed supply ran out partway through. In the best models of precision seeders, the operator can clearly see whether the seeds are dropping and how many are left.
- *It includes a dependable row marker.* The next row is marked by an adjustable

marker arm while the previous row is being seeded. It is important to keep the rows spaced evenly. When rows are arrow-straight and equidistant, between-row cultivations go much faster. The blades on the cultivator can then be set for the exact row width and the cultivator used with the assurance that there are no sections out of line.

Sowing with a single-row precision seeder.

Using the Seeder

The Earthway seeder, a plate model (address given in the tool appendix), has been my choice to meet these criteria. The one flaw that I and other growers have noted is that the plates are not stiff enough. Some small, hard seeds can wedge themselves behind the plate and bend it out from the wall, thus inhibiting seed pickup and delivery. My solution, with the plate I use for clover green manures, for example, is to redrill the holes at a blunter angle so there isn't as much slope to force the seeds behind the plate. It might also be possible to use Super Glue and attach some stiffening ribs to the plates.

Another difficulty may arise with some seeds and some weather conditions where an electrostatic charge builds up and holds the seeds to the plate. I solved that problem by fabricating a small wooden crossbar with a toothbrush attached below it. It sits across the seed hopper and brushes the seeds off the plate and down the seed tube. The manufacturer suggests washing the seed plate in soapy water and leaving a little soapy residue on it. The residue will prevent static cling. They also recommend periodic careful washing of the plates and the seed hopper to maintain the smooth and efficient functioning of the machine.

It is good policy to calibrate the seeder before using it for all the different seeds and other adjustments involved. This is most easily done by measuring the circumference of the driving wheel (let's say it is 36 inches). Turn the wheel a number of times (say three) by hand, with the seed hopper filled. The number of seeds that drop out of the seed tube (say 54) are the number that would be planted in 3 (revolutions) times 36 inches (circumference), or 108 inches of linear travel; 108 inches divided by 54 seeds is a seeding rate of one seed every 2 inches. If that is the desired seeding rate, then note the cup, plate, or belt number on the seed packet for future reference. If not, make an adjustment and go through the process again.

Fudge Factor

Now, just because it is possible to place a single seed at the precise spacing you desire, that doesn't always mean it should be done. Germination percentages must be considered. Seeds are sold with the germination percentage printed on the package, which was determined by a controlled laboratory test. Field germination will usually be lower than the stated percentage. Allowing for a fudge factor of 50 to 100 percent is wise when planning seeding rates. For example, if you want to end up with a plant every 4 inches, the seeder could be set to drop a seed every 2 inches. Less-than-perfect germination will do some of the thinning for you. Further thinning is quickly done with a hoe, because the seeds will be evenly spaced and not in a thick row or clump.

Marking

When seeding, a string should be stretched tightly to guide the first row. All subsequent rows will be marked with the row-marker arm on the seeder. Be sure to aim the seeder as straight and true as you can with each pass. When hand-seeding, the string or tape measure will need to be reset for each row. For larger areas, an adjustable rolling marker or marker rake can be used.

Rolling marker for crops planted on a grid.

Rolling marker for widely spaced crops.

Hand-Seeding

Hand-seeding is used for the cucurbit family—cucumber, pumpkin, summer squash, and winter squash. These are relatively large seeds that can be easily picked up with the fingers. The quantities and areas to be planted are not excessive for hand-seeding. Under poorer soil conditions these crops will benefit from being planted on small, soil-covered mounds of compost or manure for an extra fertility boost.

DIRECT SEEDING CHART

	Machine-Seeded	Hand-Seeded	Spacing (inches)		Also Transplanted
			Plant	Row	
Bean	*		4	30	*
Beet	*		3	18	*
Carrot	*		1	12	
Chinese Cabbage	*		12	12	*
Corn	*		12	30	*
Cucumber		*	12	30	*
Kohlrabi	*		6	12	*
Parsnip	*		3	18	
Peas	*		2	30 or 60	*
Potato		*	12	30	
Pumpkin		*	24	120	*
Radish	*		2	4	
Rutabaga (Swede Turnip)	*		4	18	
Spinach	*		3	12	*
Swiss Chard	*		6	12	*
Summer Squash		*	24	60	*
Winter Squash		*	24	120	*

13 TRANSPLANTING

Transplanting is the practice of starting seedlings in one place and setting them out in another. In this way large numbers of young seedlings can be grown in a small area under controlled cultural conditions before they are taken to the field. Whether the seed-starting facility is indoors under lights or outdoors in a cold frame, poly tunnel, or greenhouse, the space must be kept clean and well maintained. Since conditions in any covered area cannot be completely natural, I take precautions by carefully removing all plant debris in the fall and making sure it is empty of growing plants by early winter, so as to allow the low temperatures to do their work in freezing out pests. I recommend the use of a thermostatically controlled bottom-heat propagation mat to maintain optimum germinating temperatures when starting warm-weather crops.*

Transplanting has traditionally been used for those crops (celery, lettuce, onion, and tomato) that regrow roots easily. These crops don't suffer much from being transplanted, although they obviously grow better the less their roots are disturbed. Transplanting is also of value for many crops (cucumber, melon, and parsley) that are less tolerant of root disturbance, but it must be conducted in such a way that the plants hardly know they have been moved. The best transplant system is one that does not disturb the roots, is uncomplicated, can be mechanized, and is inexpensive.

The best source for information on all topics such as germination temperatures, numbers of seeds or transplants required for a given acreage, and any agricultural tables and lists ever compiled, is Knott's Handbook for Vegetable Growers, 3rd Edition by Oscar A. Lorenz and Donald N. Maynard (New York: John Wiley & Sons, 1988).

Greenhouse to Field

Transplanting should be understood as three separate operations: *starting, potting on,* and *setting out.*

Starting involves its own three subdivisions—type of containment, soil mix, and controlled climate. The seeds are sown in some sort of prepared bed or container. The container usually holds a special soil mix or potting soil. This mix differs from garden soil by being compounded of extra organic matter and drainage material, so the seedlings will thrive despite the confined conditions. A controlled climate is provided by growing the plants in a greenhouse, hot-

Setting out a tomato plant grown in a 4-inch soil block.

bed, cold frame, or sheltered area to enhance early growing conditions for the young seedlings.

Potting on means transferring the seedlings from the initial container to a larger container with wider plant spacing. With soil blocks, this isn't always necessary from a practical point of view, except with those crops that are grown for a longer time or to a larger size before being set out. Potting on is always valuable from the perspective of the highest plant quality, however, since only the most vigorous of the numerous young seedlings are selected.

Setting out is the process of planting the young plants in the field or in the production greenhouse where they are to grow. The greater the efficiency with which this transfer can be accomplished, the more cost-effective transplanting becomes as a component of vegetable crop production.

A Sure Harvest

Transplants assure the grower of crops throughout the growing season at the times and in the quantities required. A seed sown in the field is a gamble, but a healthy three- to four-week-old transplant set out in the field provides an almost certain harvest. Transplanting is the most *reliable* method for obtaining a *uniform* stand of plants with a *predictable* harvest date.

Transplanting is *reliable* because the grower has better control over the production environment. The germination and emergence variables that can be so unpredictable in the field are more certain in the greenhouse. The crops are *uniform* because there are no gaps in the rows. No land is wasted from a thin stand due to faulty germination. Vigorous transplants set out at the ideal plant density for optimum yield have a very high rate of survival. The harvest is *predictable* because the greatest variability in plant growth occurs in the seedling stage. Once they are past that stage, an even maturity and a dependable harvest can be counted on.

It is far easier to lavish extra care on thousands of tiny seedlings in a small space in the greenhouse than over wide areas in the field. During the critical early period of growth, when ideal conditions can make such a difference, the grower can provide those conditions with less labor and expense in a concentrated area. Transplanting also allows for far more productive use of a green manure program to maintain fertility. Whereas many direct-seeded crops germinate poorly in a soil containing newly incorporated green manure residues, transplanted crops can thrive and grow quickly. (In the early stages of decomposition, compounds are formed which inhibit seed germination.) Thus, green manures can be left to grow longer before setting out transplants. Rather than having to turn under a green manure the recommended three to four weeks before a direct-seeded crop, green manures can be left to grow until two weeks before a transplanted crop. Depending on the age of the transplant, that can increase the growth period of the green manure by up to five weeks. Under these conditions, green manures are a viable option before many early crops.

Cheating Weeds and the Weather

When crops are sown in the field, weeds can begin germinating at the same time or even before. Direct-seeded crops may also need to be thinned, and they must contend with in-row weeds while young. Transplant crops start out with a three- to four-week head start on any newly germinating weeds, because the soil can be tilled immediately prior to transplanting. Further, since transplants can be set out at the final spacing, they do not require thinning and are much easier to cultivate for the control of any in-row weeds that may appear.

Transplants can measurably increase production on the intensively managed small farm, because they provide extra time for maturing succession crops. This is done by starting the succession crop as transplants three to four weeks before the preceding crop is to be harvested. Immediately after harvest, the ground is cleared, the plants are set, and the new crop is off and growing as if it had been planted three or four weeks earlier (which, of course, it was). The result is the same as if the growing season had been extended by three to four weeks. Transplanting allows less land to be used more efficiently for greater production.

Earlier maturity is another obvious advantage to transplanting. Plants started ahead inside and set out when the weather permits have a head start and will mature sooner than those seeded directly. In many cool climates, tomatoes, melons, peppers, and others are only successful as transplanted crops.

Transplanting Methods

In earlier days, vegetable growers relied heavily upon *bare-root* transplants, seedlings dug up from a special bed or outdoor field and transplanted with no attempt to retain a ball of soil around the roots. Uniform results and good survival rates are difficult to achieve with this method. Most of the fine root hairs that supply the plant with water are lost upon uprooting. This reduces the absorbing

Transplants in peat pot.   *Transplants in traditional wooden flat.*   *Root circling in a plastic pot.*

surface of the root system and markedly delays the reestablishment and subsequent growth of the plants. This "transplant shock" can be avoided by moving plants without disturbing their fragile root systems.

Many types of containers have been used to keep the root ball intact—clay pots, plastic pots, peat pots, wood or paper bands, wooden flats, plug flats, and others. The plants and soil are either removed from the container before planting or are planted outside, container and all, if the pot (peat pot, paper band) is decomposable. Unfortunately, most containers have disadvantages. Peat pots and paper bands often do not decompose as intended and inhibit root growth. They are also expensive.

Traditional wooden flats grow excellent seedlings, but some of the seedling roots must be cut when removing the plants.

Individual pots of any type are time-consuming and awkward to handle in quantity. The plug-type trays that contain individual cells for each plant solve the handling problem by combining the individual units. But they share a problem common to all containers—root circling. The seedling roots grow to the wall of the container and then follow it round and round.

Plants whose roots have circled do not get started as quickly after they are put out in the field. An attempt has been made to improve on this situation by designing the tray cells with a hole in the bottom for air pruning and ridges in the cell walls.

Fortunately, there is another kind of "container" better than all of the above. That container—the soil block—is the subject of the next chapter.

TRANSPLANT CHART

	Optimal Spacing (inches)		Transplant Age in Weeks	Also Direct-Seeded
	Plant	Row		
Beet	4	12	3–4	*
Broccoli	24	30	4	
Brussels sprouts	24	30	4	
Cabbage	18–24	30	4	
Cauliflower	18–24	30	4	
Celery	12	12	8	
Celeriac	12	12	8	
Chinese Cabbage	12	12	3	*
Corn	12	30	2–3	*
Cucumber	12	30	3	*
Eggplant	24	30	8	
Kale	12	12 or 18	4	
Kohlrabi	6	12	3–4	*
Leek	6	12	4–8	
Lettuce	12	12	3–4	
Melon	12	60	3	
Onion, Bulb	3	12	4–8	
Onion, Scallion	1	12	4–6	
Parsley	6	12	6	*
Peas	2	30 or 60	2	
Pepper	12	30	8	
Spinach	3	12	2–3	*
Summer Squash	24	30	3	*
Swiss Chard	6	18	3–4	*
Tomato	24	60	8	

14 ❧ SOIL BLOCKS

It is always satisfying to find a technique that is simpler, more effective, and less expensive than what existed before. For the production of transplants, the "soil block" meets those criteria. The Dutch have been developing this technique for some 80 years, but the human experience with growing plants in a cube of "soil" goes back 2,000 years or more. The story of how cubes of rich mud were used to grow seedlings by the Aztec horticulturalists of the *chinampas* of Xochimilco, Mexico, makes fascinating reading.[1] A related technique is the old market gardener's practice of using 4- to 5-inch cubes of partially decomposed inverted sod for growing melon and cucumber transplants.

How Soil Blocks Work

A soil block is pretty much what the name implies—a block made out of lightly compressed potting soil. It serves as both the container and the growing medium for a transplant seedling. The blocks are composed entirely of potting soil and have no walls as such. Because they are pressed out *by* a form rather than filled *into* a form, air spaces provide the walls. Instead of the roots circling as they do upon reaching the wall of a container, they fill the block to the edges and wait. The air spaces between the blocks and the slight wall glazing caused by the block form keep the roots from growing from one block to another. The edge roots remain poised for rapid outward growth. When transplanted to the field, the seedling quickly becomes established. If the plants are kept too long in the

Transplanting soil blocks.

133

blocks, however, the roots do extend into neighboring blocks, so the plants should be transplanted before this happens.

Despite being no more than a cube of growing medium, a soil block is not fragile. When first made, it is bound together by the fibrous nature of the moist ingredients. Once seeded, the roots of the young plant quickly fill the block and ensure its stability even when handled roughly. Soil blocks are the answer for a farm-produced seedling system that costs no more than the "soil" of which it is composed.

Commercial-scale hand soil-block makers.

1½-inch soil blocks

Advantages

The best thing about the soil-block system is that everything that can be done in small pots, "paks," trays, or plugs can be done in blocks without the expense and bother of a container. Blocks can be made to accommodate any need. The block may have a small depression on the top in which a seed is planted, but blocks can also be made with a deep center hole in which to root cuttings. They can also be made with a large hole in which to transplant seedlings. Or they can be made with a hole precisely the size of a smaller block, so seedlings started in a germination chamber in small blocks can be quickly transplanted onto larger blocks.

Blocks provide the modular advantages of plug trays without the problems and expense of a plug system. Blocks free the grower from the mountains of plastic containers that have become so ubiquitous of late in horticultural operations. European growers sell bedding plants in blocks to customers, who transport them in their own containers. There is no plastic pot expense to the grower, the customer, or the environment. In short, soil blocks constitute the best system I have yet found for growing seedlings.

2-inch soil blocks

The Soil-Block Maker

The key to this system is the tool for making soil blocks—the soil-block maker or "blocker." Basically, it is an ejection mold that forms self-contained cubes out of a growing medium. Both hand and machine models are available. For small-scale production, hand-operated models are perfectly adequate. Motorized block-making machines have a capacity of over 10,000 blocks per hour. But they are way overscaled for a 5-acre vegetable farm.

There are two features to understand about the blocker in order to appreciate the versatility of soil blocks: the size of the block form and the size and shape of the center pin.

3-inch soil blocks

The Form

Forms are available to make ¾-inch blocks (the mini-blocker), 1½-inch blocks, 2-inch blocks, 3-inch blocks, and 4-inch blocks (the maxi-blocker). The block shape is cubic rather than tapered. Horticultural researchers have found a cubic shape to be superior to the tapered-plug shape for the root growth of seedlings.

Two factors influence choice of block size—the type of plant and the length of the intended growing period prior to transplanting. For example, a larger block would be used for early sowings or where planting outside is likely to be delayed. A smaller block would suffice for short-duration propagation in summer and fall. The mini-block is used only as a germination block for starting seedlings.

Obviously, the smaller the block, the less potting mix and greenhouse space is required (a 1½-inch block contains less than half the volume of a 2-inch block). But, in choosing between block sizes, the larger of the two is usually the safer choice. Of course, if a smaller size block is used, the plants can always be held for a shorter time. Or, as is common in European commercial blocking operations, the nutrient requirements of plants in blocks too small to maintain them can be supplemented with soluble nutrients. The need for such supplementary fertilization is an absolute requirement in plug-type systems, because each cell contains so much less soil than a block. The popular upside-down pyramid shape, for example, contains only one-third the soil volume of a cubic block of the same top dimension.

My preference is always for the larger block, first because I believe it is false economy to stint on the care of young plants. Their vigorous early growth is the foundation for later productivity. Second, I prefer not to rely on soluble feeding when the total nutrient package can be enclosed in the block from the start. All

A cube contains three times the volume of a pyramid.

that is necessary when using the right size block and soil mix is to water the seedlings.

Another factor justifying any extra volume of growing medium is the addition of organic matter to the soil. If lettuce is grown in 2-inch blocks and set out at a spacing of 12 by 12 inches, the amount of organic material in the blocks is the equivalent of applying 5 tons of compost per acre! Since peat is more than twice as valuable as manure for increasing long-term organic matter in the soil, the blocks are actually worth double their weight in manure. Where succession crops are grown, the soil-improving material added from transplanting alone can be substantial.

The Pin

The pin is the object mounted in the center of the top press-form plate. The standard seed pin is a small button that makes an indentation for the seed in the top of the soil block. This pin is suitable for crops with seeds the size of lettuce, cabbage, onion, or tomato. Other pin types are dowel- or cube-shaped. I use the cubic pin for melon, squash, corn, peas, beans, and any other seeds of those dimensions. A long dowel pin is used to make a deeper hole into which cuttings can be inserted. Cubic pins are also used so a seedling in a smaller block can be potted on to a larger block; the pin makes a cubic hole in the top of the block into which the smaller block is placed. The different types of pins are easily interchangeable.

Cubic pin

Seed pin

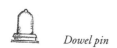

Dowel pin

Pin options.

Blocking Systems

The ¾-inch block made with the mini-blocker is used for starting seeds. With this small block, enormous quantities of modular seedlings can be germinated on a heating pad or in a germination chamber. This is especially useful for seeds that take a long time to germinate, because a minimum of space is used in the process.

Mini-blocks are effective because they can be handled as soon as you want to pot on the seedlings. The oft-repeated admonition to wait until the first true leaves appear before transplanting is wrong. Specific investigations by W.J.C. Lawrence, one of the early potting-soil researchers, have shown that the sooner young seedlings are potted on, the better is their eventual growth.[2]

The 1½-inch block is used for short-duration transplants of standard crops (lettuce, brassicas) and as the seed block for cucumbers, melons, and artichokes by using the large seed pin. When fitted with a long dowel pin it makes an excellent block for rooting cuttings.

Potting on.

The 2-inch block is the standard for longer-duration transplants. When fitted with the ¾-inch cubic pin, it is used for germinating bean, pea, corn, or squash seeds and for the initial potting on of crops started in mini-blocks.

The 3-inch block fitted with a ¾-inch cubic pin offers the option to germinate many different field crops (squash, corn, cucumber, melon) when greenhouse space is not critical. It is also an ideal size for potting on asparagus seedlings started in mini-blocks.

The 4-inch block fitted with a 1½- or 2-inch cubic pin is the final home of artichoke, eggplant, pepper, and tomato seedlings. Because of its cubic shape, it has the same soil volume as a 6-inch pot and can grow exceptional plants of these crops to their five- to eight-week field transplant age.

Other Pin Options

In addition to the pins supplied with the blocker, the grower can make a pin of any desired size or shape. Most hard materials (wood, metal, or plastic) are suitable, as long as the pins have a smooth surface. Plug trays can be used as molds and filled with quick-hardening water putty to make many different sizes of pins that allow the integration of the plug and block systems.

Blocking Mixes

When transplants are grown, whether in blocks or pots, their rooting area is limited. Therefore the soil in which they grow must be specially formulated to compensate for these restricted conditions. For soil blocks, this special growing medium is called a *blocking mix*. The composition of a blocking mix differs from ordinary potting soil because of the unique requirements of block-making. A blocking mix needs extra fibrous material to withstand being watered to a paste consistency and then formed into blocks. Unmodified garden soil treated this way would become hard and impenetrable. A blocking mix also needs good water-holding ability, because the blocks are not enclosed by a nonporous container. The bulk ingredients for blocking mixes are peat, sand, soil, and compost. Store-bought mixes can also work, but most will contain chemical additives not allowed by many organic certification programs. If you can find a commercial peat-perlite mix with no additives, you can supplement it with the soil, compost, and extra ingredients described below.

In the past few years commercial, preformulated organic mixes with reasonably good growth potential have begun to appear on the market. However, shipping costs can be expensive if you live far away from the supplier. To be honest,

I have yet to find any of these products that will grow as nice seedlings as my own homemade mixes.

Peat

Peat is a partly decayed, moisture-absorbing plant residue found in bogs and swamps. It provides the fiber and extra organic matter in a mix. All peats are not created equal, however, and quality can vary greatly. I recommend using the premium grade. Poor-quality peat contains a lot of sticks and is very dusty. The better-quality peats have more fiber and structure. Keep asking and searching your local garden suppliers until you can find good-quality peat moss. Very often a large greenhouse operation that makes its own mix will have access to a good product. The peat gives "body" to a block.

Sand

Sand or some similar granular substance is useful to "open up" the mix and provide more air porosity. A coarse sand with particles having a ⅛- to 1/16-inch diameter is the most effective. I prefer not to use vermiculite, as many commercial mixes do, because it is too light and tends to be crushed in the block-making process. If I want a lighter-weight mix I replace the sand with coarse perlite. Whatever the coarse product involved, adequate aeration is the key to successful plant growth in any medium.

Compost and Soil

Loam is made by stacking layers of sod from a grass field upside-down to decompose for a year or two. The development of the old loam-based mixes is well covered in Seed and Potting Composts *by W.J.C. Lawrence and J. Newell (London: Allen & Unwin, 1939). I based my earliest mixes on modifications of their formulas by using soil and compost to replace the loam.*

Although most modern growing mediums no longer include any real soil, I have found both soil and compost to be important for plant growth in a mix. Together they replace the "loam" of the successful old-time potting mixtures.* In combination with the other ingredients, they provide stable, sustained-release nutrition to the plants. I suspect the most valuable contribution of the soil may be to moderate any excess nutrients in the compost, thus giving more consistent results. Whatever the reason, with soil and compost included there is no need for supplemental feeding.

Compost is the most important ingredient. It is best taken from two-year-old heaps that are fine in texture and well decomposed. The compost heap must be carefully prepared for future use in potting soil. I use no animal manure in the potting-mix compost. I construct the heap with 2- to 6-inch layers of mixed garden wastes (e.g., outer leaves, pea vines, weeds) covered with a sprinkling of topsoil and 2 to 3 inches of straw sprinkled with montmorillionite clay (see page 115). The sequence is repeated until the heap is complete. The heap should be turned once the temperature rises and begins to decline so as to stimulate further decomposition.

There are no worms involved in our composting except those naturally present, which is usually a considerable number. (I have purchased commercial worm composts [castings] as a trial ingredient, and they did make an adequate substitute for our compost.) Both during breakdown and afterwards the heap should be covered with a landscape fabric. I strongly suggest letting the compost sit for an additional year (so that it is one and a half to two years old before use); the resulting compost is well worth the trouble. The better the compost ingredient, the better the growth of the plants will be. The exceptional quality of seedlings grown in this mix is reason enough to take special care when making a compost. Compost for blocking mixes must be stockpiled the fall before and stored where it won't freeze. Its value as a mix ingredient seems to be enhanced by mellowing in storage over the winter.

Soil refers to a fertile garden soil that is also stockpiled ahead of time. I collect it in the fall from land off which onions have just been harvested. I have found that seedlings (onions included) seem to grow best when the soil in the blocking mix has grown onions. I suspect there is some biological effect at work here, since crop-rotation studies have found onions (and leeks) to be highly beneficial preceding crops in a vegetable rotation.[3] The soil and compost should be sifted through a ½-inch mesh screen to remove sticks, stones, and lumps. The compost and peat for the extra-fine mix used either for mini-blocks or for the propagation of tiny flower seeds are sifted through a ¼-inch mesh.

Extra Ingredients

Lime, blood meal, colloidal phosphate, and greensand are added in smaller quantities.

Lime. Ground limestone is added to adjust the pH of the blocking mix. The quantity of lime is determined by the amount of peat, the most acidic ingredient. The pH of compost or garden soil should not need modification. My experience, as well as recent research results, has led me to aim for a growing-medium pH between 6 and 6.5 for all the major transplant crops. Those growers using different peats in the mix may want to run a few pH tests to be certain. However, the quantity of lime given in the formula below works for the different peats that I have encountered.

Blood Meal. I find this to be the most consistently dependable slow-release source of nitrogen for growing mediums. English gardening books often refer to hoof-and-horn meal, which is similar. I have also used crab-shell meal with great success. Recent independent research confirms my experience and suggests that cottonseed meal and dried whey sludge also work well.[4]

Colloidal Phosphate. A clay material associated with phosphate rock deposits and containing 22 percent P_2O_5. The finer the particles the better.

Greensand (Glauconite). Greensand contains some potassium but is used here principally as a broad-spectrum source of micronutrients. A dried seaweed product like kelp meal can serve the same purpose, but I have achieved more consistent results with greensand.

The last three supplementary ingredients—blood meal, colloidal phosphate and greensand—when mixed together in equal parts are referred to as the "base fertilizer."

Blocking Mix Recipe

A standard 10-quart bucket is the unit of measurement for the bulk ingredients. A standard cup measure is used for the supplementary ingredients. This recipe makes approximately 2 bushels of mix. Follow the steps in the order given.

3	buckets brown peat
½	cup lime. **Mix.**
2	buckets coarse sand or perlite
3	cups base fertilizer. **Mix.**
1	bucket soil
2	buckets compost

Mix all ingredients together thoroughly.

The lime is combined with the peat because that is the most acidic ingredient. Then the sand or perlite is added. The base fertilizer is mixed in next. By incorporating the dry supplemental ingredients with the peat in this manner, they will be distributed as uniformly as possible throughout the medium. Next add the soil and compost, and mix completely a final time.

To use this recipe for larger quantities, think of it measured in "units." The unit can be any size, so long as the ratio between the bulk and the supplementary ingredients is maintained. A "unit" formula would call for:

30 units	brown peat
⅛ unit	lime
20 units	coarse sand or perlite
¾ unit	base fertilizer
10 units	soil
20 units	compost

Mini-Block Recipe

A different blend is used for germinating seeds in mini-blocks. Seeds germinate better in a "low-octane" mix, without any blood meal added. The peat and compost are finely screened through a ¼-inch mesh before adding them to the mix.

16 parts	brown peat	4 gallons
¼ part	colloidal phosphate	1 cup
¼ part	greensand *(If greensand is unavailable, leave it out. Do not substitute a dried seaweed product in this mix.)*	1 cup
4 parts	compost (well decomposed)	1 gallon

Sterilizing the Mix

In more than 20 years of using homemade mixes, I have never sterilized them. And I have not had problems. I realized early on that damping-off and similar seedling problems, which are usually blamed on unsterilized soil, are actually a function of cultural mistakes like overwatering, a lack of air movement, not enough sun, overfertilization, and so forth. Good, fertile garden soil and well-prepared compost contain many organisms that benefit seedling growth. If you "sterilize" these ingredients you lose the benefits of a live mix without gaining the advantages that are achieved through proper seedling management. Recent university studies agree and emphasize the specific value of finished compost as a disease-suppressing ingredient in growing mixes.[5]

Nitrogen Reaction

With certain crops (mostly the more delicate bedding-plant flowers) there may be a further consideration. Where organic sources of nitrogen like blood meal or the old-time hoof-and-horn meal are included in a mix, the mineralization of the nitrogen by biological processes and the consequent production of ammonia can inhibit plant growth for a period of time after the mix is made, especially if moisture and temperature levels are high.[6] If you use a dried seaweed product instead of greensand this consideration probably applies as well. To avoid this reaction, make up the mix fresh as you need it and never store it for more than three weeks. To my knowledge I have never been bothered by this problem, but I feel it is worth mentioning. In my experience, when the mix is stored for more than three months, it actually gets better, as all the ingredients seem to mellow together.

One of the European organic farms I visited actually processed their mix for a whole year before using it by layering the ingredients—horse manure on the bottom, then leaf mold, then compost—in a cold frame and growing first a crop of cabbage, followed by melons, then mâche. After the manure, leaf mold, and compost have been "processed" for a year by the roots of those crops, they become the basis for the mix. Seven parts of the processed ingredients are mixed with three parts of peat, rock powders are added, and the mix is ready. Another grower of my acquaintance uses only pure compost for growing seedlings in flats and plug trays. I relate those stories as examples of the extremely wide variety of answers that different growers have found to the potting soil question. The formulas I have given above are the answers that have worked well so far for me. They are not the only answers.

Moistening the Mix

Water must be added to wet the mix to blocking consistency. The amount of water varies depending on the initial moisture content of the ingredients. On average, to achieve a consistency wet enough for proper block-making, the ratio of water to mix by volume will be about 1 part water to every 3 parts mix. A little over 2½ gallons of water should be added to every cubic foot of mix.

For successful block-making, be sure to use a mix that is wet enough. Since this will be much wetter than potting mixes used for pots or flats, it takes some getting used to. The most common mistake in block-making is to try to make blocks from a mix that is too dry. The need to thoroughly wetten the mix is the reason why the mix requires a high percentage of peat, to give it the necessary resiliency.

Handling Soil Blocks

Many large block-making operations set the newly formed and seeded blocks by the thousands on a plastic sheet on the floor of the greenhouse. When they are ready to go to the field, the blocked seedlings are lifted with a broad, fine-tined fork and slid into transport crates. These crates have high sides so they can be stacked for transport without crushing the seedlings. In lieu of these special crates, two other options are practical for small-scale production.

Simple three-sided wooden flats work well for soil blocks. The inside dimensions are 18¾ inches long by 8 inches wide by 2 inches high. Three-quarter-inch stock is used for the sides and ½-inch stock for the bottom. One flat holds 60 of the 1½-inch blocks, 36 of the 2-inch blocks, or 18 of the 3-inch size. These block flats are efficient to use in the greenhouse, because the benches need to be no more than 2 x 4s spaced to hold two rows of flats side by side. Low-sided flats such as these are not stackable when filled with plants. For transport, a carrying rack with spaced shelves is required.

The flats have only three sides so the blocked seedlings can be easily removed from the open side one at a time as they are being transplanted in the field. The flat is held in one hand by the long side while blocks are quickly placed in holes in the soil with the other. Similar three-sided flats (half as wide and only ¾ inch high at the sides) are used for mini-blocks. Since they are the same length as the others, they fit two to a space on the greenhouse bench for modular efficiency. Each of these flats holds 120 mini-blocks.

Bread Trays

When handling greater quantities of blocks, you can use the large plastic-mesh bread trays seen in bread delivery trucks. They can generally be bought used at a reasonable cost from regional bakeries. Since the sides on these trays are higher than all except the tallest seedlings, they can be stacked for transport. Bread trays vary in size, but on average each tray can hold 200 of the 1½-inch blocks and proportionally fewer of the larger sizes.

Results are excellent with bread trays. What with the open mesh sides and bottom plus the air spaces between the blocks, the roots of the seedlings remain poised at all five potential soil-contact surfaces. The bread trays are not as easy to handle for field transplanting as the smaller three-sided flats, but they become manageable with practice.

A plastic-mesh bread tray.

Making Soil Blocks

The wet mix should be spread on a hard surface at a depth thicker than the blocks to be made. The soil-block maker is filled by pressing it into the mix with a quick push and a twisting motion to seat the material. Lift the blocker, scrape off any excess mix against the edge of a board, and place the blocker on the

Pressing a small-scale, hand soil-block maker into the mix.

*Occasionally, if the mix is a shade too moist, some blocks may fall out when you lift the blocker. If you first tip the blocker slightly with a quick motion before lifting it, you can break the moist suction between the soil blocks and the surface beneath them, ensuring that the blocks remain inside the blocker.

❧

three-sided flat, the bread tray, the plastic sheet, a concrete floor, or other surface. The blocks are ejected by pressing on the spring-loaded handle and raising the form in a smooth, even motion.* After each use the blocker is dipped in water to rinse it. A surprising rate of block production (up to 5,000 per hour using the 1½-inch commercial-scale model) will result with practice.

Seeding the Blocks

Each block is formed with an indentation in the top to receive the seed. The handmade blocks are usually sown by hand. With the motorized blockers, the sowing as well as the block-forming is mechanized. An automatic seeder mounted over the block belt drops one seed into each indentation as the blocks pass under it. These motorized models are too large and expensive for the small-scale grower, but if a group of growers get together, there is a role for one of them in a specialized seedling operation. Small farmers always benefit from such cooperative arrangements and should consider participating whenever the opportunity arises.

Single-Plant Blocks

One seed is sown per block. There is a temptation to use two (just to be on the safe side), but that is not necessary. Germination is excellent in soil blocks because of the ease with which ideal moisture and temperature conditions can be maintained. The few seeds that don't germinate are much less of a problem than the labor to thin all those that do. Of course, if the seed is of questionable vitality, it is worth planting more than one seed per block, but obviously it pays to get good seed to begin with.

Seeding can be done with the fingers for large seeds such as cucumber, melon, and squash. Finger-seeding is also possible for small seeds that have been pelleted, although pelleted seeds are not easily available in most varieties, and naked seeds are more commonly used. The small seeds can be most accurately handled by using a small thin stick, a sharpened dowel, a toothpick, or similar pointed implement. Seeds are spread on a dish. The tip of the stick is moistened in water and touched to one seed. The seed adheres to the tip and is moved to the seed indentation in the top of a block and deposited there. The solid, moist block has more friction than the tip of the stick, so the seed stays on the block.

Another obvious technique is to crease one side of a seed packet or use any other V-shaped container and tap out the seeds by striking the container with the fingers or a small stick. The Park Seed Company sells small seeds in packets made of a heavy metal foil. If you take a pair of scissors and cut and crease an empty packet, as shown at left, the resulting "seed tapper" works exceptionally well, even for tiny seeds. Put only enough seeds in the packet at one time so they can be tapped out in a single row without bunching up.

Commercial seeding aids are available that aim to either wiggle, click, or vibrate the seeds out one by one. There are electrically operated vacuum seeders for the small-scale grower that can be adapted to seeding soil blocks.* I have experimented with a nonelectric, homemade vacuum seeder specifically for mini-blocks which gets its suction from the return stroke of a foot-powered

Single-seeding soil blocks.

*The Gro-Mor Wand Seeder has a hand-held wand featuring interchangeable tips attached to a vacuum pump. Customized wands are available. It is sold by Griffin Greenhouse Supply, P.O. Box 36, Tewksbury, MA 01876; (508) 851–4346.

pump for rubber rafts. I haven't quite perfected the suction tips yet, but I will get it right one of these days.* Instructions for a homemade, multipoint vacuum seeder are given in a recent issue of *HortScience*.[7] Growers should try such aids and decide for themselves whether they are worth it. Whichever method is used, though, the seeding should be done carefully to ensure that the seeds are accurately planted in each block.

In practice, these planting techniques quickly become efficient and precise. Remember that for many crops the soil-block system avoids all intermediate potting on. Crops are started in the block and later go directly to the field. That savings in time alone is worth the effort required to become proficient at single-seeding.

Germination

I never cover the seeds planted in mini-blocks. Oxygen is important for high-percentage seed germination. Thus, even a thin covering of soil or potting mix can lower the germination percentage. I find that to be important for all small flower seeds also. If the sowing instructions suggest the seeds need darkness to germinate, I cover the flats temporarily with a sheet of black plastic. I keep the moisture level high during the germination period by misting frequently with a fine spray of water. For the larger-seeded crops in the larger blocks, I get sturdier seedlings if I cover the seeds. I do that by sprinkling a thin layer of potting soil over the top of the blocks.

The third key to a high-germination percentage, in addition to air and moisture, is temperature. Ideal temperature for germination can best be maintained by using a thermostatically controlled soil-heating pad under the blocks. Although there are new low-watt models composed of a thin metal heating grid between layers of plastic, I still prefer the old heavy-duty model consisting of a ¼-inch-thick red-rubber pad with heating cables embedded within.** The temperature is controlled at the desired setting by a remote thermostatic probe inserted into the potting soil or in the gap between the soil blocks. I use a temperature of 70–75°F. (21–24°C.) for most crops. For asparagus, cucumber, eggplant, melon, pepper, and squash, I use a setting of 75–80°F. (24–27°C.).

**Manufactured by Pro-Gro Supply Corp., 12675 W. Auer Avenue, Brookfield WI 53005; telephone (800) 331-0590, fax (414) 781-6907.

Multiplant Blocks

Although I have stressed the wisdom of sowing only one seed per block, there is an important exception to that rule—the multiplant block. In this case 3 to 12 seeds are deliberately planted in each block with no intention of thinning. Many crops grow normally under multiplant conditions, and transplant efficiency is enhanced by putting out clumps rather than single plants.

The concept of the multiplant block is based on spatial rather than linear plant distance in the field. For example, say the average ideal in onion spacing is one plant every 3 inches in rows spaced 12 inches apart. Multiplants aim at an equivalent spacing of four onions per square foot. The difference is that all four onions are started together in one block and grow together until harvest. Since it is just as easy to grow four plants to the block as it is to grow one, there is now only one-quarter the block-making work and greenhouse space involved in raising the same number of plants. A similar advantage is realized when transplanting the seedlings to the field. When four plants can be handled as one, then only a quarter as many units need to be set out. Although bunched together, the plants will have extra space all around them. The onions grow normally in the clump, gently pushing each other aside, attaining a nice round bulb shape and good size.

Not only bulb onions but scallions (green onions) thrive in multiple plantings. Scallions are seeded 10 to 12 per block and grow in a bunch ready to tie for harvest. Weeding between the plants in the row is no longer a chore, since the wider spaces allow for easy cross-cultivation with a hoe. Obviously, multiplant blocks must be transplanted to the field a bit sooner (at a younger age) than single-plant blocks because of the extra seedling competition in the limited confines of the block.

Multiplant onions:
4 plants per foot.

Single plant onions:
4 plants per foot.

Multiplant blocks can be sown either seed by seed or in bunches. For counting out seeds, one of the wiggle, click, or vibration seeders have a place here in speeding up the seeding operation, though at the sacrifice of some accuracy. When I need to be precise, I first tap the number of seeds required into a ¼ teaspoon measure so I can be sure of the count before sowing the block. Tiny scoops or spoons or other small-volume measures can be fabricated by the grower to hold 5, 12, or whatever number of seeds. These are used to scoop up the seeds and dump them in each seed indentation. This method is not as accurate as counting, but it is a lot faster.

Multiplant blocks are an efficient option for a number of crops. In my experience onions, scallions, leeks, beets, parsley, spinach, corn, pole beans, and peas have been outstandingly successful in multiple plantings. Spinach, corn, pole beans, and peas, which are rarely transplanted, even for the earliest crop, become a much more reasonable proposition when the transplant work can be cut by 75 percent. European growers claim additional good results with cabbage, broccoli, and turnips planted at three to four seeds per block.

MULTI-PLANT BLOCKS

	Number of Seeds	Spacing (inches)		Block Size (inches)
		Plant	Row	
Beet	4	6	16	2
Broccoli	4	24	30	2
Cabbage	3	24	30	2
Corn	4	30	30	3
Cucumber	3	30	30	3
Leek	4	8	16	2
Melon	3	24	60	3
Onion, Bulb	5	12	12	1½
Onion, Scallion	12	6	12	1½
Peas	3	6	30	2
Spinach	4	6	12	1½
Turnip	4	6	12	1½

Watering

Blocks are made in a moist condition and need to be kept that way. Their inherent moistness is what makes them such an ideal germination medium. It is therefore most important that blocks are not allowed to dry out, which can result both in a check to plant growth and difficulty in rewetting. When blocks are set out on a bench or greenhouse floor, the edge blocks are the ones that are most susceptible to drying. A board the same height as the blocks placed along an exposed edge will help prevent this. Since the block has no restricting sides, the plants never sit in too much water. The block itself will take up no more water than it can hold.

To prevent erosion of the block, watering at first should be done gently with a very fine rose. If the rose is not fine enough, the mini-blocks should be misted rather than watered. Once the plants in blocks are growing, water can be applied through any fine sprinkler. Extra care in attention to watering is a general rule in successful block culture. It will be repaid many times over in the performance of the seedlings.

Potting On

Potting on is the practice of starting seeds in smaller blocks and then setting those blocks into larger blocks for further growth. Since most crops benefit from bottom heat to ensure and speed up germination, this practice makes efficient use of limited space in germination chambers or on heating pads. For example, 240 mini-blocks fit into the same space as only 36 of the 2-inch blocks.

Potting on blocks is quickly accomplished in one-third the time required for potting on bare-root seedlings. The smaller block easily fits into a matching size hole in a larger block. The mini-blocks are usually potted on to 2-inch blocks and those, in turn, to 4-inch maxi-blocks.

The 2-inch blocks are easily potted on using the fingers. For the mini-blocks, some form of transplant tool for lifting the blocks and pressing them into the cavity will be useful. One of the best implements for this job is a flexible artist's pallet knife. It provides the extra dexterity necessary to handle mini-blocks with speed and efficiency.

Keep Them Growing

Potting on should be carried out as soon as the seeds have germinated in the mini-blocks and before the roots begin growing out of the small cubes. The less

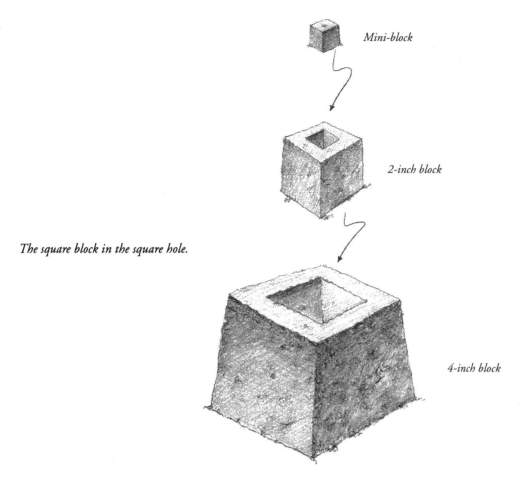

Mini-block

2-inch block

The square block in the square hole.

4-inch block

stress seedlings encounter the better. Crops like tomatoes and peppers need to be given progressively more space as they grow. They produce the best transplants when they are spaced far enough apart so that their leaves never overlap those of another plant.

For ease of moving, the 4-inch blocks can be set on pieces of tile or shallow saucers and moved in that small "flat" as necessary. Or, if they are set directly on a smooth surface, the best tool for handling them is a heavy-duty kitchen spatula. It is easy to slide it underneath, and the block can then be safely lifted and moved. There is as much soil volume in a 4-inch maxi-block as there is in a conventional 6-inch pot. It grows a first-class tomato plant.

CHART OF SOIL BLOCK AND PIN SIZES

	¾"	1½"	2"	3"	4"	PIN
Artichoke		**				S
Asparagus		**				S
Bean			**			L
Beet		**	*			S
Broccoli		*	**			S
Brussels sprouts		*	**			S
Cabbage		*	**			S
Cauliflower		*	**			S
Celery	**	→	**			S→¾
Celeriac	**	→	**			S→¾
Chinese Cabbage		*	**			S
Corn			**	*		¾
Cucumber		**	→		**	S→1½
Eggplant	**	→	**	→	**	S→¾→2
Kale		**	*			S
Kohlrabi		**				S
Leek		*	**			S
Lettuce		**	*			S
Melon		**	→		**	S→1½
Onion		**	*			S
Parsley	**	→	**			S→¾
Peas			**			¾
Pepper	**	→	**	→	**	S→¾→2
Pumpkin				**		¾
Spinach		**				S
Summer Squash				**		¾
Winter Squash				**		¾
Swiss Chard		**	*			S
Tomato	**	→	**	→	**	S→¾→2

** = Recommended   * = Alternate   → = Potted on to   *Standard Pin:* L = Large, S = Small
Cubic Pin: ¾", 1½", 2"

NOTES

[1]Michael D. Coe, "The Chinampas of Mexico." *Scientific American.* July, 1964.

[2]W.J.C. Lawrence, *Catch the Tide: Adventures in Horticultural Research* (London: Grower Books, 1980), pp. 73–74.

[3]T.E. Odland, R.S. Bell, and J.B. Smith, "The Influence of Crop Plants on Those Which Follow: V." Bulletin No. 309. (Kingston, RI: Rhode Island Agricultural Experiment Station, 1950).

[4]B. Gagnon and S. Berrourard, "Effects of Several Organic Fertilizers on Growth of Greenhouse Tomato Transplants." *Canadian Journal of Plant Science*, vol. 74, no. 1 (1994), pp. 167–68.

[5]Harry A.J. Hoitink, "Basis for the Control of Soilborne Pathogens with Composts," *Ann. Rev. Phytopath,* vol. 24 (1986), pp. 93–114.

H.A.J. Hoitink, Y. Inbar, and M.J. Baehun, "Status of Compost-Amended Potting Mixes," *Plant Disease* (Sept. 1991), pp. 869–73.

[6]A.C. Bunt, *Modern Potting Composts* (University Park, PA: Penn State University Press, 1976).

[7]J.L. Townsend, "A Vacuum Multi-Point Seeder for Pots." *HortScience*, vol. 22, no. 6 (1987), p. 1328.

15 🪶 SETTING OUT TRANSPLANTS

MOISTURE IS THE FIRST CONCERN WHEN SETTING OUT TRANSPLANTS. Soil-block plants should be watered thoroughly before being put into the ground. At first, the amount of moisture in the block is more important to the establishment of the plant than the moisture level of the surrounding soil. The moisture level of the block allows the plant to send out new roots into the soil. Only after roots are established does the soil moisture become more important. Blocks should be very wet at the start and should be kept moist during the transplant operation. The carrying flats and transport rack should be shaded from the sun and shielded from drying winds.

The second concern is soil contact. The transplanted blocks must be placed lightly but firmly into the soil. Avoid air pockets and uncovered edges. If transplanting is to deliver all the benefits we've discussed, it must be done well. I recommend irrigating immediately following transplanting, and not only to provide moisture. The action of the water droplets also helps to cover any carelessness when firming the plants in. Although the wet block planted into dry soil will support itself surprisingly well, it can eventually suffer from stress. Irrigation is stress insurance.

Consistent depth of setting is also important for rapid plant establishment, even growth, and uniform maturity. The blocks should be set to their full depth in the soil. If a corner is exposed to the air, the peat in the blocks can dry out quickly on a hot, sunny day and set the plant back. On the smallest scale, transplant holes are made with a trowel. There are a number of designs for soil-block trowels, but my preference is for what I call the "dagger" style, which has an upright handle and a right-angle blade. It is jabbed into the soil and pulled back toward the operator to make a neat hole for setting the plant.

I make my own dagger-style model using a bricklayer's trowel with a 2 x 5-inch blade. I first cut off 2¼ to 2½ inches to shorten the blade, then bend the handle down to below horizontal at about the same angle that it was above. I now have a very efficient transplant trowel for soil blocks (see illustration). The same tool can be used to lift blocks from the flat, if desired.

When setting out plants, be sure to space them correctly. Accurate spacing not only makes optimum use of the land area, but also improves the efficiency of

Making transplant holes for large blocks with a post-hole digger.

Homemade, dagger-
style trowel for setting
out soil blocks.

all subsequent cultivations. Straight rows of evenly spaced seedlings can be cultivated quickly, without the constant stopping and adjusting caused by out-of-place planting. The only way to assure accurate spacing is to measure. Stretching a tape or a knotted string is a perfectly reliable method (unless a strong wind is blowing), but it is also slow and tedious. A marker rake equipped with adjustable teeth for both lengthways and crossways marking is faster. A roller with teeth on it to mark all the plant sites in one trip is better yet.

The Studded Roller

For more efficient transplanting, the next idea is to combine the spacing and hole-making operations in one tool. If a marking roller is fitted with studs that are the size of the soil blocks, both jobs can be done at once. In newly tilled ground, this "studded roller" will leave a regular set of cubic holes in the soil.

A few design modifications can make this idea work even better. The marking studs should have slightly tapered sides (10°) to make a more stable hole. The roller should ideally be 11½ inches in diameter (you should be able to get a local metalworking shop to make one for you). That gives it a rolling circumference of 36 inches. Then, if a number of stud attachment holes are drilled in the roller, plants can be spaced at 6, 12, 18, or 24 inches in the row. The roller can be made 24 inches wide, half the width of a standard planting strip, or the full 48-inch width for the growing area in the 60-inch strip, or 30 inches wide for the growing area in the 42-inch strip (see Chapter 6). After the ground is tilled, one trip down and back with the 24-inch studded roller, or a single trip with the 30- or 48-inch roller, will prepare the entire strip for transplanting. The final step is simply to set the square block in the square hole. When placing the block, the soil should be lightly firmed around it with the tips of the fingers.

The above is an excellent system, one that I have used myself and have seen in operation on a number of European farms. It has just two small drawbacks. First, if the soil dries out between tilling and rolling, the holes will not form well. Second, the soil at the bottom and sides of the hole is compressed and could inhibit easy root penetration. These are minor points, but they do make a difference. One improvement is to replace the blocks with small (2 x 3-inch) trowel blades. These are attached to the roller at a 15° angle toward the direction of travel. The rotation of the roller causes these "shovels" to dig small holes. Since

A roller with marker blocks attached.

the holes are scooped rather than pressed, there is no soil-compaction problem.

The next step is to improve the efficiency of the system from two trips over the field to one by combining tilling and rolling in one operation. This is done by mounting a roller with blocks as closely as possible behind the tines of the tiller, after removing the back plate. In this way the holes are formed immediately in moist, newly tilled soil. Compaction is avoided because the roller has become the back plate of the tilling unit. The soil, driven against it by the tines, is falling back into place at the same time the blocks are forming the holes. The roller is attached by arms hinged to the sides of the tine cover. Metal blocks welded onto the bottom edges of the tine cover raise the roller when the tiller is lifted at the end of the row.

With this one-pass tiller/hole-maker, plus the convenience of modular plants in soil blocks, the small-scale vegetable grower now has a very efficient transplant system for all the crops in 1½-inch and 2-inch blocks. The larger blocks are transplanted into holes dug by hand. A two-handled post-hole digger is the best tool for setting out 3- and 4-inch blocks. One quick bite of the jaws leaves a hole the perfect size.

A combination tiller/ hole-maker.

WEEDS

Since the best way of weeding
Is to prevent weeds from seeding,
The least procrastination
Of any operation
To prevent the semination
Of noxious vegetation
Is a source of tribulation.
And this, in truth, a fact is
Which gardeners ought to practice,
And tillers should remember,
From April to December.

—New England Farmer, 1829

I'M ALWAYS EAGER TO SEE NEWLY GERMINATED CROP SEEDLINGS STARTING to poke through the soil. They are a sure sign that the growing season has begun. Tiny weed seedlings are another sure sign—a sign that weed competition is not far behind. I'm always quick to spot them and dispatch them while they're still small.

Weed Control

There are two conventional approaches to weed control—physical control and chemical control. Physical control involves cutting off the weeds (cultivation) or smothering them (mulching and hilling). Chemical control depends on the use of herbicides. In this production system, only physical control is recommended. I have too many objections to herbicides. For one thing, herbicide residues make it impossible to establish the undersown crops (the "deliberate weeds"), which are an integral part of the soil improvement program. There is also a great deal of evidence that herbicides have harmful effects on crop plants, weakening them and making them more susceptible to pests and diseases. But most important, herbicides pose many known and unknown dangers to the health of both humans and the environment. I believe that, over the long term, *all* herbicides will be proven to be harmful to both growers and consumers.

Physical control, principally cultivation, is the weed-control method of choice here. Not only do I emphasize cultivation, but cultivation done with hand tools. First, let me stress that this is not the same old drudgery that farm children have always shirked. The tools I recommend have been designed specifically for the job and make it quick and efficient work.

A further emphasis in this system involves more than just the design and operation of the tool—it includes the approach taken by the weeder. Weed control is often considered the most onerous of tasks, and the reasons are obvious. Not only the tools, but also the timing is often a drawback. Too many growers consider hoeing to be a treatment for weeds, and thus they start too late. Hoeing should be understood as a means of prevention. In other words: *Don't weed, cultivate.*

Cultivation is the shallow stirring of the surface soil in order to cut off small weeds and prevent the appearance of new ones. *Weeding* takes place after the weeds are already established. Cultivation deals with weeds before they become a problem. Weeding deals with the problem after it has occurred. When weeds are allowed to grow large and coarse, the task becomes much more difficult. But weeds should not be allowed to become so large. They should be dealt with just after they germinate. Small weeds are easy to control, and the work yields the greatest return for the least amount of effort. As well, small weeds have not yet begun to compete with the crop plants. Large weeds are competition for both the crops and the grower.

The Wheel Hoe

A wheel hoe combines a hoe blade with a wheeled frame to support the blade. It is the best cultivation tool for inter-row work on this 5-acre scale. There are two common styles of wheel hoe. One has a large-diameter wheel (about 24 inches) and the other has a smaller one (about 9 inches). Each style also has different means for attaching tools and handlebars to the frame. I have a strong preference for the small-wheel model. It just works better.

I remember being told years ago that the advantage of the large-diameter wheel hoe was that it could roll easily over obstacles. My reaction was that, if there were obstacles that large lying about the fields, I had more problems than the selection of a wheel hoe. The truth of the matter is that the design of the large-diameter wheel hoe is faulty. Human power is limited and shouldn't be wasted. In a well-designed tool, the force exerted by the operator is transferred directly to the working part. In the case of a wheel hoe, the working part is the soil-engaging tool, not the wheel. The low-wheel design transfers force much more efficiently than the high-wheel model. The drawings above illustrate the line of force in relation to each tool's structure.

The small-wheel model obviously allows the most efficient and direct transfer of force from the operator to the hoeing tool. Because the force is direct, a much higher percentage of the effort is applied to the cultivating blade. A further disadvantage of the high-wheel hoe is that a forward force is being used to manipulate a rear-mounted implement, thus causing torsional (twisting) forces to come into play that put even more strain on the operator. In sum, the low-wheel hoe is more accurate (easier to direct), less tiring (no force is wasted), and less cumbersome to use.

In recent years improvements have been made on this reliable tool. The heavy metal wheel of the old model, with its crude bushing, has been replaced by a lightweight rubber wheel with ball bearings. The original cultivating knives have been replaced by a far more efficient oscillating stirrup hoe, which has a hinged action and cuts on both the forward and backward strokes. When combined, these improvements result in the most efficient implement yet designed for extensive garden cultivation.

Oscillating stirrup hoes are available in widths from 6 to 14 inches. Wing models can extend the total cultivating width out to 32 inches. The wheel hoe can also be fitted with two wheels, allowing you to straddle the crop and hoe two rows at once. As is evident from the drawings below, the curved shape of the stirrup hoe blade cuts more shallowly next to the crop plants than in the middle of the row, thus sparing crop plant roots. The open center also allows rocks to pass through and even to be lifted up and out of the soil for later retrieval.

Stirrup hoes are double-stemmed; that is to say, they have a vertical support at each end of the blade. Because of this shape they are most effective when the crop is small or has only vertical leaves. To cultivate around and under the leaves of spreading crops, a single-stemmed hoe is necessary. Single-stemmed goosefoot and chevron-shaped hoes are available in widths from 5 to 10 inches.

Wing-model stirrup hoes extend the cultivating width.

A wheel hoe fitted with two wheels can straddle the crop and cultivate two rows at once.

Old-time wheel hoes were equipped with small plow attachments to turn a single furrow. I have never used one for plowing, but they are quite handy for burying the edges of plastic mulch and floating row covers. Wheel hoes can also be equipped with double-bladed plow bodies for furrowing or hilling up and with cultivating teeth for soil aeration.

Using the Wheel Hoe.   A wheel hoe equipped with an oscillating blade makes for pleasant work. The operator walks forward at a steady pace while making smooth push-pull motions with the arms. The push-pull takes full advantage of the swinging action of the oscillating blade and keeps its cutting edges free from debris. Accuracy along a row of seedlings is precise. The aim is gauged by focusing on one side of the blade (depending on whether the operator aims with the right or left eye) as it passes close to the row of seedlings. Ideally, the work should be done to a depth of only an inch or less.

A good wheel hoe will be adjustable at the front forks (A) to change the angle of attack of the blade, making it steeper for harder soils and shallower for light soils. The handles can be adjusted for the height of the operator (B). The height adjustment should be set so that the operator's hands are at about waist level and the forearms are parallel to the ground.

A further refinement makes the wheel hoe ideal for bed systems. Depending on the model, these tools are equipped with either a swivel joint or extension brackets through which the handles can be set at an angle off to one side. This feature allows the operator to walk alongside the direction of travel in order to avoid stepping on the newly cultivated soil. Thus, when crops are grown in a bed system, all cultivating can be done from the paths (see illustration).

This blending of the old and the new in modern wheel hoes results in the most efficient hand-powered cultivating implement available. It permits a high level of cultivation accuracy (to within ½ inch of rows of newly germinating seedlings) in addition to great speed of operation.

With the precision seeder or the transplant roller described earlier, you can plant straight, evenly spaced rows. With the wheel hoe you can cultivate those rows right up to the seedlings. When used in combination, these systems do away with the major part of the labor previously required for thinning and hand-weeding. The efficiency of these intermediate systems makes this scale of vegetable production just as competitive as large-scale, highly mechanized, and chemical-dependent systems.

The Long-Handled Hoe

The garden hoe that is well established in the public mind traditionally has a *wide blade,* a blade-to-handle angle of about 90°, and a *broadly curved shank* between blade and handle. The working edge of the blade is *offset* from the line of the handle. It is frequently a crude and heavy tool because it was designed for moving soil, digging, chopping, hilling, mixing concrete, and so on. It is this tool that has given hand-hoeing a bad name. A well-designed cultivating hoe, on the other hand, should have a *thin, narrow blade,* a blade-to-handle angle of 70°, *a slightly curved shank* between blade and handle, and have the working edge of the blade *in line* with the center line of the handle (a collineal design). This is a light and precise tool designed for a specific purpose—shallow cultivation. It is used as a soil shaver or weed parer rather than as a chopper or digger.

A number of considerations are important in hoe cultivation. It is undesirable to move excess soil, since this can bury seedlings or throw dirt on plants. The hoe blade should therefore be narrow and thin. The work must be accurate so as not to damage the plants. The sharp edge of the blade should therefore be intersected by the line of the handle. The work must also be shallow and not cut crop roots. The blade-to-handle angle must be set precisely. The technique is to skim, not chop, and the action should be fast and efficient, not tiring. The tool should be light, sharp, accurate, and easy to use.

Hand and Body Position.   When using a hoe, the cultivator should be standing upright in a comfortable, relaxed position. The traditional bent-over position and resultant sore back is a consequence of the chopping hoe, not the cultivating hoe. Body position is determined by hand position on the handle. There are four possible hand positions on the hoe handle: (1) both thumbs up, (2) both thumbs down, (3) both thumbs in, or (4) both thumbs out. The last one is uncomfortable. The third is a compromise. The second one, with both thumbs pointing down the handle, is the conventional chopping-hoe position and results in bending the back. The first position is the way a cultivating hoe is held.

With both thumbs pointing up the handle, the cultivator can stand comfortably upright. This is not a new technique to learn, only a new application. Most people instinctively hold a broom or a leaf rake in the thumbs-up position. If one thinks of a cultivating hoe as a "weed broom" to be used with a pulling or drawing motion, the hand position comes naturally. The hands are moved in unison to draw the hoe and are adjusted separately to idealize the working angle of the blade to the ground. These are very similar movements to those made by the hands and arms when sweeping or raking. With a little practice, the quick, accurate strokes that so effectively deal with weeds will become second nature to you.

A Razor Edge

A dull hoe blade increases the work and lessens the efficiency of cultivating to a far greater degree than you might think. I have seen a number of estimates (depending, obviously, on how dull the hoe is), but I would say that even a moderately dull edge lessens efficiency by 50 percent. Like any edge tool designed for cutting, the working edge of a hoe (hand or wheel) must be sharpened. A number of different sharpeners will do the job, but I prefer a small file. It should be carried in the back pocket and used at regular intervals to catch the edge before it becomes dull. A hoe blade should be filed to a chisel shape so the cutting edge is closest to the soil.

Tool Weight

An average field worker using a cultivating hoe will make some 2,000 strokes in the course of an hour's work. A real go-getter might do twice that. In working with a wheel hoe, about 50 push-pull strokes will be made per minute, and the

---

FITTING THE HANDLE TO THE COLLINEAR OR CULTIVATING HOE

There is normally some amount of curve in any long wooden handle. For the ideal balance or "feel" of the tool when in use, that curve must be accommodated when attaching the handle to the blade, as follows:

1. Insert the handle into the ferrule.
2. Set the hoe to balance horizontally on a narrow crossbar (for instance, the back of a kitchen chair).
3. When the tool is balanced, note the position of the hoe blade. The desired position is with the hoe blade's cutting edge down.
4. Twist the handle in the ferrule until you find the position where the hoe balances as desired.
5. Set the handle firmly into the ferrule and attach it with a screw.
6. It is helpful to have two holes in the ferrule for the handle-attachment screw. That way a new area of wood is available when the handle dries and has to be pushed into the ferrule slightly further.

direction of the tool must be reversed at the end of each row. In any such repetitious work, the weight of the tool is an important consideration. If a tool weighs even a few ounces more than necessary, the effect of moving that weight over a day's work results in the unnecessary expenditure of a great deal of energy. A well-designed cultivating hoe should weigh no more than 1½ pounds. A modern wheel hoe should weigh no more than 15 pounds.

Wide-Row Cultivating

The widely spaced row crops are cultivated most efficiently with the tiller. The choice of row spacing when planting these crops is dictated by the adjustable dimensions of the appropriate tiller model. There should be at least 2 inches clearance between the edges of the tiller and the crop rows. For example, a 26-inch-wide tiller carefully steered would just be able to cultivate rows planted at a 30-inch spacing. The depth skid for the tiller tines can be set so they run shallowly, ideally no more than 1 inch deep. For hilling potatoes, the wheels should be adjusted to the narrowest setting and the tilling attachment replaced with a furrower.

Flame Weeding

The use of flame or heat to kill weeds in row crops may seem modern, but it is not a new idea. The earliest recorded demonstration of a "weed scorcher" took place at the Royal Agricultural Show in England in 1839. The implement consisted of a wheeled metal grate (on which a coke fire was built) equipped with a fan (powered by a geared handle turned by a farm laborer), which blew the heat down to kill weeds below.

Flame weeders using liquid fuel were patented in the U.S. as early as 1852. From then until 1940, numerous models were designed and improved, principally for use in cotton and sugar cane fields. All the early models used liquid fuel, a compressor, fuel pump, and special generating burners. In the early 1940s liquid propane (LP) gas became the fuel of choice, since it burns cleanly and leaves no residue. From a modest beginning with 10 LP gas flame cultivators in the early 1940s, the concept steadily gained in popularity until, by 1963, an estimated 15,000 row crop machines were in use.

The practical and economic effectiveness of modern flame weeding depends upon a number of factors. The weeds should be less than 2 inches tall. For larger weeds, the flaming exposure time can be extended by slowing the tractor speed, but obviously this uses more fuel. Actually, a flame weeder does not burn the weeds. The heat intensity (fuel use) and time of exposure (travel speed) are adjusted so that only enough heat is applied to the weeds to cause expansion of the liquid in the plant cells and the consequent rupture of the cell walls. That requires a temperature of about 160°F. (71°C.) for a duration of one second. A simple test for sufficient heating is to lightly press a leaf between two fingers. If the leaf surface shows a dark green fingerprint, the job is done. Following flaming, the weeds continue to look normal for several hours before slowly beginning to wilt and fall over.

Flaming works best on a relatively smooth, clod-free soil, since ridges or clods can deflect the flame up against the crop plants. Flaming is more fuel-efficient when the weed leaves are dry, but it can also be done when the soil is too wet to cultivate mechanically. With the first in-row weeders flaming was delayed until the crop stem was tall or thick enough to resist accidental flame contact. Optimal speed was about 6 miles per hour. The next development was the addition of water spray shields to in-row flamers to confine the flame heat to the weeds at the base of the plant. The water shields allowed an increased cultivation speed, to 8 miles per hour. Some models combined in-row and between-row flaming, but eventually a combination of in-row flaming and between-row cultivation was found to be the most effective and economical method.

Starting in 1963 the new developments in flame weeding were reported at an annual symposium on "Thermal Agriculture" sponsored by the National LP Gas Association. These meetings continued until 1973, as the fuel crisis that year marked the end of the symposia and of most of the research projects in flame weeding. Fortunately, these ideas were being investigated independently by organic growers in Europe, and they continued to work at it. Higher gas prices inspired them to make their units more efficient. I first saw a flame weeder on a 1974 visit to organic farms in Europe. Although there were some models developed for in-row use, most of the European growers were concentrating on models for pre-emergence flaming in crops like carrots.

The technique goes like this (see chart on page 168). After preparing the seedbed the grower waits ten days to two weeks (during which time weed seeds germinate) and then drills the crop seeds. Just prior to the expected time of crop emergence the field is flamed. Timing is determined by placing a few small panes of glass over the seeded area in selected spots. These provide slightly warmer conditions, so the seedlings emerge a day or two earlier than the rest of the crop. The instant the first seedlings appear under the glass, the panes are removed and the field is flamed. The not-yet-emergent crop seedlings are insulated from the heat by the soil. A few days later they emerge through a mulch of dead weeds into a soil that has not been cultivated to bring up new weed seeds.

There are two styles of modern flame weeders—those with uncovered burners and those with burners placed under a metal cover. The cover ideally matches the width of the growing strip or bed in the production system and helps to concentrate the heat. The covered style of burner is more fuel-efficient, using 20 to 25 percent less fuel on average than uncovered burners. Flamers are available in backpack models with a single burner, hand-pushed multiple-burner models (both covered and uncovered) that roll on wheels, and tractor-mounted units. Many growers who are handy at fabricating tools have made their own flamers, since the parts are mostly off-the-shelf items. That fabrication needs to be done with care and knowledge, however, because propane is a very flammable substance. The most important design concept is to balance the number of burners with the size of the tank. The transformation of liquid propane into gas has a cooling effect. If gas use is excessive, the cooling becomes freezing and the regulator can freeze up. Some flame weeder manufacturers try to solve that problem by delivering the propane to the nozzle as a liquid, but that causes other instabilities. My recommendation to growers who wish to use this technology is to check out a flamer from a competent manufacturer. Once you become familiar with its intricacies, you can decide if you wish to fabricate your own.

I have seen many different homemade designs on small farms in Europe. Some of the small one-row models, especially those that roll on a wheel and have crop-protecting guards, seem particularly well suited to meeting specific weed-control needs in specialty crops. The future of flame-weeding technology is just waiting for the ingenuity of practical growers to modify and refine it in ways as yet unimagined. Sources for flame weeders are given in the tool appendix.

Long-Term Benefits

The emphasis on undersowing green manures in this production system obviously limits the period during which cultivation can be practiced. That is why cultivation must be done so well prior to the undersowing date. After that point the expanding leaf canopy of the crop progressively inhibits weed growth. When the additional low-leaf canopy of the undersowing is added, the inhibitory effect is even more pronounced. The few weeds that do manage to grow, however, must be pulled. The grower should plan occasional forays through the garden for this purpose.

That exhortation may seem perfectionist, but with good reason. I remember reading an old grower's book, *Ten Acres Enough,* that was published in the 19th century. The author held a weed-free philosophy similar to mine and wryly noted that the neighbors thought he was wasting his time. His conclusion, on the other hand, was that the number of new weeds was smaller every year and that his diligence paid off in the long run. My experience is the same. Ditto, Peter Henderson. In *Gardening for Profit,* published in 1879, he wrote:

> *. . . but weeds should never be seen in a garden, whether it be for pleasure or profit; it is short-sighted economy to delay the destruction of weeds until they start to grow. One man will hoe over in one day more ground where the weeds are just breaking through than six will do if they be allowed to grow six or eight inches in height, to say nothing of the injury done to the ground by feeding the weeds instead of the planted crops. Another benefit of this early extirpitation of weeds is that, taken in this stage, they, of course, never seed, and in a few years they are almost entirely destroyed, making the clearing a much simpler task each succeeding year.*

I don't worry about the weed seeds in the soil at the start. They are a given. However, I do concentrate on preventing their numbers from multiplying. Since the undersown green manure crop is a "deliberate weed" that benefits the system, it is the only weed I want. It may not be possible to attain perfection, but I will certainly approach a lot closer to that ideal if I try to prevent weeds from seeding.

H.A. Roberts and Patricia A. Dawkins, "Effect of Cultivation on the Numbers of Viable Weed Seeds in Soil," Weed Res., vol. 7 (1967), pp. 290–301.

Weeds research also confirms this observation, and details the rate of progress in ridding crop ground of weeds.* A study at the National Vegetable Research Station in England focused on the rate of decline of viable weed seeds in the top 9 inches of the soil. The rate of loss varied between 22 and 36 percent per year, depending on the amount of soil disturbance. On undisturbed soil, where no new weed seeds were brought up from below and no new seeding was allowed, scarcely any seedlings appeared after the fourth year. Again I concur from my own experience. After three to four years of diligence, your weed problems should be behind you.

System Benefits

One advantage of any system is the stability brought about by the practices involved. In a well-designed system, the practices add to that advantage by complementing each other. For example, the two planting techniques presented in an earlier chapter aid in efficient weed control. The use of a precision seeder gives evenly spaced plants in straight, evenly spaced rows. That obviously adds to efficiency and ease of cultivation. Crops grown in soil blocks and transplanted into newly tilled soil solve a number of weed-control problems. First, the crops have a head start on the weeds, which have yet to germinate. Second, the crops are set at the desired spacing, thus reducing adjustments for in-row cultivation.

A Final Word

Throughout this book I have stressed the need for the grower to develop keen powers of observation. The use of hand tools in cultivating is an aid to keeping on top of day-to-day changes. An English naturalist once made a comment in reference to Robert Burns's poem, "To a Mouse, on Turning Her Up in Her Nest with the Plough, November 1785": "Wee, sleekit, cow'rin', tim'rous beastie / O what a panic's in thy breastie! . . ." The naturalist said that, in a modern age, the poem would not have been written, because a driver of a tractor would not have noticed the mouse. The old horse farmer's advantages were not limited to mice and poetry. A grower with two feet in contact with the earth will notice more about the soil, the crops, and the general state of affairs than could ever be observed from the seat of a tractor.

Despite our modern motorized prejudices, hand tools, when designed correctly, are preferable for many operations. Good hand tools and techniques do not represent a step backward. They are, together with the other practices I recommend, a step forward to a better vegetable farm.

17 🐝

PESTS?

Let a man profess to have discovered some new Patent Powder Pimperlimp-limp, a single pinch of which being thrown into each corner of a field will kill every bug throughout its whole extent, and people will listen to him with attention and respect. But tell them of any simple common-sense plan, based upon correct scientific principles, to check and keep within reasonable bounds the insect foes of the farmer, and they will laugh you to scorn.

—Benjamin Walsh, *The Practical Entomologist* (1866)

THIS CHAPTER CELEBRATES LIFE. IT CELEBRATES THE COEXISTENCE OF growing plants, living creatures, and positive thinking. It explains why I have always found pesticides, whether "organic" or "chemical," to be the wrong answer. The systems of the natural world are elegant and logical. The idea of striving to create life-giving foods while simultaneously dousing them with deadly poisons is inelegant and illogical. Too many books focus on the doom and gloom of potential problems and eulogize the negative. I prefer to focus on the promise and practice of elegant solutions and celebrate the positive. Any supposedly "insolvable" problems are but a prelude to the next celebration.

Plant-Positive: The Other Side of the Tapestry

When faced with an insolvable problem, I stand it on its head. Then I can reconsider it from an inverted view. Very often a valid case can be made for the obverse position. The history of science records numerous examples of once sacred ideas that were shown to be backwards—the Ptolemaic concept of the sun revolving around the earth is a well-known example. Two reversals have been in the news recently. Instead of fearing the big, bad wolf, present-day wildlife managers have come to accept the actions of the predator as intrinsic to the balance of the natural world. The forest fire, once something that "only you" could and should prevent, has reemerged as a necessary component of a healthy forest.

In agriculture, most people would agree that the insolvable problem is the use of pesticides. Even with all the evidence about residue dangers, pest resistance, and environmental degradation, how do you get rid of products that are deemed so indispensable to our food supply? Well, let's turn that one on its head. Instead of the *pesticides are indispensable and we can't do without them* attitude that dominates the status quo, the reverse would be *pesticides are superfluous and intelligent agricultural systems don't need them*. That is certainly an appealing concept, but is there any evidence to support it? Hold on to your hat.

Not only is this concept documented in scientific studies, there is ample practical confirmation from farmers' experience. For over a century a small underground of farmers and researchers have rejected the idea that plants are defenseless victims and pests are vicious enemies. In their experience well-grown plants are inherently *insusceptible* to pests. They contend that plants only become susceptible to pest attack when they are stressed by inadequate growing conditions. Thus, they see pests not as enemies of plants, but as helpful indicators of cultural practices that need to be improved. Simply stated, insects and disease are bringing a message that the plant is under stress. That message is incomprehensible as long as we view pests as enemies. In essence, we have been trying to kill the messenger.

The fact that stress might have a detrimental effect on plants is not surprising in light of the similar effect of stress on humans. When we are under stress we too become more susceptible to the ills that can befall us. And, just as in agriculture, we can either choose chemical aids to mask the symptoms of our stress or we can make changes to correct the cause—changes in our lifestyle or work environment or daily habits. Any reputable stress-reduction program would recommend the latter as the intelligent course of action.

I define this thinking in agriculture as *plant-positive* in contrast to the present approach which is *pest-negative*. It makes sense. Since there are two factors involved, pests and plants, there are two courses of action: to focus on killing the pest, or to focus on strengthening the plant; to treat the symptom or to correct the cause. Since the former appears to be a flawed strategy, we might be wise to try the latter.

One way to visualize this duality is to picture the natural world as represented by an embroidered tapestry hanging from the rafters. The pesticide enthusiasts are all looking at the back side of the tapestry. From that perspective they see loose ends, stray threads, and confused patterns. Their science isn't bad, it's just that they can't see the logic of nature's woven fabric. They need to step around to the front side. From there the role of agricultural pests as de-selectors of substandard plants is clear, just as vertebrate predators like the wolf are known to target those animals stressed by illness, injury, or senescence.

History and Background

The earliest formal scientific expression of this idea first appeared in plant pathology literature during the 19th century as the Predisposition Theory[1]—that is, the host plant must first be *negatively predisposed* by unfavorable conditions before the pest can prevail. Scientific consideration of predisposition was rapidly eclipsed once plant pathology embraced the work of Pasteur, du Bary, and others, which assigned the causative role in diseases to microbes. Nonetheless, there were a few voices contending that nothing had changed. Even though the microbes could now be identified under a microscope and given names, they could still only prevail against a weakened host. Studies and review articles continued to be published. A survey of the literature on one small segment of the subject, the influence of potassium on plant health, cites 534 references, and notes that since 1950 the number of new references available has doubled every decade.[2] A study published ten years ago presenting a theory to explain the relationship between plant stress and insect abundance cites more than 300 references and has itself been cited over 200 times in subsequent studies.[3]

The general tone of these investigations lends support to what has always been a casually stated but inadequately understood tenet of the organic farming movement: "Healthy plants are not bothered by pests." Or, to put it more scientifically, *within a balanced ecosystem plants are inherently insusceptible when properly grown and only become subject to insect and disease problems when they are stressed by unfavorable growing conditions.* In other words, the pest-free plant is not the normal plant with something added, but rather the normal plant with nothing taken away.

This idea has been around for a while. In a 1793 letter to his daughter, Thomas Jefferson wrote:

> When earth is rich it bids defiance to droughts, yields in abundance and of the best quality. I suspect that the insects which have harassed you have been encouraged by the feebleness of your plants and that has been produced by the lean state of the soil.[4]

Erasmus Darwin, Charles' grandfather, speculated in 1800 that the leaves of a fruit tree damaged by insects were:

> previously out of health, which occasioned them to supply a proper situation for those insects which molest them.[5]

Thomas Green Fessenden, author of a garden book that was enormously popular in the 1830s, states:

The preventive operations are those of the best culture . . . including . . . choice of seed or plant, soil, situation, and climate. If these are carefully attended to, it will seldom happen that any species of insect will effect serious and permanent injury. Vegetables which are vigorous and thrifty, are not apt to be injured by worms, flies, bugs, etc.[6]

These comments are all expressed in a confident tone. That confidence is significant in light of today's assumption, quite obviously influenced by modern reliance on agricultural chemicals, that gardeners living in the years B.P. (before pesticides) must have had only pest-riddled produce, because they were at the mercy of continuous onslaughts of pests. It would appear this alternative understanding was more than a theory at that time but, rather, was the reality of their experience in the garden.

Even Louis Pasteur, whose name is so closely identified with the germ theory, wrote with passion about the potential of this alternative approach to forestall diseases. He was intensely interested in the importance of what he called the "terrain"—the environment within which the organism lives. His greatest fascination was not with the causative role of microbes, but rather with the "environmental conditions" that increased the "vigor and resistance" of the host.[7]

Many investigators have come to similar conclusions regarding insects:

. . . perhaps in the future more reliance will be put on correct cultural conditions than on spraying, and the conditions of the host plant be more closely watched than the presence of the insect parasite.[8]

. . . possibly the continuing need for the creation of new insecticides to hold in check greater and more destructive ravages in insect pests is aggravated by the gradual but general decline in soil fertility from year to year.[9]

. . . To sum up, the results already obtained seem to show that the search for improvement in the plant's resistance through its physiology is not just Utopian but quite practical.[10]

How Does It Work?

The most common explanation of how this works focuses on stress-initiated changes in the composition of plants. These changes increase plant susceptibility to insects and diseases. The principal change is a stoppage in the synthesis of protein within stressed plants, which results in a buildup in the plant tissues of free (unattached) nitrogen. Since availability of nitrogenous foods normally limits pest numbers in nature, their populations can explode where stressed plants increase in easily available nitrogenous compounds.[11]

In studies of a rice disease in Brazil, inadequate trace element nutrition of the plant was found to be the key stress. Where specific trace elements were deficient in the soil the disease was rampant. When the necessary minor elements were supplied, the plants were immune, even under conditions especially favorable to the disease.[12]

Research on nematodes has shown organic manuring of the soil to be important in overcoming nematode damage. The benefits that organic matter confers on the soil—improved structure, greater moisture-holding capacity, increased soil life, better plant nutrition—were all shown to be factors in preventing nematode infestation.[13]

A number of studies point out the difference between "absolute" resistance to pests, which is mostly a factor of the plant's genetic heritage, and "relative" resistance, which is a function of the conditions under which the plant grows. The opinion has been expressed that, if we could learn to nurture the mechanisms of "relative" resistance to their fullest, even practices like large-scale monoculture, often considered a causative factor of insect multiplication, would present fewer problems, because the cultural techniques would have assured the resistance of the plants.[14]

The U.S. Department of Agriculture in its 1957 Yearbook has this to say:

> *Well-fed plants are usually less susceptible to soil-borne organisms than are poorly nourished plants. Good fertility may so enhance the resistance of the* [host] *plant that the parasite cannot successfully attack the roots.*[15]

And finally, in one of the few studies specifically relating to organic farming, two Cornell researchers conclude:

> *Whatever the cause(s) for the significantly fewer insects in the organic treatments, the results support the proposition that organic fertilizers can promote crop-plant resistance to attack by insect pests.*[16]

Practical Experience

I recently sent out a questionnaire to 50 of the best commercial organic vegetable growers in the U.S. I asked if they had observed a correlation between healthy, unstressed plants and reduced incidence of pests. All but one said yes. I asked them what percentage of the pest problems that affected their chemical-farming neighbors they thought they avoided through growing healthy, unstressed crops. The average response was 75 percent. When you realize these growers have achieved that level of success with no help from the agricultural establishment, the 75 percent figure is quite impressive. It's even more impressive when you realize they are doing the impossible according to conventional agricultural thinking. The majority of these growers agree that the pest problems they still encounter only exist because they haven't yet figured out the successful cultural approach required to resolve those specific stress situations.

I have seen similarly exciting results in growing insusceptible crops on organic farms around the world. One experience stands out in particular. Back in 1979 I was visiting an organic vegetable grower in Germany along with a group of agricultural researchers from the USDA. They were working on a study, *Report and Recommendations on Organic Farming,* which was published by the USDA the following year. One member of the group was an entomologist. While the rest of us held a lively question-and-answer session with the farmer, the entomologist walked into the vegetable field. Stooping over and using his hands to sweep the air above the plants, he surveyed the insect population, looking for pests and pest damage. Eventually the conversation on the side of the field trailed off as our attention focused on the entomologist. He continued his search, becoming ever more amazed at the almost total lack of pest damage to the different crops. Finally, he stood erect, turned to the rest of us, and said in a tone of stunned admiration, "We can't even do this well *with* pesticides."

Resistance to an Idea

As you can see, there is a considerable amount of evidence—both positive scientific appraisals and successful practical examples—in support of this inverted approach to pest management. It would appear to offer a real option in the pesticide dilemma. Why, then, is this idea totally ignored by mainstream agricultural thought? Could it be that it is so revolutionary in its implications that no one dares to deal with it? Perhaps we are more constrained than we realize by the "mind-forged manacles" of which the poet William Blake wrote. The history of science records numerous instances where erroneous ideas have persisted for decades, even centuries, because of a reluctance to change. In the August 1978 issue of *Ag World*, Lola Smith addressed this very issue:

> *I cannot understand how* [agricultural] *scientists must reject so vigorously any suggestion that chemicals may be causing more problems than they are worth as presently used. Perhaps . . . to admit that such is the case would be to admit that the system they have developed with such high hope and optimism may have to be scrapped—and thus a large part of their lives may lose value.*

When I suggested to the organizers of two recent conferences on alternative pest control that they should include at least one paper introducing an outline of this theory, the suggestion was firmly rejected. Their idea of "alternative" was obviously limited to fine-tuning the status quo. I was asking for a revolution. A paper on this subject would automatically cast doubt on the premise of all the conventional papers. If this idea were correct, much of their work would be moot. How could they deal with the fact that I and other organic vegetable growers have been able to establish systems where conventional pest *control* is not the issue? This revolution deals in realities that are outside the present framework of acceptable entomological thought.

But in order for this idea to gain acceptance, the first step must involve *etymology* (the study of words) rather than *entomology* (the study of insects). It is immensely significant that we have no popular word to express a plant-positive approach. Everyone knows what the Department of Plant Pathology deals with, but does any university have the opposite, a Department of Plant _____? What would the word be? Health? Vigor? Vitality? For applying this concept to human beings, two British medical researchers have proposed "ethology," which they suggest:

> *. . . could be regarded as the study of that state of order and ease forming the background against which disorder and disease become manifest . . . . How lost health can be patched and palliated presents a different challenge to the scientist from how health can be cultivated—grown . . . . These two aspects—pathology and ethology—involve two different scientific adventures.*[17]

Ethology, as currently defined, refers to the study of animal behavior in the natural environment. Perhaps "euology" (from the Greek *eu-*, 'good,' 'well') might be coined for reference to plants. A new science of Plant Euology would focus on health rather than sickness; on "plant enhancement" rather than "pest control." Unfortunately, for the present, our minds are trapped in a pest-negative world. We can't even begin to seriously consider a concept for which we have no commonly accepted word.

We also encounter a powerfully influenced resistance to this idea based on fear—our fear and mistrust of nature. John Stuart Mill's statement from the 19th century expresses that attitude in unmistakable terms:

> *No one, either religious or irreligious, believes that the hurtful agencies of nature, considered as a whole, promote good purposes, in any other way than by inciting human rational creatures to rise up and struggle against them.*[18]

And T.B. Colwell confirms Mill's sentiments for the present day:

> *But though part of Nature, man's unique function . . . lies in controlling and transforming the natural world, not piously seeking its guidance. How profoundly we believe this today. How could we help but believe it; the entire edifice of our civilization is built upon it.*[19]

That control mentality extends to the words we use. Since insects "attack" the plant and "ravage" the crop, we do "battle" with them in order to "conquer" the "enemy." We use bug "killer" in a spray "gun" to "blast" them. In *The Pesticide Conspiracy*, Robert Van den Bosch paints a compelling verbal picture of the modern pesticide applicator as a swaggering, macho, Western gunslinger "pumping the lethal load of his Colt .44" into the bad guy.[20] Our primary view of nature and natural systems is negative. Only rarely do we consider the improved partnership with the natural world that could result from investigating, understanding, and, yes, "piously seeking its guidance."

Because we see enemies in nature, even our "alternative" practices are often misapplied. Supplementing the numbers of beneficial insects is one example. As stated earlier, I believe plants are inherently insusceptible when growing optimally in a balanced ecosystem. I try to encourage a balanced ecosystem by planting hedges of selected species and leaving meadow areas interspersed with the vegetable fields, in order to provide habitat for all the beneficial components which help create the balance.* If that ecosystem becomes imbalanced, such as by the accidental introduction of a new insect, then searching for and attempting to introduce parasites of that new insect are logical steps toward reestablishing balance. But that practice can be carried too far. Since beneficial insects exist as part of a balanced natural ecosystem, the thought has occurred to use them as a kind of biological SWAT team. Although it may be effective in some cases, the

*Meadow seed blends whose blooms provide nectar, pollen, and habitat for predatory wasps, lacewings, ladybugs, and other beneficial insects are sold under brand names such as Good Bug Blend and Border Patrol (see tool appendix). Of course, the same plantings can also provide habitat for pest insects. Researchers have investigated a number of management strategies for enhancing the effect of the beneficials. There are scientific references in Mary Louise Flint's Pests of the Garden and Small Farm *(Davis, CA: University of California, 1990) that provide more information to growers interested in exploring that option.*

❧

importation and dispersal of predatory insects is based on the same antagonistic thinking as is the use of pesticides. A recent advertisement from an insectary made that quite clear—"Get Revenge with Beneficial Insects." Bringing in mercenary bugs is still pest-negative, still focuses on the "enemy," still treats the symptom, and still attempts to kill the messenger and protect sick plants.

The genetic engineering approach shows less understanding yet. Moving resistant genes from one plant to another is purely defensive and assumes that the natural system is poorly designed. On the contrary, the design is impeccable—it is just poorly understood. A sick plant, even though equipped with a resistant gene, is still a sick plant. When healthy plants are grown under conditions that optimize their well-being, their resistance comes naturally through the proper functioning of all their systems. Genetic manipulation is still a negative rather than a positive solution.

How did we create an agricultural mentality that distrusts and disregards the workings of that very same natural world upon which it should be based? In the final analysis it comes down to the fact that we have made nature in our own image. We see natural processes as projections of our own aggressive actions and our revenge-dominated thought patterns. Thus we see malevolence in the relationship of one organism to another and in nature's relationship to us. We don't notice the beneficial balances between predator and prey that are maintained throughout the natural world. We miss the obvious logic of tipping that balance in our favor by creating optimum growing conditions for the plants. We need to shift our thinking.

Making It Work

When I first began trying to create ideal growing conditions, I didn't have to look far for a model to follow. The clues are written on every piece of uncultivated field and forest. The plants growing successfully on a natural site are those whose physiological needs are best met by the soil and climate conditions of that site. Since I wanted the site of my farm to favor a wide range of vegetables, I needed to learn how to make that site as amenable as possible to the needs of each specific crop.

I started with the obvious. I ensured that plant and row spacing were adequate for crop growth, maximum photosynthesis, and sufficient air movement. I avoided planting shade lovers in full sun or moisture lovers in dry soil or acid lovers in alkaline soil and vice versa. Then I dealt with each crop on a step-by-step basis. I would divide a field into strips. Each strip was fertilized differently (say, one with manure, the next autumn leaves, seaweed, compost, etc.), or each strip received different soil preparation (like rototilling, chisel plowing, mulching, no-till green manure, etc.) The crops (I usually included more than one variety of each) were planted across the strips.

Where differences were noted, new trials were laid out. The following year saw strips of cow, horse, pig, and chicken manure or beech, maple, oak, and ash leaves or clover, vetch, buckwheat, and rye green manures. Soil that had been deeply aerated was compared with undug; mulch type or depth or time of application was varied. I sent off soil samples for testing to try and pinpoint the beneficial factors involved, and how I might duplicate them by other means. In short, I ran my own experimental farm and developed techniques specific to its conditions. Every year crops grew better and I had fewer problems.

General experience has shown that practices which stimulate the biological activity of the soil are the most widely effective and least expensive in maintaining the insusceptibility, the yield, and the quality of the produce. These practices include adding organic matter; adjusting the balance, the amount, and the rate of availability of both the major and minor nutrients; correcting the soil pH; aerating the soil to prevent compaction; providing adequate moisture and drainage; using shallow tillage; growing mixed green manure crops for soil improvement and to modify soil biology; and employing well-designed crop rotations. All things being equal, if I were to suggest just one practice it would be to make as much first-class, well-decomposed compost as possible and use it liberally. If your efforts are not successful at first, don't give up. You need to adapt your actions to your soil, your climate, and your crops.

In 30 years of growing vegetables I have never found any need for pesticides once I succeeded in creating the best growing conditions for the crop. The optimum conditions are not the same for all crops, and they are easier to create on some soils than on others. The ideal crop rotation can make a world of difference. So can growing the right variety. I continue to observe and experiment. But in no case does the creation of those ideal conditions require more than the minimal resources of a small farm, nor more than a reasonable understanding of soil science and agronomic principles. What it does require, however, is a thought pattern that approaches the problem from a *plant-positive* rather than a *pest-negative* point of view—from a desire to correct the cause rather than just treat the symptom.

Biological Diplomacy

This cause-correction approach to pests is fundamental to organic agriculture. The hard truth is that if you don't understand this approach, you won't be able to understand how organic agriculture really works, nor will you have any idea of its potential. Without this understanding, organic agriculture continues to be constrained by an imitative type of thinking that merely substitutes "organic" for chemical inputs. Too many organic farmers unconsciously accept the framework of industrial agriculture, while employing natural ingredients—blood meal for nitrate of soda, bone meal for superphosphate, rotenone instead of DDT. When done that way, organic farming works reasonably well, because the new ingredients are more harmonious with the natural system than the old ones were. But it hasn't even scratched the surface.

What I am proposing is a totally revised way of thinking. In order for us to gain a proper understanding of agriculture, we need to develop a biologically oriented thinking that sees our agricultural efforts as *participatory* rather than as *antagonistic* vis-à-vis the natural world. This isn't a question of whether pesticides, either "natural" or "artificial," are good or bad. This theory bypasses that unwinnable debate by suggesting that pesticides are superfluous; that they were devised to prop up an agro-industrial framework which was misconceived from the start. When you abandon that framework, you can abandon its negative thinking pattern. The published research and the experience of organic growers around the world demonstrate clearly that when we accentuate the positive, we simultaneously eliminate the negative.

I would be remiss at this point if I did not tentatively extend the discussion one link further up the food chain to include human beings as consumers of plants. Are we humans also governed by these concepts? As in the case of plants, is our health, vigor, and resistance, our "biological quality," determined by our "growing conditions" and the physiological suitability of our inputs? If we have followed this positive approach to plant health and have optimized all factors of the plant's growing conditions in order to turn out a plant of the highest biological quality, will the consumption of that plant be a factor in optimizing our nutrition and subsequent well-being? The answers to these questions suggest implications of this plant-positive thinking that extend far beyond the field of agriculture.

Almost 500 years ago, while contesting the mistaken Ptolemaic concept of an earth-centered solar system, Galileo realized that he would have "to mold anew the brains of men" in order to establish another understanding. The change I am proposing—from a preoccupation with pest *destruction* to a focus on plant *construction*—requires a similar remolding. But it is a change that will allow us to eliminate all pesticides and simultaneously grow more nutritious crops.

NOTES

[1]C.E. Yarwood, "Predisposition," in *Plant Pathology*, vol. 1, ed. by J.G. Horsfall and A.E. Dimond, (San Diego: Academic Press, 1959), pp. 521–62.

[2]S. Perrenoud, *Potassium and Plant Health*. (Worblaufen-Bern, Switzerland: International Potash Institute, 1977).

[3]T.C.R. White, "The Abundance of Invertebrate Herbivores in Relation to the Availability of Nitrogen in Stressed Food Plants." *Oecologia* 63 (1984), pp. 90–105.

[4]R.C. Barron, ed., *The Garden and Farm Books of Thomas Jefferson*. (Golden, Colorado: Fulcrum, 1987), p. 156.

[5]E. Darwin, *Philosophy of Agriculture and Gardening*. (London: J. Johnson, 1800).

[6]Thomas Green Fessenden, *The New American Gardener*. 13th edition. (Boston: Otis, Broaders, and Co., 1839), p. 169.

[7]Cited in Rene Dubos, "An Inadvertent Ecologist," *Natural History* 85:3 (1976), pp. 8–12 .

[8]A.H. Lees, "Insect Attack and the Internal Condition of the Plant." *Annual Biology* 13 (1926), pp. 506–15.

[9]S.H. Wittwer and L. Haseman, "Soil Nitrogen and Thrips Injury on Spinach." *Journal of Economic Entomology* 38:5 (1945), pp. 615–17.

[10]F. Chaboussou, "Cultural Factors and the Resistance of Citrus Plants to Scale Insects and Mites," in *Fertilizer Use and Plant Health*. Proceedings of the 12th Colloquium of the International Potash Institute. (Worblaufen-Bern, Switzerland: Intl. Potash Inst., 1972) pp. 259–80.

[11]White, *op. cit.*

[12]A.M. Primavesi, A. Primavesi, and C. Veiga, "Influences of Nutritional Balances of Paddy Rice on Resistance to Blast," *Agrochemica* 16:4–5 (1972), pp. 459–72.

[13]P.A. Van Der Laan, "The Influence of Organic Manuring on the Development of the Potato Root Eelworm, *Heterodera rostochiensis*," *Nematology* 1 (1956), pp. 113–25.

[14]Von H. Thiem, "Uber Bedingungen der Massenvermehrung von Insekten." *Abr. Physiol. Angew. Entomol.* Berlin-Dahlem 5:3 (1938), pp. 229–55.

[15]United States Department of Agriculture. *Soil: The Yearbook of Agriculture* (Washington: USDA, 1957), p. 334.

[16]T.W. Culliney and D. Pimental, "Ecological Effects of Organic Agricultural Practices on Insect Populations." *Agricultural Ecosystems Environment* 15 (1986), pp. 253–66 .

[17]G.S. Williamson and I.H. Pearse, *Science, Synthesis and Sanity* (Edinburgh: Scottish Academic Press, 1980), p. 315.

[18]Cited in T.B. Colwell, "Some Implications of the Ecological Revolution for the Construction of Value," in *Human Values and Natural Science*, ed. by E. Laszlo and J.B. Wilbur, (New York: Gordon and Breach, 1970), p. 246.

[19]*Ibid.*, p. 247.

[20]Robert Van den Bosch, *The Pesticide Conspiracy*. (Garden City, NY: Doubleday, 1978), p. 19.

18 🜋

PESTS:
TEMPORARY PALLIATIVES

IN CHAPTER 17, "PESTS?," I ARGUED THAT THE EMPHASIS IN FARMING must be redirected toward practices that enhance the vitality of the crops rather than toward methods to destroy the pests. I believe that concept is key to understanding the processes of an ecological agriculture. But, as I know quite well, it will be seen only as an "ideal" of pest control by many people who would rather I had concentrated on providing lots of "magic organic solutions" for instant relief. Those in need of such help will find many books specializing in that approach. One quite well-done volume is *The Organic Gardener's Handbook of Natural Insect and Disease Control,* edited by Barbara Ellis and Fern Marshall Bradley, (Emmaus, PA: Rodale Press, 1992).

I emphasize preventive thinking because I have no interest in palliatives (from the Latin *pallium*, a "cloak"). Palliatives are actions which conceal or hide a problem by using a temporary expedient. But I must also consider the opinion of a friend who said to me, "OK, Eliot, I agree with your plant-positive thinking, but let's get real for a moment. What does a grower do at the start when the systems are not yet together or at those times when things go amiss?" My friend has a valid point. Since very few people have been consciously looking to solve problems from a plant-positive point of view, there is relatively little detailed information available for those facing difficulties with specific crops and specific situations (different soils, climates, seasons of the year.) And, until such time as attitudes change, individual growers will have little help in a plant-positive quest outside of their own experience.

So, for my part, I will suggest below a few pest-negative techniques I have used in those times of need. In my opinion these are the best of a bad lot. I always use them with the caveat that they should be regarded as temporary stopgap measures rather than as long-term solutions. I make no apology for treating "natural" pest-control practices so cavalierly. They don't solve the basic problem. Like chemical techniques, they treat the symptom rather than correcting the cause.

Nutritional Approaches

* There are quite a number of both seaweed-based and non-seaweed-based "plant enhancing" nutrient sprays used by organic growers. An extensive selection of them is available from Peaceful Valley Farm Supply. Their address is given in the tool appendix.

❧

** A good study with which to begin investigating this subject is Heinrich C. Weltzein, "Some Effects of Composted Organic Materials on Plant Health," Agriculture, Ecosystems, and Environment, *vol. 27 (1989), pp. 439-46.*

The Compost Tea Manual 1.1, *by Elaine Ingham and Michael Almes, is available for $15 U.S. from Growing Solutions, Inc., 255 Madison St., Eugene, OR 97402, (888)600-9558. It provides a clear explanation of the compost tea idea as well as information on production methods and formulas for enhancing the effect of compost teas in different situations.*

❧

These nutritional approaches to pest control are actually based on a plant-positive philosophy, and I have no objection to them except for the cost of the materials. In times of plant stress I have seen benefits from using foliar nutrient sprays to increase the plants' resistance to pests. But the results are not always consistent. In regard to seaweed-based sprays specifically, I think the explanation lies in the cytokinin content of the seaweed product. Cytokinin is a hormone produced by the roots of plants. It has an important function in protein synthesis in the plant. Plants under stress stop producing cytokinins, and thus protein synthesis is inhibited, resulting in insect and disease problems as postulated in Chapter 17. Cytokinins applied as a spray to the leaf surface seem to be able to ameliorate this situation. I suspect the inconsistency of results is a function of variation in the time of application (these foliar feeds may be more effective at certain times of day and during certain periods in the plant's development) or the quality of different liquid seaweed products; I cannot say for sure. But I do recommend that growers who plan to use liquid seaweed might want to look for brands that guarantee cytokinin content.*

A watery fermentation extract of well-finished compost, used as a foliar spray, has proven very effective against a wide range of plant diseases, including potato and tomato blight, cucumber powdery mildew, and botrytis on strawberries. The length of fermentation time appears to determine its effectiveness on different crops. These ideas are developing rapidly, and you should check at the library for the latest research results.**

The Walkover sprayer is powered by its rolling wheel.

The best tool I have found to apply liquid seaweed or any other nutrient spray is an ingenious wheeled sprayer called the Walkover. The spray tank and nozzle arms are supported by a lightweight wheelbarrow, the rolling wheel of which powers the pumping mechanism. When you walk forward, it sprays at whatever rate you set; when you stop walking, it stops spraying. By walking down the path you can spray the beds on either side simultaneously. For addresses of manufacturer and dealers, see the tool appendix.

Physical Controls

The floating row covers described in the season extension chapter (Chapter 21) work quite well as a physical barrier to keep pests away from the crop providing they are placed over the crop before the insects arrive. Special lightweight weaves designed specifically for pest exclusion, and which have only a minimal temperature-raising effect, are your best bet if the weather is warm. On my dry sandy soil I have not yet found a plant-positive answer to preventing flea beetle holes in arugula leaves during the warmer months, and a floating cover has helped a lot.

A floating row cover can act as a physical barrier against insects.

Vacuum collection of insects is an effective measure against both light-bodied pests (like squash bugs and cucumber beetles) and heavier bugs (like the Colorado potato beetle.) In 1979 I conducted pest-control trials using a 5-gallon shop vacuum, and I can recommend it highly for spot treatment of a wide range of insects, especially Japanese beetles.

Back in the 1940s there were two different manufacturers in Texas producing vacuum insect-collecting machines. These machines were attached to the front of a tractor and were driven by a belt running off the PTO. The machines employed the combined effects of both air blast and suction; an air blast from

Single-row, walk-behind insect vacuum.

outside of the row and a suction intake manifold at the center. Two rows could be cleaned of insects at once, with air blasts from the outside blowing the insects to a centrally mounted vacuum unit. In practice these machines were judged to be as effective as pesticides in controlling cotton insects.

Commercial-scale, multirow, tractor-mounted insect vacuums have recently reappeared on the market. So have single-row, walk-behind models that are powered by small gasoline engines. Experienced growers suggest that the best time to vacuum is in the early morning, when the insects are sluggish. Addresses for walk-behind models are given in the tool appendix.

Plain water can remedy some problems. Strong, fine sprays of water, especially if they can be directed toward the undersides of the leaves, have been shown to be effective at washing between 70 and 90 percent of aphids and spider mites off of plants.

Natural Pesticides

If you read the toxicity data on many natural pesticides, you will learn that it is hard to defend them as safer for humans. Both rotenone and nicotine products are toxic to most animals. Diatomaceous earth contains high levels of free silica, which damages the lungs and can cause silicosis. Precautions should be taken when using any of them. The safety factor with natural products is that they do occur in nature, do not persist, and do not leave human-made chemical residues in the environment. However, that residue-free safety may be compromised by the additives which are used as carriers and sticker-spreaders for the natural materials. I recommend considering the residue issue for any products you intend to apply.

I have used rotenone to control potato beetles, and it works reasonably well. The different Bacillus thuringiensis (Bt) strains are also effective at the present time against their target insects. I have used finely ground rock powders like basalt dust as an inert pesticide by dusting them over the plants.* (Basalt is safer to use than diatomaceous earth because it contains almost no free silica.) These finely ground powders are very effective in dry weather. In contact with the insect, they either adsorb or wear off the wax layer that covers the insect's exoskeleton, and the insect dries out. There are no residue problems, since basalt dust is also used as a slow-release soil amendment. Unfortunately, most of these materials are not selective and will kill non-target as well as target insects. However, that may be less of a concern if you are treating a one-time problem.

*Walter Ebeling, "Sorptive Dusts For Pest Control," A. Rev. Ent., 16 (1971), pp. 123–58.

Pest Resistance

There is a built-in Achilles heel with any pest-negative product or technique. Its action automatically selects for resistant members of the pest species—those whose unique genetics or behavior make them less susceptible to that particular control. The ability of insect evolution to evade our pest-negative control measures is a far more irresistible force than most people realize. For example, even the most effective insect traps select for those individuals who are not attracted to the trap. Their descendants inherit that ability. Our more "technological" practices fare no better. An entomologist friend explained to me recently that the sterile male technique, which had been considered foolproof, is breaking down in the face of the evolution of populations with mating behaviors that exclude the released sterile males, and with the appearance of parthenogenic females. The truth is pretty clear! Pest-negative practices are short-term solutions. The long-term solution involves learning how to grow the plants correctly, so you won't need to resort to palliatives the next time around.

19 ❧

HARVEST

Now that time and effort have been expended to grow first-class, top-quality vegetables, there is one last important step—harvesting. A good harvesting system involves more than just getting the crops out of the field. It must also concentrate on preserving the high quality of the produce until it reaches the customer. And it must do so efficiently, both from a practical and an economic perspective. This is the grower's final exam. All efforts up to this point can be wasted by a careless and slipshod harvesting program.

Preserving Quality

Vegetable crops continue to respire after they are harvested. That is to say, their life processes proceed as if they were still growing. Unfortunately, since they no longer have roots in contact with the soil to maintain themselves, harvested crops have a limited keeping span. The length of time depends on the individual crop, but the process involved is universal. The higher the temperature, the higher the rate of respiration of the crop and the shorter the keeping time. The grower's aim is to slow respiration in order to maintain all the quality factors—sweetness, flavor, tenderness, texture—that have been achieved by careful attention to cultural conditions during growth. This is best achieved by picking the crops efficiently and cooling them rapidly to slow down the rate of respiration.

There are two parts to the harvesting operation: the efficient organization of the actual harvest and the post-harvest treatment.

Tools and Equipment

Efficiency and economy of motion are important in all phases of the physical work of vegetable growing, but nowhere are they as vital as at harvest. Speed is essential. It keeps quality fresh and, as we have noted, quality determines the market. If the crop is grown well but is not harvested or handled properly, the earlier work was all for naught. Harvesting speed is initially a function of organization beforehand. The grower must ensure that there are adequate tools—knives, baskets, containers—on hand. The key tool is a good harvest knife. Some growers prefer the California field knife with its large, broad blade. Others use shorter styles with a hook-shaped blade like a linoleum knife or a belt sheath knife with a 3-inch blade. In many cases, the choice of knife depends on the crop to be harvested. For example, I use a field knife for broccoli and cauliflower but a lighter knife for harvesting butterhead lettuce. I also like to have a wrist loop attached to the knife so it remains on my wrist even when I let go of it with my fingers.

Harvest baskets or crates are most efficient if they are of regular size and sturdy enough to be filled in the field and stacked for transport. You may need to make your own crates for unfamiliar crops like mâche, which is traditionally harvested into shallow boxes in single layers set with the leaves upright. Many food co-ops like to have attractive crates in which to display and sell local produce. A well-designed farm logo burned into the wooden side adds distinction and farm recognition. You can deliver in these easily identifiable boxes to co-ops and restaurants and arrange for their return when you deliver the next order. For many crops, plastic crates with an open-mesh design are desirable because they can be dunked in ice water to quick-cool the produce.

The truck, trailer, or harvest cart for collecting or transporting the produce must be suited to the job. A well-designed harvest cart will have the wheels and support legs spaced so they straddle the growing strips. For this system the wheels would be set on 42- or 60-inch centers, depending on strip width. Heavy-duty cart wheels can be purchased from garden-cart makers. The wheel diameter should be at least 24 inches or more. The best "body" for the cart is a

A well-designed harvest cart with provision for shading.

flat bed for holding crates. The pickers can then cut and crate produce directly onto the cart as they move down the row. This can be the same cart used for carrying flats of soil blocks during the earlier transplanting operation. It is imperative that temporary shade over the cart or a fine cool mist be provided until the harvested crops reach the permanent storage area.

On a 1989 trip to Europe I saw some interesting designs for pedal-powered harvest aids. Models had been designed for single workers and for two or three people working in unison. These pedal carts are supported on fat pneumatic tires, like the tire on a wheelbarrow, which roll in the paths or wheelings between the beds. A form-fitting seat, close to the ground, allows the worker to reach efficiently to left or right. Since the seats make for such a comfortable working position, these rigs are an ingenious alternative to the stooping and bending involved in picking low crops like bush peas, strawberries, or young salad greens. The units are designed with pedals, chains, and gears for high power and slow speed. They enable the workers to progress along the beds at whatever speed is appropriate to the work being done. Crates and boxes are stacked on the frame. Logically, the units are also valuable for hand-weeding and transplanting.

At a recent farm conference I was pleased to see two new and improved models that are presently being manufactured in the U.S. There are a lot of ingenious people on farms, and these designs reflect that fact. One model was equipped with lightweight seeders and cultivators. That made me think about the enormous potential of such a simple idea. It is not difficult to visualize a grower on level land being able to perform every operation from seeding to harvest with an efficient pedal-powered rig. Addresses are given in the tool appendix.

Planning

Harvesting involves a great deal of repetitive work. Repetitive work is made much easier and more pleasant when economy of motion is understood and an efficient working rhythm can be maintained. To satisfy those criteria you must evaluate the job from top to bottom. What is going to happen? How is it to be done? What hand and body motions are involved? Is it simpler from left to right or vice versa? It is always possible to find an easier, quicker, and more economical way to do a job. The benefits of such improvements are important in reducing drudgery for the farm crew.

Thus, the keys to simplifying farm work, especially harvesting, are to:

- Eliminate all unnecessary work.
- Simplify hand and body motions.
- Provide a convenient arrangement of work areas and locations for materials.
- Improve on the adequacy, suitability, and use of equipment needed for the work.
- Organize work routines for the full and effective use of labor and machines.
- Involve the workers in the process. When people become more conscious of the way they perform work, their interest increases and their attitude toward the work changes. They begin to notice other things and make valuable suggestions for further improvements.

Minor Details

Let's take tomato picking as an example. Studies have shown that the average worker does not need to work harder, but rather more efficiently. Comparative trials have demonstrated the difference in worker productivity that can result from very simple changes. A comfortable handle on the picking basket so it can be moved with one hand rather than two may seem like a small detail, but the increase in efficiency is considerable. Picking with both hands and keeping them close enough together so the eyes can control them simultaneously without moving the head speeds up the process. The hand motion itself is more efficient if two tomatoes are grasped instead of just one. Since 40 percent of the picker's time is spent moving the hands to the basket, the picking rate can almost be doubled by learning the finger dexterity needed to pick two fruits at once. The technique is to pick a tomato in each hand, shift the tomatoes back into the palm of the hand, and pick a second tomato in each hand before moving the hands to the basket.

Using both hands to pick tomatoes efficiently.

The upshot of approaching the physical aspects of harvesting in such a planned and organized manner is not just an increased speed of one particular task such as tomato picking, but improved efficiency of all harvest work. Further, once the grower and the harvest crew become aware of the possibilities for making the harvest easier and more pleasant by focusing on everything from individual motions to overall organization, the improvements carry over into other aspects of the farm day. Any work that can be done in less time and with less effort is more pleasant and relaxing. Any time spent thinking about and reorganizing for work efficiency is time well spent.*

A good (although dated) book on farm work efficiency is Farm Work Simplification by L.M. Vaughan and L.S. Hardin (New York: John Wiley & Sons, 1949).

Post-Harvest Treatment

The best and most complete information on post-harvest treatment of all crops is contained in the excellent publication on the subject by the USDA—*The Commercial Storage of Fruits, Vegetables, and Florist and Nursery Stocks* (Agriculture Handbook Number 66). I have followed their guidelines for many years, with great success.

Harvested produce should be neither immature nor overmature, because in either case eating quality and storage life are impaired. Any nonedible portions such as carrot tops or extra cabbage leaves should be removed unless they are absolutely required for dressing up a sales display. Such large, leafy expanses present extra evaporative surface, hastening the water loss and loss of overall quality. The leafy vegetables that wilt the fastest, such as lettuce and spinach, should be harvested during the early morning hours and taken into cool storage immediately.

The first step after harvest is to precool the crops. Precooling refers to the rapid removal of field heat. Crops harvested early in the morning, before the sun warms things up, have less field heat to remove. Since any deterioration in crop quality occurs more rapidly at warm temperatures, the sooner field heat is removed after harvest, the longer produce can be maintained in good condition. Precooling can be done by immersion in or spraying with cold well water. The colder the better. A superior method, although it is more expensive, is to place crushed ice within containers in direct contact with the produce or spread over the top of it. Freezing units to make crushed ice sometimes can be bought used from restaurant suppliers.

After precooling, any produce to be stored should be kept cool in a spring house, root cellar, or refrigerated cooler. A temporary homemade "refrigerator" cooled by evaporating water can be set up quickly by using a fan to draw air through a water-soaked cloth into the storage area. This will also increase the humidity around the stored crops. High relative humidities of 85 to 95 percent are recommended for most perishable horticultural products in order to retard softening and wilting from moisture loss. Since most fruits and vegetables contain between 80 and 95 percent water by weight, wilting can seriously lower quality.

At times it may be necessary to store different products together. In most cases this is no problem, but with some products there can be an unwanted transfer of odors. Combinations that should be avoided in storage rooms are apples or pears with celery, cabbage, carrots, potatoes, or onions. Celery can also pick up odors from onions. Ethylene damage is another consideration. Lettuce, carrots, and greens are damaged when stored with apples, pears, peaches, plums, cantaloupes, and tomatoes because of the ethylene gas that is given off by the fruits as they ripen in storage. Even very low concentrations of ethylene may produce adverse effects on other crops.

20 ❧ MARKETING

There are many marketing options for the quality-conscious small grower. The standard possibilities are restaurants, farm stands, and farmers' markets. These are all tried-and-true outlets, and there are excellent real-life models available to study. At one time or another I have used all of them.

Plan to Succeed

To do successful business with restaurants, the grower needs hustle and dependability. Hustle, in order to find potential restaurant customers and convince them to buy from you, and to offer new crops, extended-season production, and gourmet items in order to increase the business once it is developed. Dependability, to keep that business once you have it by never defaulting on a promised order. Good chefs love good ingredients. You should let them know how nice your crops are by hosting an open-field day at your farm and inviting the chef of every local restaurant. Or else pack a gift basket of your choicest items and deliver it to them with a clear list of what is available and when. If you have exceptional produce, you will not be begging for customers. In fact, you will be doing them a favor by letting them know it is available.

The secrets to success at farm stands and farmers' markets are attractive surroundings, ease of access, cleanliness, orderliness, cheerful service, and early produce. Access to the parking lot must be open and inviting. The general level of cleanliness, neatness, and organization will be the first thing a customer notices. Make sure it speaks well of you. The employee or family member on duty at the stand must be friendly and informative. Make sure it is a pleasure for customers to shop there. Say "yes" to special requests whenever possible. Always make amends for any customer complaint. Our guarantee was ironclad. We gladly offered money back, replacement of the vegetables, even double money back without argument. It is important that customers know you stand behind the quality of what you sell. That policy never cost us more than $10 a year, and it gained us priceless customer goodwill. Nothing is more expensive for a retail business than unhappy customers.

We planted perishable crops such as lettuce in the fields closest to the stand so customers could choose their lettuces and have them cut fresh on the spot. Free copies of the vegetable recipe of the day were posted to whet our customers' appetites. Customers were encouraged to wander along the harvest paths and view all the crops. Their presence encouraged us to keep up on our cultivation so the place looked orderly and presentable. A prominent herb garden inspired gourmet cooks. We also had our own "green stamps"—a cut-flower garden free for the picking to anyone who purchased vegetables.

Clean surroundings, attractive presentation, and a friendly staff make a market stand irresistible to customers.

We wanted our operation to stand out from all the others. We established a reputation for having everything all the time. We pursued that policy by raising the broadest possible range of crops and by using succession plantings. The broadest range of crops meant some 40 different vegetables. Succession plantings meant planting as often as necessary to ensure a continuous supply of each crop from the time it first matured till the end of the growing season. One year we succeeded in selling fresh peas every day but one from when they first matured in June till we closed in October. I won't say we made money on the peas. In fact they were a loss leader. But just having them every day enhanced our reputation and our business.

All of these efforts paid off. New customers would often tell us they had been assured by friends that if anyone would have this or that crop (whatever they were looking for), we would. No other local growers bothered with minor crops like scorzonera or fennel. We did, and we gained a lot of customers by doing so. In addition, all our fields were very neat, trim, and well-cultivated. Customers loved the "look" of the place and would come twice as often and bring friends just because of that. A typical comment was, "Our friends the Smiths came to visit us, and we told them one of the first things they had to see was your farm. You make vegetables look so beautiful."

Another marketing approach is to specialize in high-demand crops such as mixed salads or in a specialty such as winter-season production—two areas we are involved in at the moment. I think the new awareness of vegetables and salads as integral parts of a healthy diet is a movement that will continue to grow. Local salad production can be especially lucrative with an extended season of availability. Once I get customers interested, I want to be able to keep supplying them. More than anything else, local salad vegetables bespeak freshness, crispness, and purity. What a successful drawing card that is for any small-farm operation.

Whatever the style of marketing, presentation is crucial. Potential customers will quickly become aware of the quality of produce you offer if your high production standards are matched by the inviting way you present your produce. The following paragraph from a 1909 book, *French Market Gardening* by John Weathers, shows the timelessness of this good agricultural advice:

> *Perhaps one of the most difficult problems connected with commercial gardening is the disposal of the produce at such a price as to yield reasonable profits. In this connection much depends not only upon the way the "stuff" is grown, but also upon the way it is prepared for sale. It is well-known that the very finest produce in the world stands a very poor chance of selling at all, unless it is packed in a neat, clean, and attractive way. . . . Originality,*

combined with neatness and good produce, very often means remarkably quick sales.

Subscription Marketing

This is a very innovative approach. It has the potential to be quite economically successful for the small farm, more satisfying to the customer's needs, and less costly in terms of farm labor. I initially called my own subscription program a "Food Guild." I choose the word "guild" because it is defined as a voluntary association for mutual benefit and the promotion of common interests. That is an accurate description of this idea. This marketing system is a farmer-consumer symbiosis, a relationship that benefits both parties.

I first heard of this concept in 1980 from a member of the USDA Organic Farming Study Team who had recently returned from an information-gathering tour of organic farms in Japan. It seems that many Japanese organic producers, who farm on the scale that we are talking about here, found that the best market was a limited group of loyal customers. The farm unit becomes the complete food supplier to whatever number of families the farm production can accommodate—not just for a few products, but to supply all the vegetables and any other farm foods over the course of the year. The customer families, who sign up in advance, were encouraged to become involved with the farm. Everything from choosing varieties of lettuce to determining the number of roasting chickens per year was done in consultation with the customers. Thus they became aware of the source of their daily food, to the degree that many would voluntarily show up in their spare time to help out on "their" farm. The farmer benefits because marketing is no longer a time-consuming process.

Obviously, if one requires this sort of devotion from consumers, they have to receive an equal value in return. And they do. The Japanese use the poetic phrase, "food with the farmer's face on it." I have heard other people state that the only way to be sure of eating pure food is to know the first name of the grower. Local organic producers offer customers safe food in an increasingly chemicalized world. Customers will sign up because they can be sure that the farm's food is pure and grown with meticulous attention to detail. They can relax and enjoy eating, free from concern about problems of chemical residues.

A few years ago I met with a German grower who operated a subscription program for 600 households: "From our garden to your house." He spoke about what it meant to him as a farmer to market in this manner. There was the obvious advantage of knowing the crops were sold ahead of time so he could concentrate on the part he loved best—growing exceptional produce. But even more important than that was the implicit recognition by the customers of his skill at growing. By signing up with his farm, consumers were choosing his services on the basis of their assessment of his professional competence, in the same way they selected a family doctor, lawyer, or other purchased professional service.

Producer-Consumer Copartnerships

The Japanese name for this marketing concept is *teikei*, or producer-consumer copartnerships. The British call it a "box scheme." I have learned of many examples of this style of marketing in European countries, where the idea has a long history. The first farm employing this concept in the U.S. was a product of the European influence. Its founders coined the name *community-supported agriculture* (CSA for short), a name now often applied to all marketing schemes along these lines. Although in most cases the basic concept is the same—the farm has contracted with a group of customers to provide them with a broad-based diet of as many farm foods (usually vegetables, but sometimes also eggs, milk, and poultry) over the course of the year as the farm wishes to produce— the ways in which that idea is presented and marketed can be very different.

The European model that inspired the first CSA in the U.S. arises from a background of social and philosophical concerns about food, food systems, participation, and human responsibility. People who share those concerns are logically attracted to that model. But there is a huge pool of potential customers whose participation may be inhibited by a focus that goes beyond food shopping. All they want is dependable access to a supply of fresh, wholesome food. Since the first rule of marketing is to give customers what they want, I suggest that there are many diverse ways in which this concept can be presented and marketed in order to expand its potential.

What's in a Name?

For marketing success and to better capture the essence of what they are selling, different plans may want to use a more precise name than CSA. My original term, "Food Guild," is one example. Or it might be better to key the name to a familiar concept. Since people commonly start or join clubs for group enjoyment of a limited resource, the "Organic Food Club" might catch their interest. People with money to invest but no skills in the investment world often turn to a mutual fund. Maybe people with a hunger for local organic vegetables but no skills in the farming world, might be enticed by a "Mutual Farm." Who wouldn't love to have their own private gardener like the lord of the castle? Well, an operation called "The Estate Garden" could advertise its service and produce quality as the equal of having a private gardener, yet be no more expensive than the food store since the cost is spread among many members. Possibly just a local town or region name may be all that is needed: "Mountainside Home-Grown Vegetables, Inc.—sign up now and reserve your share."

The variations, refinements, and possibilities of a guild marketing program are unlimited. There are some approaches that may initially seem more workable than others, but the real determinant will be the desires of the guild participants. Some areas of the country and some groups will require entirely different arrangements than others. What we have here is a system of marketing in harmony with the biological diversity of farming itself. There are as many marketing choices as there are agricultural choices to accommodate different soils, climates, and locations. It is refreshing to think that this program could potentially be as individual to the farm as are the production practices themselves.

The Possibilities

A program can be set up for any degree of participation or non-participation by the customers, depending on the desires of a particular group.

- The customers could help with harvesting and distribution as in a food co-op, or the farm could hire interested customers or outsiders for picking and packing.
- The vegetables can be made available "as picked," or the farm can wash and bunch for a more professional presentation.
- The customers could come to the farm (say, twice a week) to pick up their food supplies, or the farm could deliver to a centralized pick-up spot (in a town or city) or to individual customers on whatever schedule was selected.
- The farm could provide just the raw materials, and the customers would be responsible for any processing. Or the farm could freeze or can the storage items for the customers and provide them with the finished products.
- The customers could store out-of-season foods in their own freezers and cellars, or the farm could provide bulk facilities for freezing and storage that the customers could then draw upon as needed.
- There could be a specified list of products supplied each week throughout the year, and customers could have the flexibility to request greater quantities of one or the other item, either by paying more or by trading off against something else: more Chinese cabbage, less lettuce; more chicken, less pork.

- The length of the fresh produce season can vary. Growers in a summer-vacation-home area may find a perfect match between the outdoor production season and when potential customers are in residence. If customers are available, the production season can be doubled with simple greenhouse protection at either end. Obviously, the longer the season of availability, the more attractive the program is to potential customers.
- A program could also be conducted in partnership with another organization. Back in the late 1970s we set up such an arrangement with a nearby food co-op. We called it the "organic grab-bag." It was a bag of vegetables at a fixed price, but with no guarantee of the contents other than that it represented a great value for the money. People would sign up in advance and we would fill the bags with whatever kinds of crops were plentiful that week. We deducted an additional 10 percent when the co-op began supplying the pickers (who received co-op work credit for their participation). It was a wonderful arrangement. We got paid for excess crops that might otherwise have gone unsold. The buyers got a great value and took care of the harvesting, packaging, and delivery. All we had to do was show them where to pick and provide a minimal amount of instruction. The opportunity exists to make similar arrangements with any organized group.
- From my marketing experience I would suggest that the more services a subscription program provides, the more attractive the program will be in a world ever more attuned to supermarket convenience. Although as a producer I know that quality is my first consideration, I realize that for many potential customers—those who are not yet aware of differences in quality—service and convenience rank higher. If I want their business, I must take account of that reality.

Pricing

The choice of the either-ors above will determine the price of the food and the level of service. Logically, the more services the farm provides, the more the food will cost. With the exception of the most personalized service, the cost should be similar to standard store prices for comparable items. And that is another benefit of this concept. Organic foods are often criticized as being too expensive for most budgets. That is often a function of the laws of supply and demand in the marketplace. But because of the benefits that accrue to the farm and farmer through this prearranged system of marketing, organized consumer groups can obtain the best organic produce at standard food-store prices.

However, in those cases where items are more expensive to produce, their sale price must cover the increased costs. Since this is a mutually beneficial relationship, the customers will be cognizant of the vital importance of a local farmer to their own happiness and well-being. A price must be agreed upon that will allow the farmer and farm workers a realistic income for providing such an important ingredient in the lives of their customers.

The biological production technologies I recommend are designed to keep small producers in business by lowering their costs. The resultant higher quality of the crops should further aid small producers by increasing their income. Food prices should reflect quality, just as prices do in other consumable goods. There has to be a premium paid for quality and the skill and caring that creates it or it won't exist. The small farmer who is turning out a premium product must demand a fair return.

Stay Small

These days, when a business succeeds there is always the tendency to multiply the success by getting bigger. I have one word of advice—don't. That admonition may sound heretical given the dictates of modern economics, but my experience confirms it. I have seen too many successful producers make the expansion mistake. Without exception, they have each become just another company trading on the reputation they established before expanding. If demand exceeds supply, bring the two back into line by raising prices. Income will increase just as it would by expansion, but quality will not be compromised.

21

SEASON EXTENSION

WE LIVE IN AN AGE OF SUPERMARKET THINKING WHERE CUSTOMERS HAVE come to expect out-of-season produce. The supermarket sells tomatoes in April and peas in October. In order to compete, local growers should attempt to come close to those goals for the period of the year when their marketing operation is open. For almost all vegetable crops, a longer growing season is desirable if it can be attained economically. Vegetable growers can capture and hold new markets and receive higher prices by having produce available as early or as late as possible compared to unprotected outdoor crops. The grower meeting a local demand or running a market stand will find that a policy of "everything all the time" pays off handsomely.

The secret to success in lengthening the season without problems or failures is to find the point at which the extent of climate modification is in balance with the extra amount of time, money, and management skill involved in attaining it. When planning for a longer season, remember the farmer's need for a vacation period during the year. The dark days of December and January, being the most difficult months in which to produce crops, are probably worth designating for rest, reorganization, and planning for the new season to come. In any season extension, the aim is always to keep the systems as simple and economical as they can be without relinquishing the dependable control necessary to ensure the success of the protected cultivation. A broad range of options are available. This review will run through most of them and then recommend those that fit best into a small-scale vegetable operation.

Climate Modification

When considering the possibilities for extending the growing season, we should be aware of options other than building a greenhouse or moving south. There exist many low-cost or no-cost practices that can make a significant contribution to modifying climate conditions in the grower's favor. Any human modification of climate involves altering the existing natural parameters in order to achieve more than those parameters would otherwise allow. As a rule of thumb, the more we wish to modify the climate, the more energy we must expend in doing so. For example, growing tomatoes in January in New England obviously requires a far more expensive and extensive effort than merely speeding up the ripening of summer tomatoes by setting out the plants in a particularly warm and sheltered spot.

The simplest way to improve the growing conditions for early crops is to find, create, or improve such warm and sheltered spots.* We can temper the climate with minimum energy expenditure if we work with natural tendencies and try to augment their effects. Three common natural parameters that are logical candidates for modification are the degree and direction of slope of the land; the amount of wind exposure or protection; and the heat-absorbing potential of the soil (soil color). If your land does not slope to the south, a practical approximation of a southern exposure can be created on a flat field by hilling it up in east-west ridges with the southern surface sloped at approximately 40°. This gives the effect of many small south-facing slopes. Calculations have shown an average 30-percent gain in total heat absorption by the soil from this practice. Early crops planted just up from the base of the southern slope of these ridges have a significant head start in the spring over similar crops planted on the flat.

Windbreaks of hedges and trees require long-term planning if such shelter does not already exist. Fortunately, effective short-term protection can be had by using temporary shelters. Two parallel lengths of snow or dune fencing 4 feet high and 60 feet apart can increase air temperature by 1° to 4°F. (roughly 1° to 2°C.). The slightly more substantial protection of a snow or dune fence combined with a hedge can mean an average air temperature increase of 5°F. (3°C.) in April and 7°F. (4°C.) in May. Even a temporary 2-foot hedge of spruce boughs can keep the air temperature of the protected plot 2° to 3°F. (1° to 2°C.) higher than that of nearby open fields.

On small European farms I have seen temporary windbreaks of woven mesh materials placed on the edges of fields perpendicular to the prevailing wind and also within fields to create smaller protected areas. A number of companies sell these specialty windbreak fabrics, which have securing grommets already set into the fabric edges. They are usually made in 4- or 6-foot widths and come in lengths of 100 to 300 or more feet. They are attached by the grommets to wooden posts set at a 6- to 10-foot spacing depending on the wind conditions. In really windy conditions the fabric should be secured to the post with a full-length batten. These windbreaks provide part of the advantage of a greenhouse. You have the walls and not the roof, which means that irrigation and ventilation are still provided by rain and natural air movement. Yet the temperature around the plants has been raised substantially. The closer together the vertical walls are placed, the more protection they give. Temporary 2- to 3-foot-high walls of

*Some interesting books on microclimate are: Climates in Miniature by T. Bedford Franklin (London: Faber, 1945); Shelterbelts and Windbreaks by J.M. Caborn (London: Faber, 1955); and Climate and Agriculture by Jen-Hu Chang (Chicago: Aldine, 1968).

translucent plastic between tomato rows, for example, will raise the daytime temperature 10°F. (5° to 6°C.) on average with no worry about overheating as in a covered greenhouse.

Soil color is a third factor that adds to the effects of the first two. The beneficial out-of-season growing conditions created by the combination of a southern slope and wind shelter can be augmented even more by darkening the soil. Certain soils warm more rapidly than others, and this natural power of absorption can be increased. Dark colors absorb more heat than light colors, and soils are no exception. Charcoal, carbon black, and coal dust have all been used successfully to darken and increase the heat absorption of soils.

In an experiment conducted to test the way in which soil color affects the rate of heat absorption, three plots were prepared on a natural sandy loam. The first was covered with soot to make it black, the second was left with its normal soil color, and the third was dusted with lime to whiten it. Thermometers were placed at a 4-inch depth in each plot. By midafternoon, on a sunny day in early May, the blackened surface had raised the temperature at the 4-inch level 7°F. (4°C.) above the temperature of the normal soil and 12°F. (7°C.) above that of the whitened surface. The darker soil also retained the heat gained by a few degrees at night. The emissive power of radiation of the longer wavelengths radiated by the earth is not affected by color, so the black soil did not lose heat more rapidly than the others.

Depending on the speed of growth and type of crop, the heat-absorbing effect of a darkened soil will diminish over a four- to ten-week period as the plants grow and their leaves shade the soil. This is a harmless development, since it is only in the spring that soil temperatures need to be raised.

Plastic Mulch

The next logical step beyond charcoal dust is a simple sheet of material laid on the ground as a mulch to aid in warming the soil. Polyethylene plastic is the standard material. Plastic strips 4 to 6 feet wide and as long as convenient are laid on the soil with the edges buried to anchor them against the wind. Four things contribute to the popularity of plastics as a commercial mulch. Plastic mulch retains moisture, warms the soil, can prevent weed growth, and is readily adaptable to mechanization for application and removal. Both tractor-mounted and hand-cart–mounted implements are available.

Growers have long known that clear plastic will warm the soil more effectively than black (the clear acts like a low greenhouse). However, black plastic was more commonly used since it also shades out weeds. The latest developments in infrared-transmitting (IRT) plastic mulch provide the best of both worlds. The infrared rays (which make up about 50 percent of the sun's energy) pass through to warm the soil as well as under clear plastic, but the light waves are blocked to prevent weed growth. Warm soil temperatures are vitally important for an early start with heat-loving crops. Ground-covering plastics have been available in smooth-surfaced, textured, biodegradable, and perforated styles. The perforated style allows moisture to pass through to the soil.

Low Covers

The next step beyond mulches is some sort of low covering or structure over the plants. The advantage of these simple, low structures is their flexibility. They can be moved or erected to cover specific crops as necessary. Whereas plastic mulch used alone will justify its cost in earlier maturity of warm-season crops, in practice it is usually combined with a low plastic cover for even more improved results.

Lightweight, translucent, low plant covers have been used in horticulture for as long as the materials have been available. The problem that arises with any plant covering during the changeable weather of a typical spring is the need to ventilate the structures when the weather is too warm and close them up again as

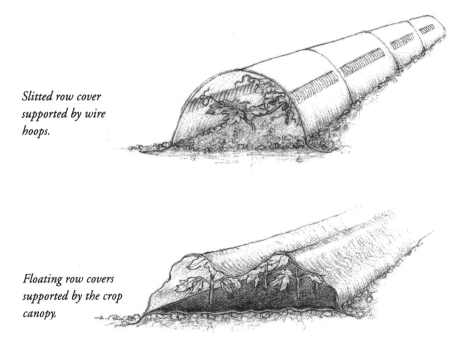

Slitted row cover supported by wire hoops.

Floating row covers supported by the crop canopy.

temperatures cool off. The extra labor and attention needed for such ventilation control can be a strain on the grower's resources. Recent modifications and new products have been aimed at combining cover and ventilation in one unit through slits or holes that allow the passage of air. These designs do not give as much frost protection as unperforated covers, but the difference is small, and the tradeoff benefit in the form of self-ventilation makes this idea very practical.

There are two common types of self-ventilating covering materials. The first is a clear polyethylene plastic 5 feet wide and 1½ to 2 mils thick, with slits or holes for ventilation. These are popularly known as *slitted row covers*. The second idea is a spun-bonded or woven translucent plastic cloth that permits the passage of air and water without the need for additional slits. These are referred to as *floating covers*. This is a rapidly developing field, and new products appear every year. I expect that future developments will supersede the design, but not the intent, of these covers.

The slitted row cover is laid over hoops made of No. 8 or No. 9 wire with the ends inserted in the ground on either side of the black plastic mulch. The structure stands about 16 inches high in the form of a low tunnel. The floating covers are laid directly on the plants, which raise the cover as they grow. In both cases, the edges of the covering material are buried in the soil as an anchor against wind. Since these structures are low and don't easily allow for cultivation inside the cover, a weed-inhibiting plastic mulch is usually considered indispensable for weed control. For crops where a plastic mulch is inappropriate (such as early direct seedings of carrot, radish, and spinach) the cover must be removed periodically for cultivation once the crop seeds have germinated.

Benefits.   Low covers offer much more than just frost protection. In my opinion, frost protection is probably their least valuable contribution, since it amounts to only a few degrees at best. What low covers do well is create a protected microclimate beneficial to crop growth that does not otherwise exist outdoors early in the season. Low covers shelter the plant like a horizontal windbreak. They inhibit the excessive evaporation of soil moisture, allow both soil and air to warm to a more favorable temperature during the day, and maintain that improvement, albeit in a smaller way, at night. They also provide protection against insects and birds.

Slitted row covers are labor-intensive. I prefer the floating covers, which don't require hoops, are more resistant to wind, and maintain a more moderate temperature range. With reasonable care they can be used a second year. They are also available in widths of up to 50 feet, which allows large areas to be covered quickly, with fewer edges to bury to hold them in place.

Spring Use. Low covers can be used as early as the grower dares, depending on the crop. Since the covers provide only a few degrees of frost protection, tender crops like tomato transplants are more of a risk than hardy seed crops like carrot and radish. Many growers successfully sow extra-early carrots under floating covers, which are removed periodically for cultivation.

Removal. Covers are usually left on for four to six weeks, or until outdoor temperatures rise. Removal of the covers must be done as carefully as any hardening-off procedure. Partial removal and replacement for a few days prior to total removal is recommended so that all the advantages gained are not lost. If possible, final removal of the covers should be done on a cloudy day, ideally just before rain. Definitely avoid bright sunny periods accompanied by a drying wind, as those conditions will worsen the transition shock for the plants.

The floating covers are worth reusing over fall crops. This sometimes involves modifying the technology. When floating covers are used for spring crops, the covers will be removed before the crops mature, while with fall crops the covers remain on the mature plants. In windy conditions this sometimes results in abrasion of the plant leaves, which can mar the appearance of a leafy crop. In that case, the fabric could be supported on wire hoops like the slitted row covers, or on bowed fiberglass rods, so it no longer rubs against the vegetable crop.

Cold Frames

Traditional low structures such as glass cold frames and their improved variants (Dutch lights, continuous cloches), with which I have had experience over the years, are not recommended in this system. Much as I like glass for frames be-

Dutch light cold frames propped open for ventilation.

cause it lasts longer and (to me at least) is prettier than plastic, its disadvantages in extra work and initial high cost outweigh its benefits in better frost protection and ventilation. While I will probably continue to use a range of glass frames as well as plastic covers, I recognize that this is more for nostalgia and familiarity than efficiency or economics.

If you want to extend the season further than is possible with low covers, a large protected growing area can be enclosed most effectively and economically by increasing the size of the hoops and the plastic sheet to make it a walk-in tunnel.

Walk-in Tunnels

By walk-in tunnels, I mean most unheated structures consisting of a single layer of plastic supported by spaced arches or hoops tall enough to walk and work under. In design they vary from very lightweight units on the one hand to structures indistinguishable (except for the lack of supplementary heat) from a greenhouse. I have seen tunnels 200 feet long, although 100 feet is a more common length, and 50 feet may be more manageable in climate requiring close attention to ventilation. Six feet is the usual minimum width and 17 feet the maximum, although most are 12 to 14 feet wide. In practice, the width is a function of the materials used, the planting layout, and the range in styles, from simple to complex.

Walk-in tunnels are similar to a Quonset-shaped, bowed-pipe-frame greenhouse. The materials, however, are usually lighter and less permanent, since tunnels are designed to be moved. Fiberglass rods, plastic pipe, metal rod, reinforcing bar, electrical conduit, and even bowed strips of wood can be used for the structure. In the lightweight models (up to 15 feet wide) the arches are made like large versions of the wire hoops used to support the slitted row covers. Their ends are inserted into the ground. Larger walk-in tunnels are anchored by pipes driven into the ground to provide support for the arch frame. The arches are usually spaced 4 to 6 feet apart.

The plastic covering is secured in a number of ways. For the 6- to 8-foot-wide units, the plastic can be pulled tight at each end and attached to a stake driven into the ground. The plastic just touches the soil on each side of the tunnel and is not buried. The arches hold the plastic up, and stretch cords run over the top of the plastic from one side to the other to hold the plastic down. Ventilation is provided by raising the plastic sheet up along the bottom edge.

The friction between the arch and the cord keeps the plastic at the desired height above the ground. Ventilation, up during the day and down at night, can be accomplished quickly with a little practice. Since a larger growing area is being ventilated per unit of labor, the extra management involved is more justifiable than for the low structures. Access to the tunnel is gained by raising the plastic along one edge and ducking under.

As walk-in tunnels become wider the design changes. The ends are usually framed up separately and include a wide door. In some cases the plastic covering is secured by boards attached 3 feet above the ground, along either side of the arches, and extends down to a long board lying on the ground. In this system, the plastic can be rolled up for ventilation on either side by means of the long boards. At night the cover is rolled down and the board is held in place on the ground by rocks or concrete blocks.

At the upper end of walk-in tunnel design, the plastic is attached to baseboards as in a conventional pipe-frame greenhouse. The baseboards are bolted to foundation pipes spaced 4 feet apart and driven 18 inches or so into the ground.

The interior diameter of the foundation pipe is slightly larger than the outside diameter of the pipe arch. The pipe arch is erected by inserting the ends of it into the foundation pipes. The arch rests on the upper of the two bolts that secure the baseboard (see detail drawing on page 212).

In models without roll-up sides, ventilation is provided by large doors or roof vents. The doors are framed up as large as the tunnel width permits. The roof vents can be opened and closed by hand or by automatic temperature-activated spring openers. The roof vents are an interesting construction in themselves. The desired vent sections are framed out in the roof of the tunnel, either with the same material used in the structure or with wood. The most common spacing is one vent for every four hoop sections. The plastic covering is secured around the edges of the roof opening, most easily with a two-part

The basics of a plastic-covered structure.

fastener (a hard plastic channel and an insert strip) attached to the edges of the vent opening to hold the plastic. The two parts snap together and provide a strong, reliable grip on the edge of the plastic (see detail drawings at left). A lightweight frame for the roof vent hatch is covered with plastic, hinged at one end, and attached to the temperature-activated opening arm.

In protected areas, where wind is not excessive, a far simpler roof-venting system can be tried. Instead of putting the plastic on the tunnel the conventional way (lengthwise), the cover is put on side to side. For example, if you are using 25-foot-wide plastic, there would be a cross seam every 25 feet (actually, every 24 feet, since a 12-inch overlap to cover the edge from the prevailing wind is recommended). Venting hot air through the roof or sides is made possible by spreading the two seam edges apart and holding them open with a prop. Fancier systems use pull cords and pulleys to open and close a number of these seam vents along the length of the tunnel. Horizontal support wires (as shown in the drawing at the bottom of page 213) should be added to the structure to provide extra support for the plastic in this system.

With any plastic structure, even when conventionally covered, wind whipping and abrasion can be a serious problem. No matter how carefully the cover is tightened when it is first put on, it always seems to loosen. There are two ways to deal with this. The simplest is to run stretch cord over the top of the plastic from one side to the other, as with the 6- to 8-foot-wide tunnels. One cord between every fourth rib is usually sufficient. The tension of the stretch cord will compensate for the expansion and contraction of the plastic due to temperature

Channel and insert strip for securing plastic.

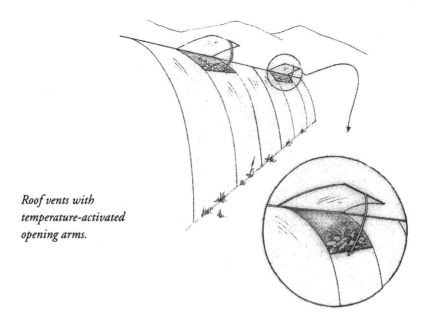

Roof vents with temperature-activated opening arms.

changes and will keep the cover taut at all times. The second solution is to cover the tunnel with two layers of plastic and inflate the space between them with a small squirrel cage fan. This creates a taut outer surface that resists wind and helps shed snow.

The final step beyond these advanced walk-in tunnels is to add a source of heat other than the sun. At this point you have a greenhouse, so it might be better to deliberately build one from the start.

Venting hot air by spreading the plastic seams.

Using pull cords and pulleys to open plastic seams for venting a tunnel covered with a single layer of plastic.

Greenhouses

The simplest greenhouse is only a stronger and slightly more complicated walk-in tunnel. The major differences are that the greenhouse has greater structural stability and provides supplementary heat. A greenhouse can be built of 2 x 4s and will look very similar to a house frame. Or it can be constructed in the same bowed-pipe Quonset design as the walk-in tunnels using a heavier-gauge tubing. I prefer the latter style. Bowed-pipe arch greenhouses can be home-built or purchased in modular units that are simple to erect, lengthen, or move as desired. Pipe, being less massive and less numerous than wooden structural members, casts almost no shadows and allows a maximum amount of light to enter.

The two layers of air-inflated plastic mentioned above are commonly used for greenhouses. This air-inflation idea adds strength and stability and makes the greenhouse more rigid. The outer plastic skin remains tight in all temperatures and is not subject to flapping, abrasion, and tearing that single layers experience during windy weather. Furthermore, the stressed curve of the surface sheds snow better and, except in the heaviest storms, it will not need to be swept or shoveled off. When inflated, the two layers are separated by about 4 inches of air, providing an insulation layer that results in a 25- to 35-percent savings in heating costs compared to an identical greenhouse covered with a single layer.

Supplementary heat for the greenhouse can be provided by burning any number of fuels, but the most popular small greenhouse heaters, and the ones I recommend, burn natural gas or propane. They come equipped with a fan blower and are vented to the outside. Installation is relatively simple, and the units can be moved along with the greenhouse.

Energy is an important issue. Some growers may want to explore the greenhouse heating potential of wood, decomposing organic matter, passive solar storage, or some other fuel. I heartily concur with this concern. All I suggest is that you postpone solving the energy problem for a few years. My goal is to present a farming system that works, and you must decide at the outset where your priorities lie. Is this a horticultural unit or a forum for experimenting with new energy technologies? For beginners it is always a wise practice to use a dependable conventional technology, because most of the problems have already been worked out by others.

Along with the provision of heat comes the need to mechanize the ventilation system. Thermostatically controlled fans and automatic shutters do the best job and are conventionally used in greenhouse temperature-management systems. Two-stage thermostats allow for different quantities of air to be moved, depending upon temperature demands, and will prove most effective in precisely regulating the ventilation system.

Another piece of advice is appropriate here. Although the idea of two-stage thermostats, automatic shutters, and ventilation fans may seem overly technological and complicated, they emphatically are not. A greenhouse structure can quickly overheat to temperatures that are deadly to plants. A dependable ventilation system is crucial. Occasionally, such mechanisms may malfunction, and, yes, they are more expensive than hand-operated vents or roll-up sides. But they are parts of a successful system, and that system works reasonably well. Any questions should wait until you have gained some experience with greenhouses. Once you are involved with greenhouse growing, you'll see the system makes sense. The rest of the vegetable farm will be demanding enough so that you will appreciate having some automatic assistants to look after a few details.

Cover, Tunnel, or Greenhouse?

I've presented a wide spectrum of technologies, from the use of southern slopes to automatic greenhouses, to help define all the options available for lengthening the season. What follows are selections from that spectrum that best meet the needs of the small-scale grower.

The growing area used for early and late production should have as ideal a microclimate for plant growth as you can create. If it can be located on a south slope with an effective windbreak to the north and unimpeded cold-air drainage downslope, those qualities will add to the effectiveness of the structures. Most important is a windbreak. The temporary shelter from a snow fence or windbreak netting can be used until it is certain where and what ought to be planted for more permanent shelter.

Low Covers

In my opinion, the floating covers are the best of the low-cover options for general crops, while slitted row covers are preferred for cucurbits (especially melons). When used in conjunction with a black plastic mulch they offer dependable season extension for transplanted crops. When floating covers are used without mulch they can provide significantly earlier harvest for the following direct-seeded crops: carrots, beets, parsley, radish, scallions, spinach, turnips, beans, and potatoes. Floating covers used in spring and fall over early and late crops of transplanted lettuce can justify their cost on this crop alone.

Large floating covers (20 to 50 feet wide) are more efficient to use than the narrower single-row models. There are fewer edges to bury in order to secure them. Burying the edges can also be avoided by laying 20-foot lengths of ½-inch rebar on top of the edges. The weight and the rough surface of the bar effectively hold the cover against wind lifting. The rebar can be removed as needed, and the cover edges do not become as soiled or torn as they do when they are buried. This helps extend the life of the cover for future use.

In extended-season production, each crop requires a decision by the grower as to whether an earlier maturity justifies the additional cost. When growing for a local, multiple-crop market (as opposed to a wholesale, single-crop market) it makes most sense to use covers to advance the harvest just enough for each crop to supply the demand until the earliest unprotected crops mature. Once the outdoor crops become available, the economic benefit of protected cultivation disappears. When approached within that framework, the amount of land to be covered is not excessive, even when many crops are involved.

Walk-in Tunnels

The recommended walk-in design is as follows. The width should be 12 to 15 feet and the length no longer than 48 feet for better control of ventilation. A farm-fabricated structure can be made of bowed 20-foot lengths of ½-inch fiberglass rod, ¾-inch Schedule 20 PVC pipe, or 1-inch-thick heavy-wall electrical conduit bent on a jig.* The fiberglass rod is the simplest to set up and remove. One 20-foot length can be formed into a half circle with a diameter of 12 feet or a flatter half circle with a diameter up to 15 feet. Each bow makes one supporting arch. The ends of the rods are pushed into the soil to the depth of about a foot. The arches are set 4 to 5 feet apart and are connected by a ridge purlin.

I make a ridge purlin from other fiberglass rods by tying them to the apex of the arches with strips of rubber inner tube. The ridge purlin can be neatly finished

Those growers wanting to fabricate their own tunnels or lightweight greenhouse structures from bowed metal pipe will be interested in the inexpensive pipe bow-bender and U-stake ground-anchoring system from W.W. Manufacturing Co., 60 Rosenhayn Ave., Bridgeton, NJ 08302, telephone (609) 451–5700.

Making a temporary tunnel structure with fiberglass rods.

off at the ends of the tunnel with plastic T connectors used to join plastic plumbing pipe. The cross of the T is slid over the end hoop, and the end of the purlin is inserted into the stem of the T. The minimum-protection version of this fiberglass-rod tunnel can be covered with 20-foot-wide floating material. For a heavier covering use regular polyethylene. The edges are held down by burying them with soil. The ends can be closed by pulling the covering material together and securing it to a stake with strips of inner tube as in the smaller hoop tunnels illustrated on page 217. For a more permanent tunnel, the ends can be framed up with wide doors for easy access and maximum ventilation. These doors are covered with a single layer of poly attached to the door frame at the top and to a board at the bottom so it can be rolled up for ventilation. A section of the two-part hard-plastic channel and insert-strip fastener mentioned earlier can be used on the side of the door frame to close the plastic tight in windy conditions.

If you decide to upgrade this tunnel, there are three logical steps to take. First, a small portable heater and fan can be included for frost protection at night and extra ventilation during the day. The fan is also useful when the greenhouse is not being vented, to move inside air around the plants and prevent stagnation. Second, a conventional greenhouse heater can be installed and run with the thermostat set low (40° to 55°F.—4° to 13°C.). Fuel costs will be minimal, and this sort of arrangement will prove useful for growing cool-temperature crops in spring and for extending the fall season on tomatoes through October and lettuce to late November.

Third, if the heater is to be run for warm-temperature crops (55° to 70°F.—13° to 21°C.), then it pays to add a second layer of poly with an air-inflation blower to save on fuel costs. Unless the tunnel is to be run warm, however, a single layer is preferable. The second layer will cut out an additional 10 percent of the light and will not help retain the heat radiating back out from the soil at night. There are new infrared reflecting plastics on the market that claim to hold in the radiated heat. I have not yet found them to be worth the extra cost.

Greenhouses

Of course, by the time you add air inflation and a heater, you almost have a greenhouse. For commercial vegetable production, a 17- to 33-foot-wide, 50- to 100-foot-long bowed-pipe arch model covered with double-air-inflated polyethylene plastic best meets the needs of the small-scale producer.

The smaller houses are an efficient size to grow in and are manageable enough to move when desired. Wider houses are even more convenient, as long as they fit a grower's production system. Three points will need to be considered.

An efficient small greenhouse.

One possible cropping layout for a 17-foot-wide greenhouse.

For a manual of general information on all aspects of greenhouses, see Greenhouse Engineering by Robert A. Aldrich and John W. Bartok, Jr. (Storrs: University of Connecticut, n.d.). Other books are listed in the bibliography.

First, in a multicrop production system there is greater flexibility with two or more smaller houses than with one large one. Since there will be different crops grown, each requiring a different temperature regime, a whole house can be given over to one crop or a group of crops with similar cultural needs. Second, if something does go wrong, it will threaten only a part of the production rather than all of it.*

Growing in a Greenhouse

The aim of a greenhouse is to create *climatic conditions* that are optimum for plant growth. The same should apply to *soil conditions*. Plant growth is intensified in the greenhouse, so extra care must be taken with soil preparation. All the factors that were stressed in the chapter on soil fertility are triply stressed here. Applications of well-finished compost are required for successful greenhouse culture. Greenhouse tomatoes and cucumbers are two of the most demanding crops and they need exceptional fertility, not only for soil preparation but also as a compost top-dressing applied once every six weeks. Lettuce, the other major greenhouse crop, will do well in a rotation with either tomatoes or cucumbers without further soil amendment.

Heated greenhouse production of high-demand crops is a valuable magnet to attract customers to the rest of the farm's produce. It can also be a highly

---

CROPS FOR SEASON-EXTENSION STRUCTURES

Floating cover plus black plastic mulch:
Cucumber, eggplant, melon, pepper, summer squash, tomato

Floating cover:
Bean, beet, broccoli, cabbage, carrot, corn, lettuce, parsley, potato, radish, scallion, spinach

Walk-in tunnel (early crops):
Beet, carrot, celery, cucumber, eggplant, lettuce, parsley, pepper, radish, scallion, tomato

Walk-in tunnel (late crops):
Celery, cucumber, lettuce, mâche, parsley, radish, scallion, tomato

Walk-in tunnel (overwinter crops):
Carrots, mâche, lettuce, parsley, scallion

Greenhouse (principal crops):
Cucumber, lettuce, tomato

Greenhouse (subsidiary crops):
Celery, parsley, pepper, radish, scallion, summer squash

lucrative area of specialization in its own right. But don't jump into it without first giving the matter considerable thought. Growing high-quality greenhouse vegetables demands a real commitment to management and an attention to detail. Serious commercial-greenhouse production should be postponed until the farm is well established and more capital can be acquired. Then I would recommend it. Books with detailed information about greenhouse vegetable production are listed in the bibliography.

Tomorrow's Answers

The progressive grower always keeps one eye on doing a job and the other on how it could be done better. You should always be alert to improve both the practical and economical aspects of your present production technologies, not in order to follow the future, but rather to lead it. The future can often be predicted based on today's patterns of development. The trend in season extension is quite clear. The pattern runs in the direction of making the structures lighter, simpler to manage, and more mobile.

The old-style cold frames had heavy glass covers and permanent concrete bases. Lighter-weight glass covers and wooden frames followed. The development of the continuous cloche added mobility by making the structure out of glass panes held rigid by a wire frame. In the next development, plastic was substituted for glass, and widely spaced wire hoops became the framework. All of the above had to be ventilated by hand. The slitted row covers simplified the ventilation problem through the use of slits in the plastic. The floating covers go two steps further. They eliminate the structure and incorporate the ventilation into the construction of the material itself. In view of these trends, it is safe to assume that the future will see even more refinements in floating covers. These might include better anchoring, more positive ventilation, and improved performance in light transmission and frost protection.

The trend in greenhouses has followed a similar path. The early heavy-framed glass houses needed a strong structure to support the glass covering. When houses began to be designed for plastic, the rafters could be spaced much farther apart because the covering was so much lighter. The metal-pipe arch frames are lighter yet, both visually and substantially. This minimal framework blocks very little of the incoming sunlight and is easy to put up and take down, something that cannot be said for an old-time greenhouse. The logical continuation of this trend is toward an even lighter, simpler, and more mobile superstructure coupled with an even more stable (and easier to put on) air-inflation cover.

One fact that cannot be ignored in all of this is the temporary nature of plastics as opposed to the greater permanence of glass. Greenhouse plastics last three years, at best, before they need to be replaced. They must also be disposed of. If the use of plastics in horticulture continues to expand, concerned growers should make three demands of the manufacturers: recycling programs should be initiated so these materials do not end up in a landfill; biodegradable forms of plastic should be developed that decompose safely when their practical life is over; and resource-efficient forms should be developed that are made from cornstarch or other renewable plant products rather than petroleum. If extend-

EXPECTED HARVEST DATES FOR SELECTED CROPS GROWING UNDER SEASON-EXTENSION STRUCTURES

A Sample List Compiled for Mid-Vermont

Date	Greenhouse	Tunnel	Cold Frames or Low Covers	Outdoor
2/28	Lettuce	Mâche* Carrot*		
3/5	Parsley			
3/10	Radish			
3/15	Scallion			
3/20				
3/25				
3/30		Parsley* Scallion*		
4/5				
4/10				
4/15				
4/20		Lettuce*		
4/25		Radish	Scallion* Mâche*	
4/30	Tomato Cucumber		Spinach*	
5/5	Zucchini			
5/10		Lettuce	Parsley*	

*wintered over

ing the vegetable season has to result in perennially expanding the plastic-waste problem, then the old-time permanence of glass for cloches, cold frames, and greenhouses becomes a more responsible, though expensive, solution.

Today's ideas were yesterday's improvements. Tomorrow's ideas will rise from today's problems. The best new concepts come from experienced practitioners and were devised to answer their needs. Once you gain experience, the next improvement for you as a small grower, and for countless other food producers, is just around the corner.

Date	Greenhouse	Tunnel	Cold Frames or Low Covers	Outdoor
5/15		Spinach		
5/20			Lettuce Radish	
5/25			Spinach	
5/30				Lettuce
6/5	Celery			Radish Spinach
6/10				
6/15		Tomato Cucumber		
6/20		Zucchini Carrot		
6/25			Tomato	
6/30			Cucumber Zucchini	
7/5			Carrot	
7/10		Celery		Tomato Cucumber
7/15				Zucchini Carrot

SPECIFICATIONS FOR SEASON-EXTENSION STRUCTURES

	Floating Covers	Slitted Row Covers	Walk-in Tunnel	Greenhouse
Shape	Flat	Quonset	Quonset	Quonset
Support	none	#8 or #9 wire	electrical conduit, PVC pipe, fiberglass rod	1½", 17-gauge galvanized steel pipe bows
Source	—	homemade	homemade or purchased	purchased
Width	4'	4'	12' to 14'	17' to 33'
Length	100'	100'	48' or 96'	48' or 96'
Covering	porous spun-bonded cloth	2-mil poly	6-mil UV-resistant poly	6-mil poly UV-resistant poly
Layers	1	1	1	2
Insulation	none	none	none	air inflation
Heat	sun	sun	sun plus portable heater for frost protection	propane or natural gas greenhouse heater
Ventilation	open weave	slits	large doors, vents, small fan	exhaust fan, automatic shutters
Alignment	conforms with garden rows	conforms with garden rows	E-W	E-W
End Construction	cover buried in soil	cover buried in soil	framed for large door and covered with poly	framed for door and vents, double poly covered
Door	none	none	roll-up 6-mil plastic	wide opening double doors
Season	spring & fall	spring & fall	Mar. 1 to Nov. 15	year-round

22

THE MOVABLE FEAST

THE IDEAL GREENHOUSE SYSTEM FOR ORGANIC GROWING WOULD BE AS forward-thinking in terms of "natural" protected cultivation of vegetables as the leading-edge developments of organic growers over the years have been in terms of "natural" field cultivation. The temporary plastic tunnel greenhouses come close. After covering the ground when needed, they can be disassembled and moved to another location. They can be preceded or followed by a green manure. They avoid difficulties like pest and disease buildup and soil nutrient excesses often encountered with permanent greenhouses. It would be nice to have that periodic outdoor exposure of the soil allowed by temporary structures, in addition to the benefits of a full-function, permanent greenhouse. Fortunately, that combination is possible. The answer is a greenhouse that moves.

The Mobile Greenhouse

A mobile greenhouse, by which I mean a fully equipped greenhouse that can slide or roll to one or more alternative sites, combines the climatic benefits of a permanent greenhouse with the soil-cleansing benefits of a temporary tunnel. The idea of a greenhouse that could be moved without being dismantled became a reality at the end of the 19th century. Its development was a response to the search for a better solution to greenhouse soil sickness. The options at that time—removing and replacing the soil to a depth of 12 to 16 inches or sterilizing the soil with steam—were considered less than satisfactory because of high labor costs and/or the soil fertility problems following sterilization.

The early mobile greenhouses of a hundred years ago were quite a piece of work. I'm sure the idea of building something as fragile as a glass greenhouse to be strong enough to move from one site to another without self-destructing posed a challenge to the original innovators. Nevertheless they persevered. The houses they built looked like conventional greenhouses on the surface—a wood or steel frame that was covered with glass. But instead of being attached directly to a foundation, the frame of the mobile house was supported by metal wheels which rolled on metal rails. The rails were solidly attached to a conventional foundation. The end walls were planned so the bottom part could be raised to pass above crops when the house was rolled to one or more alternate sites.

Some models took a different approach. They were designed so only the roof moved. In those cases the roof trusses made a stable triangular structure which rolled on rails set on top of the side walls. That style offered extra value in a windy location. Even when the site was uncovered the walls alone served as a translucent windbreak and provided considerable climate enhancement. Despite the initially higher costs of mobile greenhouse designs, many innovative growers thought this a worthwhile experiment and quite a few were built.*

I saw my first mobile greenhouse while visiting an organic market garden in Holland during the early spring of 1976. Although newly constructed, it was just like the classic models I had read about. The metal frame covered with glass was 40 feet wide by 120 feet long. It sat on metal wheels running on railroad rails long enough so three different sites could be served. The morning I arrived the house was being moved. Even though I was familiar with the idea I will admit my surprise at seeing such a huge structure trundling slowly towards me, pushed by workers on each rear corner. The irrigation, heat, and electricity inputs had been disconnected prior to moving and then were reconnected to new outlets at the second site. The early crop of lettuce which the house had been covering was now advanced enough to finish its growth outdoors. Tomato transplants, ready to be set out in the newly protected site that afternoon, were waiting alongside.

I was told that, except for certain special situations, such as out-of-season strawberry and flower crops, very few mobile houses were still being built. Most Dutch growers had shifted to solving their greenhouse soil problems with chemicals or by growing in artificial media. However, my hosts believed the mobile technology made great biological sense for their organic operation. The same reasons that inspired its initial development, i.e., preventing pest buildup and soil fertility problems, still applied to those growers using natural methods. And although in this case the cost averaged about 20 percent higher than a static glass house, the returns were also 20 percent higher. My hosts also stressed another virtue of mobility. The capital cost of the greenhouse could be recovered more quickly because it could effectively cover more crops in a year than could be protected by a stationary greenhouse.

The Advantages of a Mobile Greenhouse

First, I want the same thing that the early mobile greenhouse pioneers wanted—more natural soil conditions. By exposing the soil to the outdoors—rain, wind,

*The only history of mobile greenhouses I have been able to find is a 1960 study done by an English garden writer with funding from a Royal Horticultural Society trust: I.G. Walls, Design, Cropping, and Economics of Mobile Greenhouses in Britain and the Netherlands (R.H.S. Paxton Memorial Bursary, 1960). It proved so difficult to locate that I eventually begged a copy of the manuscript from the author. Photocopies of that manuscript are presently available from ATTRA (for address, see page 286).

snow, direct sunlight, and serious subfreezing temperatures—I can bring into play many natural cleansing and balancing processes that are denied to a permanently covered, full-function greenhouse. Second, and this point expands on the first, mobile houses permit me to use a wider crop rotation. I can now include long-term green manures without sacrificing any greenhouse cropping potential, because I grow them on the uncovered site. Soil-improving crops are a definite plus, not only for their physical and biological effects on the soil, but also to reduce the amount of compost that needs to be brought into the greenhouse. The greenhouse soil can now become as self-supporting in fertility as the rest of the farm (see Chapter 11). Third, I find that mobility allows me to avoid the more artificial and palliative-centered approaches (for example, steam sterilization, grafting of tomatoes to resistant rootstocks, constant pest monitoring, trapping, and supplementation of beneficial insects) to which other organic greenhouse growers are turning as the problems of continuous greenhouse cultivation intensify year after year. I readily admit to a lack of enthusiasm for palliatives. I prefer to look for ways to encourage natural processes to do what they do so well if I just let them do it.

The fourth advantage is the saving of money and energy for both heating and cooling. For example, I start planting many winter harvest crops in midsummer and continue on through early fall. These winter crops are planted on the uncovered site, where they grow vigorously until the shortening days and cooler temperatures of late fall slow their growth. I then move the greenhouse over them to provide protection for winter harvesting. If I had started these crops in a stationary greenhouse, I would have needed an expensive cooling system. Even with the vents open and doors removed to provide as much passive cooling as possible, the summer greenhouse is too warm for starting winter crops. But the summer greenhouse is an ideal place to grow heat-loving crops. And so I do. For example, sweet potatoes not only thrive in the summer greenhouse but also add further diversity to my crop rotation.

The only cost for all these biological advantages is the additional expense of making a static house mobile. If that additional expense is reasonable, the idea becomes very attractive. So, when I became serious about building a real mobile greenhouse, I began by checking the prices of the mobile plastic greenhouses offered by European manufacturers. Unlike the economic figures given me by my Dutch friends years ago, these new houses are no longer 20 percent more expensive. I received a quote from one manufacturer that was *triple* the initial price of the house. Of course a lot of that price differential relates to the difference in initial cost between glass and plastic houses. But it still seemed way out of line. My goal was to find a mobile greenhouse technology that would add no more than 10 percent to the cost of a plastic greenhouse, and yet would be strong enough to be used on a 30 by 96-foot house. Further, since I already owned stationary plastic houses, I wanted a system that could make them mobile without too many added parts. During the occasional frustrations that inevitably occur while trying to develop any new idea, I asked myself more than once, "Do I really need mobile houses? Can't I do just as well with ones that don't move?" Every time, one after another of the reasons stated above would come up as a justification to continue my efforts. I'm glad I did.

The Mobile Plastic Tunnel

There are two basic parts to a pipe-frame, plastic-covered greenhouse—the hoops and purlins, which make up the structure, and the ground stakes, which serve as a foundation. The key to a mobile greenhouse is to separate the hoop structure from the foundation so the structure can be moved. There are obviously a lot of potential solutions.

When I built my first greenhouses—three 17-foot-wide by 50-foot-long hoop houses—I took a partial approach to mobility. Since these 17-foot-wide houses were simply constructed with single-piece bows and a single center purlin, I planned to dismantle and move them every three years when the plastic cover needed replacing. I laid out the utilities—electricity, water, and propane—so they would be detachable and reattachable when the houses were moved across the path to their alternate location. The layout is shown on page 229.

Due to a change in plans for the land on the alternate site, these houses were never moved. Consequently I took the opportunity to experiment with continuous crop rotations within the greenhouses. I tried to provide as much crop variation as possible. The crops included long-season tomatoes, cucumbers, melons, lettuce, winter salad greens, and spring bedding plants followed by fall tomatoes. Speaking from that experience, I think rotations can prevent a lot of greenhouse problems. But I retained my interest in mobile houses because I want more biological variability in my greenhouse soil management program than I can get from crop rotation alone.

A good friend with whom I had been discussing mobile greenhouse designs decided to ponder no longer. He jumped right in and built two models: one was a wooden-framed 20 by 50-foot house, and the second a 30 by 100-foot plastic tunnel greenhouse. He used what I call a *rail and skid* system. The rail for his wooden house was a 2 x 6 attached flat on top of wooden foundation posts. A second 2 x 6, the skid, was built into the base of the house and sat on top of the first. The 2 x 6s were bolted together when the house was in place. For moving,

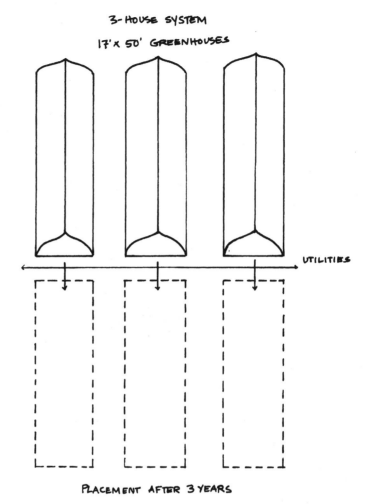

they were pried apart, and short sections of 2-inch diameter pipe were inserted to serve as rollers. Two people could push this house, but they had to be careful to push evenly so as to keep the rail and skid aligned.

For the 30 by 100-foot tunnel he made the rail from U-channel mounted open side up and welded to pipe foundation posts. The skid was a solid metal bar which fit into the U-channel. The greenhouse hoops were welded to the skid. In order to move this tunnel, he would loosen the attaching clamps and progressively pry the metal bar up enough to place a couple dozen used golf balls underneath it along each U-channel. More golf balls were placed in the U-channel section over which the house was about to be moved. Two people, each with a come-along attached to a front corner, pulled the house to the new site. Once the house was in place the golf balls were removed. Ball bearings could have reduced the rolling friction, since golf balls deform slightly under pressure.

Sliding Rails

After considering these and a lot of other fanciful schemes I put up my first experimental mobile tunnel, 17 feet wide by 32 feet long, using a simple system I refer to as a *double sliding rail*. I decided that, since I was planning to move my houses only once a year (see mobile greenhouse cropping plans in the next chapter), I could get by without wheels or rollers. The bottom rail is a 2 x 6 attached to the foundation pipes that I purchased with the tunnel. The upper rail consists of two pieces—a 2 x 4 riding on top of the 2 x 6 rail, and a 2 x 8 bolted alongside, into which the greenhouse hoops are set.

I lessen the friction before moving this house with a low-technology solution—I paint liquid soap on the rails. The house can be moved easily by four people—two pushing on the back corners and two pulling ropes at the front. When the house is in position the 2 x 8 is bolted through to the 2 x 6 at 12-foot intervals. This system is very successful and seems perfectly adequate for houses up to 50 feet in length.

For larger houses, say 30 feet by 96 feet, I speculated on the possibility of a double metal rail system using angle iron for both rails. I planned to grease the surfaces of the angle iron to reduce friction and pay particular attention to keeping the uncovered section of the rail greased so it would not rust. I thought a pair of come-alongs could provide the motive power, but I was afraid there might be too much friction.

At this point in the development process I began to rethink everything. I wondered if this wasn't a perfect example of restricting my options. If I didn't need wheels, why did I need rails? The first mobile houses, skinned with glass, were both heavy and fragile. Thus, a solid system of wheels and rails was necessary to move them. I had subconsciously imposed that thinking pattern on moving plastic-covered hoop houses, which are not only much lighter than a glass house, but also quite flexible. Why not put even 30 by 100-foot houses on skids and forget the wheels and rails? I didn't think there would be any more friction between skid and soil than between the two metal rails I had just considered.

First I put up a 12 by 20-foot tunnel on pipe skids. Two people could move it, and it eventually became a poultry house (see page 272). But the pipe was

Double-sliding rail.

expensive, so my design for a 30 by 96-foot mobile plastic greenhouse had it resting on wooden 4 x 6 skids, made by bolting 2 x 6s together in a staggered pattern. It would be moved by a tractor or with come-alongs. Fortunately, I built a 20-foot-long by 14-foot-wide prototype first. I thought that, if I were planning to move this greenhouse frequently, I might add a thin metal shoe to the bottom of the skid to reduce friction. In truth, it would probably need better friction reduction than that. Moving even this small prototype required a lot of power, because the friction between wood and soil was much greater than I had found with the pipe skid. Further, there is an additional problem with large houses on skids. Without rails, there is no guidance to keep the edges running straight. Depending on the stresses exerted on them, they can either toe in or splay out. I returned to thinking about wheeled designs.

The lessons I learned from the tunnels on skids suggested the next step in design development. When the rail was attached to the bottom of the hoops it made a very sturdy structure. With the rail in that position, wheels could be attached to the ground foundation posts. That's an appealing concept because the design is cleaner and less expensive. There is no need to invest in rails extending twice the length of the greenhouse. All that's needed is the rail on the bottom of the house and the wheel units it rolls on. A 96-foot house with ground stakes at 4-foot intervals along each side has 26 hoops and would require 52 wheel units. I wouldn't even need more wheels than the house actually sits on, since they could be picked up and moved ahead as each post was uncovered. Only the ground posts would remain on the alternate site after the house had been moved.

Wheels and Rails

Since other people's experience is an inexpensive teacher, I continued my quest by investigating how the latest European models were solving the mobility question. The lightweight mobile plastic houses presently being manufactured are moved on wheel-and-rail systems similar to the old mobile glasshouses. But instead of railroad wheels, they use wheels much like those used for the sliding gates on industrial pipe-frame fences. The wheel units are mounted on the bottom of each greenhouse rib, and roll on a pipe used as the foundation rail. They work well, but are very expensive.

As I inquired further into the wheel-mounted European designs, it became obvious that much of the high cost was attributable to the fancy wheels and the special brackets for the rails. It appeared as if the designers had gone with the expensive option without trying hard enough to make it affordable. In my experience, affordable usually means simple. I have always agreed with the design criterion expressed so well by Antoine de Saint Exupéry in *Wind, Sand, and Stars:*

> [For] *the production of a thing whose sole and guiding principle is the ultimate principle of simplicity . . . perfection is finally attained not when there is no longer anything to add, but when there is no longer anything to take away. . . .*

So in my initial wheel design I took away everything I could. I wanted a unit that I could fabricate easily in the shop with common tools. I settled on using ¾-inch rod as an axle and a short section of 1-inch pipe as a roller. I made the

European mobile greenhouse design.

Homemade rollers on notched axles.

Mobile glass house perimeter-sealing system, with bristle.

axle with short projections on either end that fit into slots I cut in the top of the foundation pipes. The tools required were a hacksaw, a vise, and a disc grinder.

This roller worked well, but I still wondered if a more professional "wheel" might make the house move even easier. Since I wanted to find something inexpensive and "off the shelf," I went to the local university library and looked through the *Thomas Register*. The *Thomas Register* is a multivolume publication which lists seemingly every manufacturer and every manufactured item available in the U.S. I looked under headings like wheels, rollers, and casters. I soon located a manufacturer of 1¼-inch ball casters designed with a base stem that can be inserted into the top of a foundation pipe. I ordered samples, and they fit the bill in every particular. Now that I had a couple of suitable rolling systems, the next step was to find a rail.

The Rail

I decided to make the rail out of U-channel mounted upside down. That way the two edges would guide the rail to keep it from sliding off the wheel unit while the house was being moved (see Figure 1).

Since the rail is the base for the greenhouse, I had to make provision for securing it to the hoop superstructure of the tunnel. For this I chose to weld short pieces of rod to the top of the rail every 4 feet. The greenhouse hoops, also set at 4-foot intervals, would be slipped down over these rods (see Figure 2).

The baseboard, which is attached to the ground posts in conventional greenhouse construction, would in this case be attached to the base of the greenhouse by bolting it through both the rod and the greenhouse rib, thus securing them all together (see Figure 3).

So far so good. However, when a house sits above the ground on rails or wheels, there is necessarily an open space between the bottom of the house and the surface of the soil. The modern designs of European mobile glass houses solve that problem with a complicated but effective form-fitting skirt and flexible-bristle brush sealing strip that closes the gap without inhibiting movement.

The mobile houses on skids and my double-rail model have an advantage here over wheeled designs. Their foundation is already in close contact with the soil. Many of the European plastic-covered wheel-and-rail mobile designs use a strip of greenhouse poly attached to the bottom of the baseboard and buried in the soil to close off the gap (see Figure 4). That's an effective measure, but the poly must be freed from the soil before the house is moved and then must be reburied. I hoped to come up with a system that didn't require that extra step.

Figure 1: Basic U-channel rail.

Figure 2: Greenhouse hoops inserted in rods

Figure 3: Baseboard securing greenhouse rib to rail unit.

Figure 4: Use of poly to close gap at soil line.

Figure 5: Using aluminum flashing to close gap at soil line, and to control rodents.

The labels in the figure:
AIR-INFLATED DOUBLE POLY

GREENHOUSE HOOP

POLY LOCKING SYSTEM

ROD WELDED TO ANGLE IRON TO RECEIVE GREENHOUSE HOOP

BOLT THROUGH BASEBOARD, GREENHOUSE, HOOP AND ROD

U-CHANNEL

ACME BALL CASTER

BASEBOARD

FOUNDATION POST

FLASHING

SOIL LEVEL

Learning from Mistakes

When I built my first double-rail design I assumed the gap would be closed by the 2 x 6 rail because it made contact with the soil. All was well until the hard freezes of winter. Since the house was unheated, it froze around the edges. The expansion of the frozen soil was enough to raise the rail and anchor posts slightly, and they remained elevated when the soil subsided in the next thaw. The gap was back. I solved that problem by intentionally leaving the rail slightly above the soil and adding an 8-inch strip of aluminum flashing attached to the bottom edge of the 2 x 6 and extending down into the soil. The frost couldn't get enough of a grip on the thin flashing to raise it (see Figure 5).

That flashing simultaneously solved a second problem—rodents. I had a real battle in one of my greenhouses with voles, our local meadow mouse. These small furry creatures tunneled in during late fall and created havoc. Under most conditions the flashing alone will keep them out. However, in particularly difficult spots where determined rodents tried to tunnel under the flashing, I stymied them by backfilling the flashing with ¾-inch crushed stone—a size that is too big for them to move and too small for them to squeeze between.

Flashing not only keeps out the voles and seals the perimeter airspace. It has the further plus of providing a flat surface along the length of the foundation. That offers a way to close the gap between the bottom of the greenhouse and the top of the foundation. I do that by using a wider baseboard, so it extends below the bottom of the house and presses against the flashing, thus providing a seal. That same baseboard inspired my next refinement. I originally wanted to use angle iron as the rail since it is less expensive than U-channel, but I chose the channel instead, because the two edges could guide the house as it rolled. But with the baseboard extending below the house, the baseboard now served as the outer edge guide. I could now use an angle-iron rail, as shown in Figure 6.

The wider baseboard also led to solving the final and probably most important consideration with mobile houses—the need to connect them securely to the foundation when they are in place and to disconnect them easily for moving. You only have to be unprepared for a windstorm once to appreciate how much power the wind can pack. The prototype mobile greenhouse on 2 x 6 skids I

Figure 6: Use of angle iron instead of U-channel.

Figure 7: Bolting through the baseboard and ground stake.

GREENHOUSE HOOP

AIR-INFLATED DOUBLE POLY

POLY LOCKING SYSTEM

ROD WELDED TO ANGLE IRON TO RECEIVE GREENHOUSE HOOP

ANGLE IRON

ACME BALL CASTER

FOUNDATION POST

BASEBOARD

BOLT AND STRAPPING (EVERY FOURTH POST) TO SECURE GREENHOUSE TO FOUNDATION

FLASHING

SOIL LEVEL

mentioned earlier (the one that was so difficult to move) was skidded dizzily across a field by a sudden windstorm after I had decided to wait until the following day to put in the ground stakes.

With the baseboard extending below the greenhouse, I can now secure the house to the foundation by bolting through the baseboard and the ground stake. I find it adequate to do this at every fourth stake. For extra strength in case the wood cracks or weakens, I attach a 6-inch length of flat bar to the upper baseboard bolt. It extends down to where the foundation bolt goes through it, the baseboard, the flashing, and the ground stake. That metal reinforcement provides an extra-secure anchorage, and I can now sleep comfortably on windy nights (see Figure 7).

Now let's see if all of this has been done within the limit of 10 percent additional cost I set for myself at the start. In order to make a 30 by 100-foot house mobile I need the following new parts: 200 feet of angle iron, 50 short lengths of 1¼-inch rod, 52 ball casters, 16 flat bars (each 6 inches), and 16 extra bolts. Any other materials (such as the flashing for vole prevention) would have been used in a static house anyway and are not considered extra expenses for mobility. At the time this chapter was written the cost of a 30 by 96-foot tunnel averaged around $1.50 per square foot. That gives $450 as an average budget for making it mobile. All of the above materials can be purchased for that price.

I assure you that this design is not my final word on the subject. I suspect there are still some things to "take away." I have related my journey through these design considerations to pass on my starts and stumbles to those of you who will refine and improve the idea to meet your own needs. I haven't even mentioned some of the more extreme options I considered. When chasing new ideas I always try to let my mind roam freely and then simplify afterwards. Many totally off-the-wall concepts have eventually inspired some small refinement. Even when I finally decide upon a design, I always know it can be improved. I believe in a simple law and corollary. The law states, "There is always a way." The corollary states, "Once you find a way, there is always a better way."

23

THE WINTER GARDEN

In addition to the information presented here and in Four-Season Harvest, *I encourage market growers to see my latest book,* The Winter Harvest Handbook: Year-Round Vegetable Production Using Deep-Organic Techniques and Unheated Greenhouses *(Chelsea Green Publishing, 2009). It includes extensive and up-to-date information regarding use of row covers in unheated, as well as minimally heated, greenhouses, such as temperature survivability of various greens and a crop list with a seeding schedule.*

❧

Part of my fascination with greenhouses and greenhouse systems arises from a desire to supply food to my customers for as much of the year as possible. I think I benefit their health by growing vegetables of an exceptional quality. I know I help support a vibrant local economy by keeping the money circulating within my community. And, as I mentioned in the marketing chapter, I have an important advantage over the large wholesale shipper. As a local grower I provide *fresh* vegetables. So I don't care if the trucked-in crops can claim they were grown with pure stardust by elves and fairies. Any vegetables picked in bulk and shipped through the wholesale system are not fresh. Mine were picked today and are on the customer's table tonight or tomorrow. I can compete on that fact alone.

If I'm going to stress that freshness angle I want to make it happen for as much of the year as possible so as not to disappoint my accounts—whether stores, restaurants, co-ops, or subscribers—or lose them to another supplier. But I want to do this without excessive expenditure of energy. Well, for many years I have been harvesting fresh vegetables for beautiful salads and main dishes every day of the winter from a small, unheated greenhouse in my home garden. I call it the "winter garden." The simple system I use to protect the crops is described in my book *Four-Season Harvest*. I think the concepts behind that idea are not limited to the home garden. I believe that energy-efficient, commercial, four-season harvesting can be a reality all across the country. In fact, I even talk about reversing the standard farming year, selling vegetables from September to May, and taking my vacation in the summer.

The winter garden succeeds by combining the *technology* of climate modification with the *biology* of the vegetable world. The technology of my home garden system consists of two layers of protection to temper the harsh blasts of winter; the plants grow under cold frames inside a poly-tunnel. My temperature records over the years indicate why that passive technology is so successful. Each layer of covering effectively moves the covered area 1½ USDA zones to the south. For example, here in Zone 5 the growing area under an unheated tunnel is really in Zone 6½, and the area protected by the cold frame inside the tunnel is Zone 8. When the outside air temperature has dropped to -15°F. (-26°C.), the lowest temperature inside the protected cold frame has been 15°F. (–9°C.)—warm enough in the short term to protect cold-hardy crops from damage.

The biology involves the selection of cool-season vegetable varieties. There are 20 or more different crops I can harvest in the winter garden. Familiar vegetables like spinach, carrots, leeks, parsley, scallions, kale, chard, mustard, chives, escarole, endive, and turnip greens share space with the less familiar arugula, claytonia, dandelion, kohlrabi, mâche, minutina, mizuna, radicchio, watercress, and sorrel. These traditional winter crops don't mind the short days, nor are they harmed by freezing or by remaining frozen for periods of time. Whereas they would not survive if left unprotected, they not only survive but even thrive in the double coverage because they are safe from the desiccating wind chill and alternate wetting and drying that are the real plant killers of the outdoor winter.

Claytonia.

Commercializing the Winter Garden: Technology

I needed to modify my home-garden system for commercial production, because what I can and am willing to do in my backyard would be too expensive and labor-intensive if practiced on a large scale. In my backyard system, cold frames provide the second layer of protection inside the plastic tunnel. As I mentioned in a previous chapter, much as I love the simple technology of cold frames and owe them a debt for inspiring this system, I realize that the age in which they were a commercial horticultural option has mostly passed.

The discussion to follow is mainly pertinent for growers in USDA hardiness Zones 3 to 6. Those south of Zone 6, or those in the coastal regions of California, Oregon, and Washington whose climates require some winter protection, should not need a second layer, even for the less freeze-tolerant crops. A mobile plastic-covered tunnel greenhouse, either single-layer or air-inflated, will suffice. In situations where an inner layer may occasionally be desirable, one of the floating row covers will serve well and is quick to apply, since the edges won't have to be anchored. There is no wind inside the tunnel.

Passive Protection

My first thought for the inner layer of an efficient commercial system for Zones 3 through 6 was to put smaller plastic tunnels inside a larger one—say, two 14-footers side by side within a 30-footer. I later learned that this is done commercially for specific crops in some countries; winter strawberries in Japan and winter tomatoes in northern Africa are two examples. For interior greenhouses you don't need the galvanized pipe-frame tunnels you would erect out-of-doors.

That's just as well, since they could be awkward to vent or move or store during the summer season. Since the indoor tunnels are completely protected from wind and snow, the least expensive versions of the temporary tunnels we discussed in the previous chapter work just fine, They can be very lightly constructed with hoops up to 8 feet apart, so as to be easy to set up and take down.

Another thought I had was to make the second layer more heat-retentive. I had always suspected the cold frames were successful due to their low height; the second layer they provided was close to the ground. Maybe low protection was better at holding in the soil heat at night, since there was less convection in the confined space. So I designed a system using the night-curtain technology from heated greenhouses. *Night curtains* are made of a heat-reflective material and are drawn overhead inside the greenhouse on supporting cables to reduce heat loss at night. But I planned to place them at the height of cold frames, about 12 to 16 inches above the soil. A supporting monofilament runs the length of the greenhouse above each bed. This option is appealing because the protection is still basically passive and yet easily removable when not needed. These systems are usually automatic and are triggered by light-sensitive switches. Unfortunately the cost for these refinements is higher than I would like. But the use of a low second layer rolled out at night and rolled back in the morning is a definite possibility.

Another passive solution, one adopted by some Mediterranean area growers, is to place water-filled containers in the greenhouse to collect and store more of the sun's heat. According to their experience, the most efficient way of doing that is to make tubes out of clear polyethylene plastic that are 12 inches in diameter and as long as the greenhouse. These are filled with water and laid on the soil between the rows of crops. I have never tried that because we have so many cloudy winter days and I plant my rows so close together. But if my winter weather were sunnier, that low-tech, low-cost idea would have a lot of merit.

All of the second layers I have tried thus far provide "adequate" but not "perfect" protection in the colder zones of the country for all of the winter crops I hope to sell. I raise the issue of "perfect" because of the importance I place on crop quality. Were I to judge the crops in my home system by my critical standards for commercial production, only four of them—spinach, carrots, mâche, and scallions—would pass all the time. Those four are the least affected by winter cold. With the others there is often a bit of leaf or stem damage or discoloration due to extreme cold that I need to deal with. That extra cosmetic preparation time is no problem in the home kitchen, but it would not satisfy me as a commercial grower.

The slightly less-than-perfect quality I'm talking about is not universal, nor is it glaring. But it is enough to make me want to do better. The amount and kind of damage depends on the variables of how fast the temperature drops, how low it goes, and how long it lasts. It is also determined by when you want to harvest. Growers who don't plan to harvest during the most difficult period—mid-December to mid-February—may find that a simple passive system is all that they need.

Now I could go to a third layer, say, a low cover inside the smaller tunnel inside the larger one. In fact, that is an option I'm currently exploring, although at times it begins to seem as complicated as the sentence I just used to describe it. This arrangement is further complicated by another factor that comes into play: light. Each new layer of covering cuts out an additional 10 percent of available light. Two layers have not been a problem, but with a third layer you may run the risk of losing on crop quality, due to inadequate light, what you are trying to gain in crop quality through more protection.

One way to solve that dilemma is to take a step I have been reluctant to take with this system and replace the passive inner layer with an active one, supplying minimal heat. Not enough heat to make crops grow, just enough to prevent freezing damage. I have hesitated to do this because, along with my passion for growing crops, I have a passion for simple, passive solutions. My backyard winter garden meets my simplicity criteria admirably. The move from a passive to an active system can be a slippery slope. I'm subject to the same temptations as any other grower. If I have minimal heat to protect crops A and B, why not turn it up a little and grow C and D? The next thing I know, my simple, environmentally sound system has disappeared and I have Maine's only mango farm.

On the other hand, as a commercial grower I don't want to be so inflexible that I put myself out of business. For hardiness Zones 3 to 5 a little bit of supplementary heat is appealing. So I am exploring this option as well as the passive ones. It's all part of determining the biological and technical limits of a quality winter harvest. Over the next decade I expect the two parts of the ideal equation—improved passive protection and improved biological selection—will come together and I will find a commercially viable passive system for the colder zones that both meets my crop-quality criteria and avoids the need for adding heat.

Active Protection

Even though I am adding heat to some of the greenhouses, I do it to the minimum degree possible. As I said before, this active second layer is needed only to protect crops against excessive cold rather than as a stimulus for out-of-season growth. Thus, I have set the thermostat at 32°F. (0°C.). My continuing research into the low-temperature physiology of vegetables has led me to experiment with a setting of 28°F. (–2°C.), and possibly as low as 25°F. (–4°C.). But it will take the experience of many more winters before I refine this system perfectly.

A friend in Canada, who has been independently investigating some of these same ideas, told me he was reasonably content with one season's experience in a greenhouse where the temperature dropped as low as 12°F. (–11°C.). He didn't plan it that way. It happened because he had only a small heater and that was all the protection it could provide on the coldest nights. That type of accidental experimentation often opens our eyes to unexpected possibilities. However, I'm surprised by his results because 12°F. is three degrees lower than the lowest temperature (15°F.) recorded in the double-covered area of my passive system, and I thought even that was too low for commercial quality. But then, my friend was not harvesting during the depths of winter, which is certainly another option to consider. In fact, I would be perfectly content with my passive systems as they now stand if I either didn't plan to harvest from mid-December to mid-February or limited myself to just the hardiest crops. It may turn out that I am too concerned about minor cosmetic defects, or that, under the influence of different soils, crops, climates, and greenhouse sizes, the results are more variable than under my conditions. This leaves plenty of possibilities for growers to refine the system to their own conditions.

In order to minimize energy consumption I decided against the usual propane hot-air greenhouse heater and instead chose a radiant heater for my first winter trial. It proved quite successful. According to greenhouse research, radiant heaters burn 40 percent less fuel. A radiant heater consists of a long pipe with reflecting shields above it and a propane burner at one end. This unit hangs from the peak of the greenhouse, and the pipe runs its full length. The burner heats the pipe, and the reflectors radiate that heat downward. With the exception of a small fan which pressurizes the exhaust at the end of the pipe, no other fans are needed, either for delivering the heat or preventing stratification as with hot-air systems. By avoiding those fans I achieve major savings in electricity use (80 percent less) in addition to the saving on fuel.

Radiant heat is similar to the sun in that it does not warm the air but warms the surfaces it touches—in this case the plant leaves and the soil. It works best for low-growing crops, making it a perfect match with winter production. A radiant heater will cover an area 2½ times wider than the height at which it is hung. Thus, for my 30-foot-wide houses, I need to mount the heater 12 feet above the ground. Since I am growing a range of crops with varying temperature tolerances, I benefit from what might otherwise be considered a weakness in radiant heating systems—the tendency to be warmer at the burner end than at

ELECTRIC CONNECTION

AIR INLET FOR COMBUSTION

SUSPENSION BRACKET

FAN HOUSING

EMITTER TUBE

REFLECTOR

COMBUSTION TUBE

END CAP

DIFFUSER

GAS SUPPLY PIPE

BURNER/ CONTROL ASSEMBLY

A fuel-saving radiant heater.

the exhaust end and to be warmer in the center than at the edges. I can exploit these interior "microclimates" by selectively planting those different areas of the greenhouse to adapted crops.

Since this heater hangs from the peak of the greenhouse, it can move with the house. I just have to detach the power and gas lines first. Further, since the burner can fire from either end of the pipe, the utilities can be supplied to the central point of the two greenhouse sites and the burner and exhaust ends can be switched after the house is moved (see drawing on page 246). These are all small points, but they add up to efficient functioning when the system is in use.

Soil heat is another minimal heating system worth exploring. I haven't tried it yet for protecting winter salad crops (although I am planning to do so), but I am familiar with soil heat as one of the complementary heating systems for greenhouse tomatoes. Many growers use soil heat to warm the soil and improve root growth in tandem with a hot-air system, which provides the rest of the heat. Soil heat alone can provide only 25 percent of the heat needed by a winter tomato crop. However, for our purposes, where we wish to keep the minimum temperature at ground level just above or below freezing to protect the crops from excessive cold, the average of 20 Btus/sq. ft./hour that soil heat systems provide will be sufficient.

Soil heat rises from ¾-inch plastic pipes buried about 1 foot down in the soil in rows 12 to 18 inches apart. Each pair of pipes makes a continuous loop that takes warm water down to the other end of the greenhouse and then returns it. This results in an even temperature along the whole length of the paired pipes. The water, which starts at about 100°F. (38°C.), returns to the heater, where the temperature is raised again. There are special on-demand heaters manufactured for this use, but most growers I know use domestic hot water heaters. A 30-gallon model producing 30,000 to 40,000 Btus per hour is sufficient for a 30-by 96-foot house.

Either polyethylene or polybutylene pipe is used. The polybutylene will tolerate higher water temperatures. Since the pipe is the least expensive component, it makes sense to install it for both sites with the heater and controls at the center. You can drain the lines on the site that is not in use. Digging trenches to install the pipes in the soil is laborious and detrimental to soil structure. The easiest method, taught to me by a fellow grower, uses a single-arm subsoiler on a small tractor to pull each length of pipe through the soil at the desired depth. The pulling starts from a cross trench at one end which will eventually hold the supply and return pipes.

Soil heat may be a better solution than radiant heat for minimal protection in the winter garden. On the other hand, it could change the growing conditions more than I want. Warming the soil beneath the surface creates some new dynamics. The best bet may be another option, one that avoids subsurface heating of the soil. Warm-water pipe loops (down and back) are set on the soil of the paths between the beds. They are pressed into the soil with your feet. As long as you don't work in hobnailed boots, there shouldn't be any wear on the pipe. These lines are pulled up and installed on the alternate site when the house is

*"Floor Heating of Greenhouses" and "Greenhouse Floor Heating System— Drawing #161" are available from Cooperative Extension Service, Cook College, Rutgers– The State University, New Brunswick, NJ 08901.

moved. With this system, the heat is provided down low where it is needed, but not directly underneath the roots of plants. I plan to explore both soil-heating options. In the meantime, the cooperative extension service of Rutgers University in New Brunswick, New Jersey, has some pamphlets available on the topic, plus available blueprints for installing soil heat in a 30- by 96-foot greenhouse.*

Cooling Systems

Having dispensed with the need for fans as part of the heating system, I dispensed with them for all my cooling systems, too. I made that decision to save money and energy, but it also makes good practical sense. Since these houses are protecting winter crops, they will be used when cooling needs are minimal. Winter cooling can be accomplished by roof and side vents, which are opened and closed by automatic, temperature-activated arms. I have equipped my plastic-covered houses with automatic roof vents similar to those used traditionally on glass houses. During the summer months the houses will be growing a long-season, heat-loving, low-maintenance crop like sweet potatoes, or a warm-climate green manure like sesbania or crotalaria. Removing the end doors and opening the vents will provide sufficient passive cooling. The crops for the following winter, as I mentioned earlier, are planted from midsummer through mid-fall on the uncovered site and need no artificial cooling.

For growers in warmer climates, where summer heat precludes leaving the greenhouse over the tomatoes, for example, it can be moved back to the alternate site and a very heat-resistant green manure might be grown for that period. Warmer-climate growers will also want to delay moving the greenhouse over cool-season crops until later in the fall.

Your choice between all of these and many other technological options for winter cropping will depend on the skills and resources available to you and the climate demands of your region. I find it exciting that the simple backyard system of cold frames inside a hoop tunnel that stimulated my interest in the winter harvest works so well as it is. If a simple system can do that in chilly New England, the potential for all regions of the world to eat locally produced winter salads is just waiting to happen.

Commercializing the Winter Garden: Biology

Although I have experimented with 20 or more crops in winter gardening trials, I do not grow them all commercially. Choices have to be made. First, some have superior cold hardiness. The hardiest three—mâche, scallions, and spinach—

need no other protection for winter harvest, even as far north as Zone 3, than a double-covered, air-inflated tunnel. A fourth, carrots, can join the previous three if a thick layer of insulation is placed directly over the carrot beds. Some crops, like chives, respond to the cool conditions and the short day length by cutting back production in the middle of winter. Crops like kale, chard, leeks, and dandelions require more space than can be justified economically compared to other winter greenhouse crops. Some vegetables, like kohlrabi and radishes, don't hold their quality even though protected from outside conditions. And some crops will be easier to market than others.

The most promising crops in my experience for commercial winter production are listed below. I have included general comments on the cultural practices I favor. Growers either to the north or south of my Zone 5 location will need to refine my planting times for their areas.

Arugula—*Eruca vesicaria sativa*. This tangy Italian salad favorite is at its tenderest and tastiest during cold weather. Salad lovers who claim they don't like arugula have gotten a bad impression from hot-weather crops and will quickly change their opinion when they taste arugula from the winter garden. I plant arugula like the other winter salad greens in rows as close as 4 inches apart. Planting begins in late summer and extends through the winter. I aim to sow seeds at 1 inch apart. If I sow too thickly I pick an extra baby crop from the thinnings. In midwinter, when regrowth is slow, I depend on timed succession plantings. In spring I treat it as a cutting (mesclun) green as long as quality holds, and then move back to young succession plantings as the weather warms. There are different strains of arugula but no named varieties. I recommend buying from a number of suppliers to see if one particular strain matches your soil better. There is also a wild arugula, *Diplotaxis muralis* according to my sources but *Eruca sativa selvatica* according to others, which is a smaller, hardier, slower-growing plant than regular arugula. It is also slower to bolt, with a mild flavor that is definitely arugula-like, but with less bite. It is exceptionally well adapted to the winter garden.

Carrot—*Daucus carota sativa*. The winter-harvest carrots were nicknamed "candy carrots" by my children. When they arrived home on the school bus they would run eagerly to the tunnel greenhouse to pick and eat them. That's quite a testimonial to their delicious flavor. Candy carrots are a product of two cultural choices: late sowing time (August 1–15 in New England) and winter harvesting (after soil temperature drops into the mid-30s F.). When the small, tender carrots that result from late planting are left in a cold soil, which causes some of the starch to change to sugar, it produces the most consistently sweet and tender carrots I have ever sold.

Candy carrots are an intensively planted, high-yielding crop. They are planted in rows 4 inches apart and thinned to 2 inches apart in the row. In the early years we protected outdoor plantings under cold frames filled with straw for overwintering. They miraculously retained their greens, and we were able to market bunched, extra-sweet baby carrots from December through March. Nowadays we cover them with an unheated mobile tunnel and add some form of insulation over them. You can insulate with straw, bags of autumn leaves, rolls of foam, or anything else handy. If I use straw I put a sheet of plastic between it and the carrots to keep the straw from mixing with the soil when I harvest. My favorite variety is 'Napoli' for its slightly higher quality, although I have also used 'Minicor', 'Amsterdam Forcing', and 'Nelson' with equal success.

Claytonia—*Montia perfoliata.* A native California weed, this plant is sometimes listed as "miners' lettuce." European plant breeders developed this weed into a popular winter salad green which they call "winter purslane" from the partial similarity of its fleshy leaves to those of that other cultivated weed. Claytonia has such succulent, sweet, and delicious raw leaves that everyone comments on it when first encountering it in a salad mix. The leaves grow individually on long stems. Sometimes the stems can be too long (over 2 inches), and then I shorten them after cutting each handful. It is important to harvest just above the crowns so the next cutting will be clean. Sown in rows 4 inches apart and left unthinned, claytonia will produce up to three cuttings from each succession planting. I am not aware of any named varieties, nor have I noticed differences between seed lots from various suppliers.

Endive (Frisée)—*Chicorium endivia.* I use the French word *frisée* to emphasize that I am talking about the green salad endive with the beautiful, deeply cut leaves as opposed to "Belgian endive" (witloof chicory). I think frisée endive is a wonderful winter lettuce substitute because it is much hardier under cold-weather stress and offers the novelty of a seasonal special. Further, when grown in the short days and cool temperatures of winter, the heads of the "tres fine" varieties do not need to be blanched, because the bite of the leaves remains mild and the flavor is really superb. The advantage of blanching (by tying up the leaves or covering the heart for about ten days) is that the white leaves and stems from the heart of the plant make a striking contrast to green leaves in a salad. I sow from mid- to late August through mid-September and transplant at a 10- by 10-inch spacing for the smaller varieties and 12- by 12-inch spacing for the larger varieties. I like 'Nina', 'Neos', and 'Tosca' as "tres fine" varieties and 'Salad King' as a standard. 'President' is the best under very cold conditions.

Lettuce—*Lactuca sativa*. Lettuce is not successful in the passive winter garden in Zone 5 and colder because it cannot tolerate the freezing and thawing. In the home garden I substituted mâche for lettuce in winter salad mixes. There is so much other variety I never missed the lettuce. However, if the leaves of soft butterheads or crisp romaines are desired in midwinter, they should be sown in a slightly heated greenhouse with attention to the planting schedule on page 260. Since I have plenty of green in the salad and only radicchio available as a red, I favor lettuces with good red color. I continue to look for the perfect red.

Mâche—*Valerianella locusta*. The classic cold-weather salad green. Also called "corn salad" from its origin as a weed in European winter grain fields. It is the hardiest salad plant I know of, and it will actually continue to grow through the coldest weather. It is used like lettuce as the major ingredient of a salad. Its mild, nutty flavor provides a perfect background for more assertive ingredients.

Mâche germinates and grows best in cool soils. I sow from September through January. The seeds are sown 1 inch apart in rows spaced 4 inches apart. Mâche can be slow to germinate if the soil is warm because it prefers cool fall conditions. If you need to sow earlier, cover the rows with boards and keep them moist to create cool, shady conditions. Check every day and remove the boards as soon as the plants appear.

There are two types of mâche grown in Europe. The Dutch varieties (such as 'A Grosse Graine') are pale-leaved and not as winter-hardy. The smaller, darker-leaved varieties (such as 'Vit', 'Coquille de Louviers', and 'Elan') are the standard in France and Switzerland. I have grown both types and will admit to a slight prejudice in favor of the darker varieties because the leaves hold up better. But interested growers should trial them both, since the Dutch types will give more weight of crop in areas that have milder winters.

I have seen greenhouses in Europe that were growing only mâche. In order to increase yields many were transplanting this crop. They sowed mâche in 1½-inch soil blocks, three plants to the block, and transplanted them out at six blocks per square foot. I doubted the economy of transplanting such a small, short-season crop, until they explained that they could get four crops per winter from transplanting instead of only two from direct-seeding.

Even full-grown mâche plants are small; the leaves at their largest are the size of your thumb. They are traditionally harvested and served whole. Cut them just beneath their base with a sharp knife, keeping the blade parallel to the soil.

For the very highest quality I think the leaves are most tender when cut at about 75 percent of their full size, even though this means a sacrifice of bulk yield. There are a number of different named varieties that vary in leaf size and hardiness. My favorites for dependability, flavor, and winter survival even under the coldest conditions are 'Vit' and 'Ronde de Nice'.

Minutina—*Plantago coronopus*. This is one of my favorite new winter salad crops. It is a relative of the round-leaved plantain, a common lawn weed, and of a popular wild food here on the Maine coast, goosetongue (*Plantago oliganthus*). Minutina is also called buckshorn plantain from the shape of the leaves and erba stella from the starlike appearance of the plant itself. The leaves, which are included in mixed salad blends, have a mild, springlike taste (some people say salty) with a pleasing crunch. The leaf shape adds visual diversity to salads.

I plant in 4-inch rows and cut only once when the leaves are 4 to 5 inches tall. If you wish to cut the regrowth, the plants must be cut short the first time, since partially cut leaves will continue growing and are not as pretty without the tip. Plant from August to November and again in early spring. Keep the soil moist for tenderest leaves.

Mizuna—*Brassica rapa* var. *japonica*. The lovely, deeply cut, almost fernlike leaves of mizuna add unique texture and flavor to winter salads. This plant germinates and grows well under cool winter conditions. I broadcast the seeds in rows spaced 4 inches apart and harvest by cutting the young leaves when they are 4 to 6 inches tall. They regrow for additional harvest. A close relative, mibuna, has long, slender leaves rounded at the tip and is grown in the same way.

Parsley—*Petroselinum crispum*. Needs no introduction. There is always a market for bunches of fresh parsley. Parsley will produce all winter from a mid-July sowing in soil blocks. I transplant them out at an 8 by 8-inch spacing. I have always had excellent results with the curled variety 'Darki'. I find the flat Italian parsleys are not as hardy and don't produce as well in the winter.

Radicchio—*Cichorium intybus*. The number of chicories I encountered on a trip to Italy reinforced my impression that the chicory family is almost a vegetable universe in itself. Although eaten for thousands of years, many of its members have only recently been domesticated, and I seem to meet new family members and learn new practices every day. My favorite members of the family are the radicchios. I have grown both the old-style radicchios that have to be cut back before heading and the new models that form the red head directly. So far

I have found the newer models more dependable, because they produce consistently and hold well for a long period of harvest in the winter garden. However, I continue running trials of planting dates for the traditional types because I am sure they offer certain flavor or timing advantages that I haven't discovered yet.

I observed one extra virtue of chicories on a visit to European growers in 1989. All members of the chicory family seemed to be beneficial preceding crops in a rotation. A number of rotational trials on my farm since then have confirmed that hunch and given me yet another reason to grow them. I sow radicchio from early to mid-August and thin to 12 by 12-inch spacing. I use four varieties—'Giulio', 'Augusto', 'Rosanna', and 'Chioggia Red Preco'—and among them I get pretty good harvest over the winter. But I'm nowhere near satisfied, and feel that I'm just beginning to scratch the surface with this crop.

Scallion—*Allium cepa.* I use the word "scallion" to refer to a young or green onion. Scallions are so hardy in the winter greenhouse they can be harvested while frozen solid and still make beautiful bunches after they thaw. I have harvested bulb onion varieties (*Allium cepa*), bunching onion varieties (*Allium fistulosum*), and young pearl onions in winter, so I know all of them will work. My favorite onion varieties for winter harvest as scallions are 'Buffalo' and the pearl onion 'Snow Baby'. They do well on my sandy soil. Both produce a very sweet and tender scallion. I sow from mid-July to early August in rows 6 inches apart and aim for 12 plants per foot of row.

Sorrel—*Rumex acetosa.* This perennial crop can either be grown from seed every year or can be propagated by dividing and transplanting established plants (just chop them in quarters or sixths with a spade). I prefer propagation by division because it allows me to improve quality by selecting plants with the nicest leaves. Sorrel is hardy, with a weedlike vigor, and does not need to be pampered. I watched two French growers transplanting sorrel divisions into a winter greenhouse as casually and rapidly as if they were throwing dirty clothes into a hamper.

Harvest the young leaves at 4 inches to no more than 6 inches long for best quality. Yield will slow slightly in the depths of winter and will be hard to keep up with, once spring reappears. There are a number of named varieties, but personally I have had experience with only one. I started years ago with some seeds of 'De Belleville' and have been dividing those plants ever since.

Spinach—*Spinacia oleracea*. I treat spinach as a salad crop in the winter tunnels. A continuous supply of mesclun-salad-sized leaves can be harvested right through the winter. I begin sowing in mid-August and continue through October. Spinach is also succession-seeded as spaces open up during the winter. I sow in rows 4 to 6 inches apart and thin to 4 inches apart in the row. I always fertilize spinach with an extra supply of two-year-old, well-finished compost. Both 'Space' and 'Imperial Spring' have done well in the winter garden.

Watercress—*Nasturtium officinale*. I started watercress from seed in soil blocks years ago, and it grew so enthusiastically I thought why not transplant it to the garden? Well, it never succeeded in the garden (even with shade cloth, trickle irrigation, and a mulch of marble chips), but I struck gold when I transplanted some seedlings to the winter tunnel. The combination of low winter light filtered through the poly covering and cool temperatures provide ideal conditions for very successful watercress crops. I used trickle irrigation in one trial but didn't feel it added anything. The key in my experience is to spread sufficient lime for a neutral pH and to add lots of well-finished compost to the soil before transplanting. I transplant the soil-block seedlings at an 8- by 8-inch spacing and keep the beds watered, but not outrageously more so than for other winter greenhouse crops.

I have found that the planting can die away because the stems don't automatically reroot in these nonstream conditions. Thus, after I harvest the tips from beyond the point where the stems are putting out new roots, I renew the bed with a ½-inch covering of compost and a good watering. The covering helps the stems root and send up new shoots. The results are not always consistent, but I haven't yet determined whether the cause is variable compost quality, a flaw in the technique, or inadequate attention to detail on my part. But even with the best of attention weeds will eventually become a problem, and I then clean up the bed and replant to the next crop in the rotation.

If you have bench space, a very successful technique is to make timed succession sowings of watercress seed beginning in early August, on a planting schedule similar to that suggested for lettuce on page 260. Once they reach the desired size, these can be harvested in one or two cuts directly from the flats they are growing in. That should give assured harvests right through the winter. New sowings can be made early in the year to carry on till late spring.

The same can be done by rooting cuttings in soil blocks. Using cuttings allows you to progressively select and propagate your own strain of watercress from those plants that do best under your specific growing conditions. Blocks made with a long dowel pin (see page 136) work perfectly. Some bottom heat will be beneficial if greenhouse temperatures are cool.

Other winter crops presently under consideration are beet, broccoli raab, fennel, baby leek, radish, and snow pea. In my first year of trials with edible flowers, calendula was not successful; violets, on the other hand, produced flowers every month. The following herbs were harvestable all winter long: winter thyme, winter savory, and sage.

Mobile Greenhouse Crop Rotation

I have heard it suggested that nature is not more complicated than we think, but is more complicated than we *can* think. I hope that isn't true. But the saying does come to mind when planning greenhouse crop rotations, because there is now something else to keep aware of. In addition to time moving and crops moving we must add the movement and the influence of the greenhouse. I don't look at this as a complication but as a promising opportunity. The more we attempt to optimize our interaction with the biological systems affecting agriculture, the more of a fascinating mind game it becomes.

First, let's consider the summer season. Even with the end doors removed and the vents open, the greenhouse will experience summer temperatures on average 15°F. (8°C.) higher than the outside air temperature. Why not take advantage of that situation if it can be done with a minimum input of time, labor, and expense? For the summer months—June, July, August, and September—during which I am not planning to market crops from the greenhouses, I have been exploring two options—warm-weather green manures and a warm-weather, low-maintenance crop.

There are any number of interesting green-manure crops I normally don't grow in my climate because of their high heat requirements. But I have long been interested in them because I would like to explore their potential for adding heretofore unknown biological factors to my soil. Ecological studies celebrate the benefits of wide diversity, and I now have the opportunity to broaden the diversity of my greenhouse soil. The greenhouse is providing an extra-warm summer environment at no cost to me, and that is just what some exciting new soil-improving crop may like. Some of the crops I'm trialing are crotalaria, soybeans, cowpeas, and sesbania. I don't know if any of these will catch on as part of my rotation, but it is always worth a look.

For a marketable crop in the summer greenhouse I choose sweet potatoes. My experience so far has been 100 percent positive. Sweet potatoes are easy to establish, they cover the ground quickly to smother weeds, and they require almost no care other than watering. Plus there is an interesting mutual benefit. Not only do they offer me more variety in my rotation because they are a new crop unrelated to any of the others I am growing, but that same newness offers growing conditions free from the nematode and soil-borne fungus problems that can plague them on their home grounds. Because of that benefit northern growers often get higher yields than many growers do down south.

I have been told that sweet potatoes planted on rich soil will go mostly to leaf and form spindly roots. I suspect there is an imbalance in plant foods, such as an oversupply of nitrogen, when that occurs. I haven't had that problem on my composted soil. The variety 'Georgia Jet' has done well for us, although the roots will develop growth cracks under less than perfect conditions. Both the southern suppliers from whom we purchase our rooted cuttings, called slips, and other experienced northern growers have suggested 'Beauregard' and 'Jewel' may be superior choices.

I dig the crop with a hand fork as soon as I can or as late as I dare, depending on the dictates of the next crop in the greenhouse rotation. I want to make sure I harvest before the soil temperatures drop below 50°F. (10°C.), as this can impair the sweet potato's keeping quality. After harvest, the roots need to be cured at temperatures between 80° and 90°F. (27° to 32°C.) in a damp atmosphere for seven to ten days. If there is no other suitable curing area, you can put the doors back on the greenhouse to keep it warmer and cure the roots right there. The curing process, in addition to improving the protective qualities of the skin, also sweetens the roots. After curing they can either be sold in bulk or stored at between 50° and 60°F. (10° to 16°C.) and sold as long as they last. Locally grown sweet potatoes are a great attention-getting crop with which to start the fall sales season, especially where they are as unique to the area as they are here on the Maine coast.

The fall, winter, and spring seasons in the greenhouse involve a wide range of crops. I try to follow the crop rotation suggestions in Chapter 7 as much as possible. I can always manage not to grow the same crop twice in succession, but the more intensive I make the production, the more constraints there may be on crop variety in the rotation. Since the greenhouses will be replanted for a second harvest, there will be an intra-year rotation (during the same year) as well as the multiyear rotation (from year to year). Let's start with a multiyear rotation consisting of winter crops, sweet potatoes, tomatoes, green manures, and the movement of the greenhouse itself. This plan is based on using two greenhouses, No. 1 and No. 2, each having two sites, A and B. The shading indicates the site is covered by the greenhouse.

The crop-rotation year in the winter garden runs from October to October. In the example below, for the first year Greenhouse #1 is on site A and site B grows green manure, while greenhouse #2 is on site B and its site A grows green manure. When the second year begins the next October, each greenhouse is moved to its alternate site, which has previously been tilled and sown to the winter crops. The uncovered sites now grow green manure until the following year, and the sequence continues.

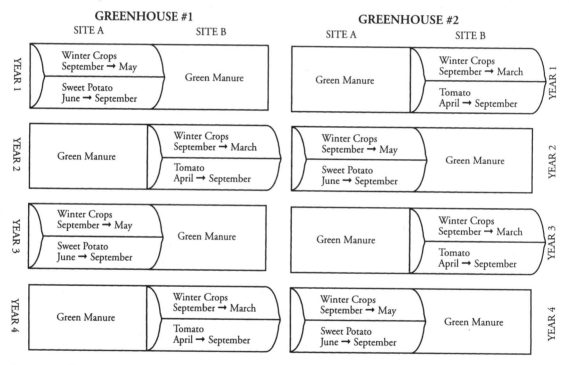

Four years of crop rotations with two moveable greenhouses.

I divide the winter into four harvest periods: Oct–Nov, Dec–Jan, Feb–Mar, Apr–May. Of course there is overlap, but those are reasonable guides. One house is planted earlier to be ready for the Oct–Nov harvest, and the other is planted later for the Dec–Jan period. As spaces open up through the harvesting of the Oct–Nov crops, those areas are replanted to crops for the Feb–Mar harvest. Similarly, as the Dec–Jan crops are harvested, they are replaced by sowing crops that will be ready to harvest during the Apr–May period.

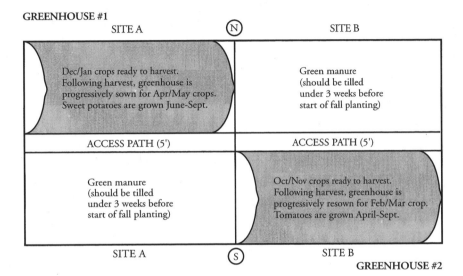

GREENHOUSE #1

SITE A · Ⓝ · SITE B

Dec/Jan crops ready to harvest. Following harvest, greenhouse is progressively sown for Apr/May crops. Sweet potatoes are grown June–Sept.

Green manure (should be tilled under 3 weeks before start of fall planting)

ACCESS PATH (5′) · ACCESS PATH (5′)

Green manure (should be tilled under 3 weeks before start of fall planting)

Oct/Nov crops ready to harvest. Following harvest, greenhouse is progressively resown for Feb/Mar crop. Tomatoes are grown April–Sept.

SITE A · Ⓢ · SITE B

GREENHOUSE #2

Another way of looking at the crop rotation cycle.

When I use the term "intra-year rotation" I am referring to this planting and then replanting of the houses. My greenhouse is divided into 30-inch-wide beds with a 12-inch path between them. As soon as part of a bed has been harvested, I re-prepare the soil. That consists of pulling any stems or roots and adding a light covering of compost, which I mix in shallowly. The soil in the winter garden remains highly productive. I have to avoid the temptation to add extra organic fertilizer. Once the crop is up, you can experiment with a liquid organic fertilizer if you think the extra plant food will help. In my experience, though, it is not needed and can easily overwhelm these cool-season crops. However, I have found the need to add extra fertility (usually some alfalfa meal) for crops following spinach. Spinach in the greenhouse can definitely have a detrimental effect on subsequent crops. Other growers share that opinion. If I can avoid replanting right after spinach, say, by using the space for flats filled with transplants, I do so. If I need to replant right away, arugula is usually my choice for the post-spinach crop.

The grower should devise a cropping plan that takes into account when the spaces to be replanted will be cleared and what crop should be planted next according to its speed of growth, the amount required, and any rotational principles that can be applied. Those are a lot of masters to serve, but the task is not as complicated as it might seem, nor is it unforgiving. In the example above, each multiyear rotation has 10 to 12 months of green manure plus either sweet potato or tomato between each winter cropping period. That is sufficient variety to allow the grower to be more relaxed with winter crop sequences. Even growing the same winter crop twice in succession would not be unpardonable, but I would avoid it if I could. The enjoyable challenge of planning rotations is that there is always some small refinement that can be made so the next crop is just a little bit better than this one.

Sowing the Winter Crop

For intensive production I use close spacing, with rows only 4 to 6 inches apart. The five-row seeder mentioned earlier (see page 73) or a six- or seven-row model can be very useful here. It is a good equivalent of the expensive European precision greenhouse seeders, but you don't have to spend a fortune importing one. I made mine ten years ago and it still works fine today.

Another seeder option I have found useful in the greenhouse is the SAALET or "So Easy Super Seeder" made in Denmark. (Address given in the tool appendix.) This is a small plastic unit for home gardeners with seed plates that adapt to most seed sizes and spacing requirements. It is inexpensive (under $25) and built well enough that I use it commercially. I have a number of them permanently set up with different seed plates for the seed sizes I use. The only modification I have made is to replace the cheap plastic handle with a wooden one.

SAALET seeder.

European greenhouse seeder.

The European greenhouse seeder models are built with rollers front and back to smooth the soil. A frame with seed dispensers hanging from it occupies the space between the rollers and connects them. Pulleys from the rollers drive the seed mechanisms. I think any handy grower should be able to make a very professional, hand-pushed gang seeder for greenhouse use by combining a number of the small SAALET seeders with rollers and a frame. The more the sowing process can be mechanized and made efficient, the more precise the grower can be in keeping up-to-date on seeding schedules.

Gauging the time from sowing to harvest is important to successful winter cropping. This is only minimally dependent on climate (average temperature). By far the most significant influence on duration of growing period in the winter months is the short length of the winter days. Shorter day length is a reality in both northern and southern growing regions. Crops take longer to mature when the days are short.

The effect is universal enough that the Dutch experience with planting dates (they are located in the mid-50 latitudes) is very useful to me (here at the 44th latitude), and friends in California (between the 36th and 38th parallel) have confirmed that the timing is similar for them. The Dutch have found that planting dates need to be bunched closely in the fall in order to achieve harvests that are spaced one week apart in the winter and spring. The Dutch data for greenhouse lettuce on the graph below is a good example.

The horizontal axis represents sowing dates from August through April. The vertical axis gives the number of days to harvest. Written along the curve of the graph are average harvest dates corresponding to the planting date directly below. As you can see, sowing dates just one month apart in the fall (say, September 5 and October 5) result in harvests over two-and-one-half months apart (November 10 and February 2).

This graph is a good guide to begin with. Although it is based on growing fully mature heads of lettuce, the ratios between date of sowing and length of time to harvest are applicable to other salad crops, even those cut young as ingredients in a salad mix. For the first year I suggest making many extra plantings to cover the options. Keep careful notes of your results. A season of experience should refine the specifics pretty well. Of course the weather can play a part, since the number of cloudy or sunny days can vary from year to year. In addition, if you transplant winter crops, the size of the soil block can make a difference. (A plant in a 2-inch block will get a better start and continue to outpace a plant in a 1½-inch block.) But in the final analysis an understanding of the

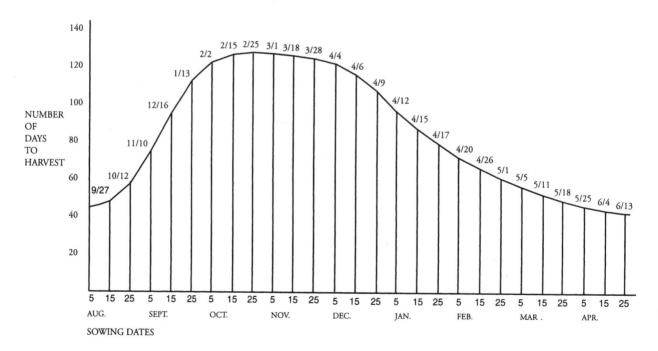

Sowing schedule for weekly lettuce harvest.

effect of day length on crop timing will be the most helpful background. It should enable you to devise a planting schedule that results in a day-to-day harvest of a wide variety of crops all winter long.

Greenhouse Soils

Greenhouse growing takes place in a relatively small area compared to acres of outdoor crops. Since yields and returns are high for this intensive, long-season production, I can afford the materials and labor to modify the soil considerably. The quality of the soil is of especial importance under greenhouse conditions. Before the first fall crops went in I did my best to achieve soil perfection. On my sandy soil I spread peat moss (a 2-inch layer) combined with montmorillonite clay (10 tons per acre or 0.5 pounds per square foot), in addition to limestone, colloidal phosphate, and greensand. (See Chapter 11 for a discussion of peat and montmorillonite; see Chapter 10 for information on soil mineral additives.) My intention was to jump-start the establishment of soil conditions that grow great crops and then maintain and improve them thereafter with compost, crop rotations, and green manures. If I saw the need, I would reapply the peat and montmorillonite a second time.

In Chapter 10 I stressed the importance of learning to make exceptional compost. High-quality compost is even more important in the greenhouse than in the field. I prefer compost made from plant waste rather than animal manures. I can't express that preference scientifically. I just think plant-waste compost has a more moderate effect and the crops are healthier. I can afford to concentrate on compost quality because in this greenhouse system I don't need enormous amounts. The long-term green manures and diversified crop rotations made possible by the movable greenhouses contribute immeasurably to keeping the soil alive and productive.

Weeds

My weed solution, as I explained in Chapter 16, is to dispatch them young and never let any go to seed. I saw a perfect example of the validity of that approach a few years ago when we built a new greenhouse. I had leveled the site by bringing in topsoil we'd removed from a ditch. The difference in weed numbers between that new house and the older houses was glaring. Whereas weeds are almost nonexistent on soil we have cultivated for a few years, they were rampant on the new soil. It made me aware just how successful my "don't let them seed" policy had been. Low-growing salad crops are particularly susceptible to weed competition and can be inadvertently mixed with weed seedlings at harvest. I can't emphasize this point enough: Get on top of weeds at the start and stick to it.

The way to achieve that goal is very straightforward. Most weeds germinate in the top 2 inches of the soil. Get rid of those seeds and the problem is solved. I have seen steam used to do the job in European organic greenhouses. Every few years the growers cover the soil with heavy tarps and pump pressurized steam under them for five minutes to raise the soil temperature in the top 2 inches to 80°C. (176°F.) and kill weed seeds. They wait two weeks after steaming for the biological life to return before replanting. The result is a very impressive, weed-free greenhouse. I have never used steam and probably won't, but I achieve the same end by encouraging weed seeds to germinate (the action of the rototiller does that very well) and then eliminating the tiny new seedlings before planting. As long as I till shallowly and don't continually bring up new seeds from lower layers, the weed seed reservoir in the top 2 inches of soil is exhausted after three to five years, and the foundation for clean cultivation has been laid.*

*See the complete citation on page 170.

Those clean conditions must be maintained by never letting any weeds go to seed. That is usually easy to do when growing short-duration salad crops, but the greenhouses often get ignored in the off-season. The summer greenhouse crops, whether commercial ones like sweet potatoes or a warm-weather green manure for soil improvement, are chosen for their ability to cover the soil and prevent weed growth. I still patrol the premises to pull any weeds that might appear before they can reproduce themselves.

When I first became involved with intensive greenhouse salad crops grown in narrow rows, I realized I needed a specialized tool to cultivate the inter-row areas. After pondering the problem and trying every hand-cultivating tool I could find, I went to the workshop. I hammered flat 4 inches at one end of a piece of No. 9 wire and sharpened one edge of that surface. I then bent the wire around and back on itself and then off at a right angle so I had a thin hoe blade with an 8-inch-long wire shank aimed at the center of the blade. I stuck the shank into a wooden file handle, bent it slightly so there would be a 35° working angle to the soil, and returned to the greenhouse. This simple homemade tool represented a quantum leap in successful greenhouse cultivation.

The short blade fits between the rows. It is strong enough for the light cultivation I need it to do. I use it with a slight vibrating back-and-forth motion. This is a perfect example of a tool designed for doing a job in the right place, at the right time, with the right touch. Whereas it would not be at home in a hard soil, the friable greenhouse soil is ideal. It would bend out of shape if I used it to chop larger weeds. It has just the right strength and precision for light cultivation when

Homemade
cultivating tool.

the newly germinated plants are small. The very thin, sharp blade cuts shallowly, just under the surface, and doesn't dump soil on the crop seedlings. Best of all it is pleasant to use. Once the crops are larger I have a number of stainless steel collinear hoes with the blades cut down to different lengths so I can work in an upright position.

Pests

I have experienced very few insect and disease problems in the winter garden. Initially I felt the greenhouse might be introducing an artificial factor that could make plants more susceptible. I am convinced now that any effect is minimal. The only disease I have seen was a little gray mold fungus (*Botrytis* spp.), which didn't surprise me, since it thrives in cool, damp conditions. I now prevent it by venting off moist air in the mornings. Prevention is a time-honored greenhouse practice. In Dutch organic greenhouses I have seen specially designed vacuum cleaners used before planting a crop to remove any leaves or other partially decayed organic residues from the soil surface so they cannot serve as substrates for disease organisms. I don't use a vacuum, but I do spend time cleaning up crop residues and keeping stems trimmed close. I try to manage the greenhouse environment so as to encourage only the plants.

European growers have a nice trick for improving airflow to prevent problems in midwinter lettuce crops. Instead of setting the soil-block–grown transplant seedlings into the soil at the usual depth, they set them on top of the soil. With a little irrigation the plants will root vigorously from the bottom of the block. Depending on block size, this keeps the lower leaves an inch or more above the soil surface, providing better air movement and less chance of bottom rot.

Aphids can appear in early spring on crops that have yielded through the winter (spinach, chard, sorrel, parsley). A thorough watering is usually all that is necessary to restore balance. Whether they appear because the soil is too dry at that stage from my minimal winter watering, or whether they depart because the water flushes extra nitrates from the soil I cannot say. I did inadvertently introduce whiteflies in one house a few years ago on some brought-in plants. They survived through the summer but did not follow the greenhouse when it moved to cover winter crops, and I have not seen any whiteflies since.

A small flock of ducks helps deal with slugs. They patrol the ground around greenhouses and eagerly dine on anything that moves. Slugs have not been a problem since putting them to work. Ducks can be fenced selectively inside the greenhouse during the winter on beds that have been harvested. We have used active foraging bantam ducks (Australian Spotted) as well as egg-laying breeds (Khaki Campbells, Welsh Harlequins) with equal success. The egg layers make sense because they turn a problem, the slugs, into a product, fresh eggs. It is necessary to shut the ducks up at night to protect them from their predators. Our duck house, which can be easily moved to any location, is a smaller version of the wheeled chicken houses described in Chapter 24. It is affectionately known as Duckingham Palace.

Fall and winter freezing may have a lot to do with the absence of pests. I have asked entomologists for information on that subject. I'm curious to know whether anyone has researched the use of selective low temperatures as a pest-control measure. I am aware that many bedding-plant growers turn off their houses in the winter to freeze out pests, but I have never heard of anyone doing it while plants were growing in the house. The idea would be to take advantage of any differential hardiness between plant and pest by allowing the temperature on a freezing night to drop to a point where the pests were killed but the plants survived.

A few entomologists, after I explained the parameters of the system—mobile houses, compost fertilization, crop rotation, green manures, winter crops—commented that, given what they knew about insect life stages and reaction to low temperatures, they wouldn't be surprised not to find any pest problems at all. I found their comments reassuring, and definitely in line with my practical experience. For whatever reason, pest control is a very minor concern for crops in the winter garden. Which is nice, because it allows me to concentrate on the most important consideration—crop quality.

Crop Quality

With the exception of some freezing injury in our unheated prototype winter garden system (when outdoor temperatures went to −15°F. and crop temperatures reached 15°F.), the quality of winter garden crops is continually high, both visually and in terms of flavor, tenderness, and just plain eating pleasure. We do everything we can to ensure optimum soil conditions, and it obviously pays off.

The major quality problem sometimes seen in winter hothouse crops—high nitrate content—is not a problem in this system. That's because none of the causative factors are present: use of soluble nitrogen fertilizers, forcing crops in low-light conditions at high temperatures, lack of trace elements, and the use of susceptible varieties. We fertilize only with well-humified, one-and-one-half- to two-year-old compost; we don't force the crops; we have plenty of trace elements in the soil and organic matter to make them available; and we are not growing special winter-forcing varieties.

Plus there are positive factors operating, thanks to the mobile greenhouse. There is no continuous buildup of nitrates or other salts in the soil as there would be in a permanent greenhouse, because this soil is uncovered for one year out of every two. In addition, the crops that we are harvesting during the lowest winter light (mid-November to mid-February) were all grown outdoors in the fall. They stopped their growth naturally as a result of low temperatures and low light. The greenhouse covering then arrived to protect them (the same as if we had moved them to a milder climate). As I have mentioned elsewhere, we have extended the harvest season, not the growing season. The conditions for these crops are the same as they would be in the more temperate winter climate around Nice, France, or Genoa, Italy. That's correct. Our latitude, 44°N., which results in cold winters on this side of the Atlantic is the same as Provence and the Ligurian coast. Winter garden crops here in Maine receive the same length of day as winter salads grown in the milder winters of those locations.

The high quality that can be achieved with winter garden crops is not solely attributable to my organic methods. I have seen problems on European organic farms that used dried blood and feather meal fertilizers to force winter crops. Blood and feather meal are just as likely as soluble chemical nitrogen to result in high nitrate levels in winter produce. High-quality winter crops are a result of understanding the constraints of winter production and taking care to create optimal, balanced conditions for plant development.

Low Winter Sun and Greenhouse Layout

The other reality of short winter days is low sun angle. Be sure your greenhouse site won't be shaded by trees, hedges, houses, a mountain, or other greenhouses. The amount of change in angle from summer sun to winter sun always surprises me. At our latitude (44°N.) the noon sun has an altitude angle of 69° on June 21, but only 22° on December 21. I have to constantly remind myself to pay attention to where the winter shadows will fall when I am laying out greenhouses.

I plan my greenhouses with the long axis running east–west to maximize winter sun. To the south of 40°N. latitude, a north–south orientation is recommended. You need to be aware that true south for greenhouse layout is not the same as magnetic south at most locations. You will need to determine your "magnetic declination" from a topographic map and adjust accordingly.

When the sun is low in the winter sky, a 10-foot-tall greenhouse running east–west will cast a shadow 25 feet long; a 12-foot-tall greenhouse will cast a 30-foot shadow. Thus, a second greenhouse behind the first should be sited at least that far away so as not to be shaded. In the past I have often used that winter-shade area to grow outdoor summer crops (they benefit from the windbreak created by the greenhouses), or I have covered that ground with temporary greenhouses in spring and summer when the sun is higher in the sky.

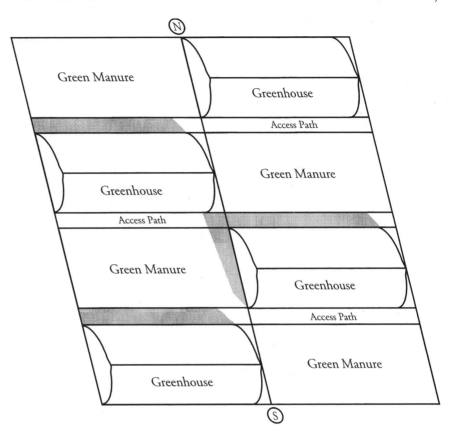

Siting greenhouses to avoid cast shadows and to provide windbreaks.

Another option is to take advantage of movable greenhouses and plan the rotation so the greenhouses are offset. That way you can place them as close together as is convenient, yet still avoid winter shadows. The sample rotations on pages 256 and 257 are planned so the winter positions will alternate between sites A and B as shown above.

There is one final reality of winter in addition to cold temperatures and low sun: snow. With heated greenhouses the standard practice is to turn up the heat during a snowstorm so as to melt off the snow. For unheated and low-temperature production I take a different approach. My greenhouses have a Gothic arch roofline and heavier pipe construction; both features make for a stronger structure that sheds snow better. Although the snow slides off the roof, it doesn't go away. A heavy snowfall remains piled up against the sides and can block sun. If you shovel by hand, pay attention. You can easily jab the snow shovel through the greenhouse plastic (I have done it more than once). If you have a lot of greenhouses, a snow blower is the tool of choice. The snow blower can remove snow from right alongside the wall of the greenhouse without creating back pressure as a snowplow would.

24 🪲 LIVESTOCK

One way to diversify the farm's potential marketing options and simultaneously improve soil fertility for vegetable crops is to include livestock in your system. Because adding livestock to the farm can increase the management load considerably, you should not acquire livestock until the basic vegetable-growing operation is firmly established. Even then, a lot of thought must be given to the added hours of work and the possible need for extra workers.

If you feel comfortable taking on these new responsibilities, the addition of livestock is the next logical step in enhancing your farm's stability and economic independence. Livestock can be considered as a part of the crop-rotation plan or as a separate operation altogether.

Free Manure

Many vegetable growers keep livestock separate from the rotation, using mainly purchased feed for their farm animals. The stock are not usually kept for profit, but rather as a source of free manure. For example, if the farm has barn space, you might decide to raise dairy bull calves to beef market weight on purchased hay and grain. As a supplementary farm activity this is not likely to yield a profit per se. The costs will likely equal the income from selling the animals. But the profitability must be calculated from the savings gained by not having to purchase manure, and the further benefit of having the quantity and quality of manure you need, produced right on the farm.

Horses

From my experience with different manures as fertilizers for vegetable growing, I would recommend horses over cattle. If the facilities were available I would choose to board horses for the winter. In many ways this may be a simpler option. First of all, winter is the slackest time in the vegetable grower's year, and the livestock responsibility would not be continued through the busier half of the year. Second, I could charge enough to feed the horses well and bed them on straw to produce a quality manure-straw mixture. Lastly, even if my return from the operation were only enough to cover expenses (I could thereby underbid other horse boarders to get the number of animals I desired), I would have produced, at no cost, a year's supply of what was long considered to be the ideal soil amendment for general vegetable crops: horse manure and straw bedding. This fibrous horse manure-straw combination has been a reliable fertilizer throughout the history of market gardening.

The size of the livestock operation can be calculated according to the farm's manure requirements. In order to manure half the acreage every year at the rate of 20 tons per acre, a 5-acre operation would need 50 tons of manure. Since a horse will produce 15 tons of manure (with bedding) per year, that would equal .066 horse per ton. For a six-month boarding operation, that factor must be doubled to .133; .133 horse per ton of manure x 50 tons = 6.65 (call it 7) horses. Boarding seven horses bedded on straw for six months would give you 50 tons of first-class vegetable fertilizer.

Managing the Manure

There would be one problem to contend with, however. On the scale of production we are considering, the grower would be faced with a great deal of work managing that manure properly (by composting it) and spreading it on the field. However, if the stalls were cleaned every day and the manure added to a steadily growing compost windrow, the composting part would be manageable. Spreading that quantity of manure is a more formidable task. I have spread 50 tons of manure by hand in a year, and I've done it for many years of vegetable growing.

Yes, it is hard work, but certainly not beyond the ability of most people. It is usually accomplished over a period of time, and in retrospect it is not all that difficult.

I will agree that spreading 50 tons of manure would be a lot easier with some machinery. Since I don't believe you can economically justify the expense of a tractor and front-end loader on a 5-acre farm, the best solution is to hire a custom operator. The difficulty, of course, is to find someone who can do the job when you need it done. If that can be arranged, hired machinery would be a viable solution.

Rotating Livestock and Crops

As I said, were I to operate such a program, I would choose horses. But there are other considerations which convince me that the first option, including livestock in the rotation, may be a better solution for the following reasons:

- Small livestock products such as fresh eggs or range-fed poultry can be valuable as a means of attracting and keeping customers for the vegetable operation. The livestock/soil-fertility combination will then contribute directly to farm income.
- The winter months are the outdoor grower's only opportunity for vacation. I guarantee that most people will be more effective during the rest of the year if they take some time off then.
- The ideal soil structure and organic matter benefits conferred by adding manure to the soil can also be achieved by growing a mixed legume-grass sod for two or three years.

Fortunately, there is a livestock choice that will make optimum use of a legume-grass sod, provide a readily saleable item, not require winter care, and effectively produce manure and spread it for you in the process.

Poultry

The best livestock to complement vegetable production are poultry ranged on sod in the rotation. Chickens or turkeys thrive when run on shortgrass pasture, known as "range." According to varying experience, pasture can provide up to 40 percent of their food needs. In this option poultry are grazed on a green manure crop that is included in the crop rotation. In that way the legume or grass crop grown for soil improvement also feeds the livestock and they, in turn, manure the field.

Studies show that grazing a green manure results in higher soil fertility than an identical green manure that was mowed with the clippings left in place. There is a significant soil-fertility benefit from the biological activity of animal manure, even though its ingredients came from the field itself and some nutrients were actually removed by the livestock. If grazing is supplemented by feeds purchased off the farm, the fertility gain will be even greater. On average, 75 percent of the fertilizer value of the feed consumed is returned to the soil in manure.

Poultry on range thrive best when the grass is kept short and succulent, a stage at which it is also highest in protein. Grass can be kept short by mowing, at the cost of time and fuel, or by grazing sheep at little expense. Determining the ideal ratio of sheep to poultry to pasture acreage requires some observation and experience on the grower's part. It usually falls somewhere around four sheep and 200 chickens (or 50 turkeys) per acre, depending on the size and breed of stock and the productive capacity of the soil. Overstocking causes crowding and bare spots and should be avoided. You can always mow a little, if necessary. The first requirement in this range system is for some sort of movable poultry house.

The Chicksha

There are many ways to house poultry on range. Range-rearing systems were used extensively prior to the 1950s, and many styles of shelter were devised. When we began with range poultry, we modified those early designs to make the houses smaller and lighter so they could be moved without a tractor. We also built them with larger wheels for easier rolling. This design was instantly christened "the chicksha." We built them 5 feet wide by 6 feet long and 30 inches high at the center. This height is more than sufficient for the chickens and allows for a heat lamp to be mounted inside the house during the brooding period. This size is large enough for 50 birds per house, since they are only kept in there at night for protection against predators.

The walls and roofs were made of a single layer of overlapping pine clapboards. The floors were made of ½-inch mesh hardware cloth so the manure could fall through at night. (Each morning the house was rolled to a new site on the pasture.) The same mesh material was used for windows to let air in. When young chicks were being started in the chicksha, the floor was covered with wood chips and the windows with plastic to keep the interior warmer. Low roost bars were added to the floor when raising layers. The houses were built in two parts—the undercarriage and the superstructure—so they could be taken apart for cleaning. The houses were strong, the management was efficient, and the chickens thrived in them.

WIRE MESH
WINDOWS

PINE CLAPBOARDS

CLOSET ROD
PUSH BAR

30"

4'

5'

2x2 ROOSTING BAR

REAR SUPPORT

26" CART WHEEL

CORNER
GUSSETS
FOR OVERLAPPING
FRAME

ACCESS DOOR

6'

WIRE MESH
FLOOR

2' X 4' FRAME

*The Chicksha.
Its door, hinged at the
bottom, becomes the
entry ramp when
open.*

It was the new, woven electric-mesh sheep fences that allowed us to make the next design innovation. The right models provide secure predator protection. They need to be 4 feet high to deter coyotes and foxes. Since this means that the nighttime predator protection is now separate from the house, we can build the house from very light materials. Our present field houses are larger and lighter than anything before and house 300 birds. They are also much less expensive. Because an electric fence provides predator protection from skunks, coons, foxes, and dogs, all the house has to provide is shelter. So what we did was to convert one of our plant-growing tunnels into a poultry shelter. The present design is basically a movable greenhouse for poultry.

The Hoop Coop

The hoop coop, as our solar hen house has come to be called, consists of a sliding base frame and a hoop superstructure covered with plastic. It is anchored to the ground with a short length of rebar driven in at each corner.

The base for the 12 by 20-foot coop consists of a pair of parallel 20-foot-long pipes or 2 x 6s set on their edges. The ends are beveled so they slide along the ground.

The superstructure is made of 20-foot lengths of fiberglass rod (it could be metal or plastic pipe) bowed into hoops the same as for the field tunnels described in Chapter 21. The hoops are erected every 4 feet into holes drilled in the upper edge of the 2 x 6 runners. The hoops are covered with a single layer of plastic.

The doors are framed at both ends. The door frames hold the sides of the coops apart. The door shape is triangular, rather than rectangular, for greater strength. These triangular door frames are best made of metal pipe welded together in the shape of an A.

After the hoops are erected, the plastic covering is put on and attached tightly to the baseboards. The plastic is held on with narrow lath strips as described for covering greenhouses.

The ends of the plastic are attached to the door frame. To do this, you can employ either the plastic inserts used around the edges of the greenhouse vents or sections of rubber pipe or hose slit lengthwise, so they can be opened up enough to slide over the A-frame pipes and hold the plastic to them tightly. The door material (composed of the same plastic covering) extends from one side of the A-frame and closes diagonally.

In the midsummer heat, two options will keep the house cooler. An opaque

The hoop coop (12 feet in width and 20 feet in length).

white plastic can be used instead of the clear plastic, but at the expense of losing some of the early-season heat gain. Or greenhouse shade-cloth can be stretched over a clear plastic to block the sun. The shade cloth mesh also serves to protect the plastic from other livestock when they graze with the poultry. The hoop coop offers the following management benefits in conjunction with a range-poultry system.

Low Initial Cost. The two 20-foot-long pipes or 2 x 6s for the base frame and the welded metal door frames are the only special components. The fiberglass rods for the hoops are the same as those used for a 12-foot-wide field tunnel. The only continuing expense is the yearly replacement of the plastic cover.

Mobility. This house can be used on a wide variety of terrain. The house should be moved to a clean site every day. The A-frame door design allows moving even with poultry inside because there are no crossbars at ground level. The house is moved by means of a rope or chain attached to the runners. If the fiberglass hoops are reinforced with a ridge purlin like the field tunnels, then feeders can be hung from the hoop frame and thus will move with the house. Waterers and any outside range feeders will have to be moved separately, but that can be done every other day.

Cleanliness. The house itself is easy to clean because there is so little structure involved. The 6-mil plastic covering should be replaced after each season. The ground underneath and around the house is changed daily. All crops and livestock benefit from a rotation where they are moved to new ground periodically. A movable chicken house prevents the buildup of disease and parasites in the environs of the shelter, which never spends too long in one place.

Flexibility. We have used this design for range poultry from start to finish. The house is intended to be the only shelter necessary from the day the chicks arrive. When used for starting baby chicks, the grass upon which the house sits should be mowed very short. Ventilation is managed by adjusting the door coverings. With the doors rolled down and a brooder hung inside, the atmosphere is warm enough for starting baby chicks once outdoor temperatures are over 50°F. (10°C.).

Simpler Feed. Studies have shown that poultry on good range will grow well on just whole grains and mineral supplements without the need for the complicated feed mixtures fed to birds raised in confinement.* The grass, worms, and insects provide extra protein, plus all the known and unknown ancillary feed factors. This can result in a savings of up to 40 percent in feed costs. If desired, the poultry diet can be supplemented from the garden with trimmings or unsold crops.

*Jim Worthington, Natural Poultry-Keeping (London: Lockwood, 1970).

Less Work. This is one poultry house that doesn't need to be shoveled out; whether day or night droppings fall onto the pasture. Since the house is moved to a new location every day, the manure ends up being spread lightly and evenly across the range. When poultry are grazed with other livestock, bird-scratching helps to incorporate all the manures into the soil. Scratching also benefits the pasture by aerating the surface of the soil and encouraging the growth of the finer grasses.

Better Health. Grass, insects, and outdoor living contribute greatly to the health of the poultry. Pasture has long been recognized as one of the most important guarantees of poultry health. Poultry raised on range do not need to be protected with drugs and medications like those raised in confinement.

Better Flavor. And do they ever taste better! I have yet to meet anyone who doesn't notice the difference. There is no meat or dairy product that the consumer associates more with poor flavor and overmedicated treatment than poultry. When they are raised on clean grass range, the improvement is so considerable it almost seems like the meat of a superior species. Growers who can provide the market with range-fed birds will find customers beating a path to their door.

Hoop-Coop Chicks

My baby chicks on range have never been bothered by owls or hawks. But if that is a problem where you live, you will want to use covered pens. There are excellent designs in Joel Salatin's Pastured Poultry Profits *(Swoope, VA: Polyface, Inc., 1993). This exceptional book also contains extensive material on feeding, slaughtering, and marketing. The author is a specialist on range poultry, and his information is very sound.*

Poultry are purchased as day-old chicks, or poults, and are housed right from the start in the hoop coop. A brooder lamp or a floor brooder is placed in the house for warmth. (Specific details about temperature and feeding needs for baby poultry can be found in many books, extension pamphlets, or from the poultry supplier.) In colder weather chicks can be started indoors, then moved to the hoop coop when the weather warms up. Or you could provide supplementary heat in the hoop coop.

There are advantages to starting in the range house. First, the chicks identify with the house and will return to it for shelter after they are let out on pasture. Second, the hoop coop allows them to have that important early access to grass. The very earliest grass area for chicks should be clean ground that has not been grazed by poultry for the past few years. That is one of the advantages of incorporating poultry into a crop-rotation system where clean, new ground can be assured.*

When poultry are on pasture, a simple but specific management schedule should be followed: in the morning sprinkle scratch feed, pull the rebar anchors, move the house a short distance, and drive in the anchors again; in the evening refill the feeders and waterers. Feed can be provided inside from hanging feeders

Hoop-coop chicks.

or outside from range feeders. Each has its advantages. The inside hanging feeder is moved automatically when the house is moved. The large, covered, outside range feeder holds more feed and needs refilling less often. The waterers are usually set outside the hoop coop and moved periodically.

Poultry Plus Sheep

As mentioned earlier, poultry on range do best when the grass is kept short. Closely clipped pasturage is higher in protein and easier to digest. To keep the grass short, either mow it from time to time or graze it with animals. Sheep will do it best. To avoid year-round livestock care, sheep should be purchased as lambs in the spring, grazed during the poultry season, and sold at the end of the year. There is not much profit here; money saved in mowing time and expense is the principal return.

When poultry are on pasture with other stock, the feed should be available from inside the range house where the other stock cannot get at it. A few bars across the A-frame door will keep the sheep out of the house. A range feeder is no proof against hungry sheep, who will often knock it over and spill it, even if it is redesigned to make access more difficult for larger animals.

Fencing

The same predator-proof, woven electro-plastic netting serves for both poultry and sheep. The simplest electric source is one of the battery-powered fence chargers. Since these fencing systems are extremely portable, the fence can follow the hoop coop to all parts of the farm. This allows any small or odd-shaped piece of the property, even lawns or brushy areas, to be grazed periodically.

Breeds

With sheep, you can use whichever breed is locally available. However, downland breeds, which are more pure grazers than part-browsing, upland breeds, may be the best bet. With turkeys, the smaller varieties are usually better rangers than the larger ones. Of the large turkeys, the bronze are better foragers than the white, in my experience. With chickens, breed is a difficult but important choice. Certain commercially popular broiler crosses, such as the Rock Cornish, may not be the best. Their nutritional requirements are so specific due to their rapid growth that they must be fed high-protein commercial feeds. Although they do well on range as long as those feeds are used, there are few savings in feed costs because they don't take advantage of the pasture.

The most desirable chicken breeds for this system are active foragers. Their only disadvantage is that, although they are a perfectly nice bird, they don't provide the unbelievably plump carcasses of the hybrid broiler crosses. If those carcasses are what the market wants, then a grower will have to try out the different hybrid strains to see which one is most adaptable. We have found the Barred Rock cross to be quite successful. For those interested in the older breeds, I recommend White Rocks, Dark Cornish, and Mottled Houdans. All of these breeds thrive on range plus a simple diet and reach market size at 12 to 16 weeks. The last two breeds are especially adapted to ranging and provide an ideal product for a market that appreciates the best in gourmet chicken.

THE INFORMATION RESOURCE

Nature is a language, and every new fact that we learn is a new word; but rightly seen, taken all together, it is not merely a language, but the language put together into a most significant and universal book. I wish to learn the language, not that I may learn a new set of nouns and verbs, but that I may read the great book which is written in that language.

—Ralph Waldo Emerson

I CAN SEE A CLEAR PATTERN IN MY DEVELOPMENT AS AN ORGANIC GROWER. I have made a conscious shift away from *product inputs* which I have to purchase and have moved toward *information inputs* which support a farm-generated production system. The more information I acquire about soil improvement, deep-rooting legumes, green manures, crop rotations, and other management practices that correct the cause of soil fertility problems, the less I need to treat the symptoms of low soil fertility by purchasing stimulant fertilizers. Similarly, as I have learned to reinforce plant insusceptibility to pests through improving soil fertility, avoiding mineral imbalance, providing for adequate water drainage and airflow, growing suitable varieties, and avoiding plant stress, I have removed the need to treat symptoms by killing the pests. It is a familiar pattern in my thinking. Information inputs help me focus on cause correction, whereas product inputs only encourage symptom treatment.

As I become increasingly proficient at working with the biology of the natural world, I learn to create crop-friendly ecosystems that mimic natural systems. I like to say that my farming is becoming ever more "biological" (a term I prefer over "organic" to describe this type of farming in general). I have also heard this trend referred to as a shift from shallow to deep organics (to borrow a phrase from the ecology movement). Whatever the name, the understanding is the same. The optimal "organic" farming system, toward which my farming techniques are progressing, is one that participates as fully as possible in the applicable biological systems of the natural world. Whether my farm-generated–input approach will succeed in attaining its ultimate goal—a time when I need to purchase no inputs at all—is yet to be determined. Given the inherent mineral deficiencies of the acid podzolic soil with which I began, that goal presents an interesting challenge. But this isn't a religious quest. I don't plan to go out of business by creating some inflexible doctrine for myself. I keep working at it because it's been so successful. With each step in this direction I find myself running ever more stable and productive systems. I like that. However, as I watch organic agriculture begin to move into the mainstream, I notice a strong trend in the opposite direction, toward more, not fewer, purchased inputs. The reasons for this are not hard to find. But first some definitions.

The Craft, Business, and Science of Agriculture

I define what I do as the CRAFT of agriculture. I am a grower. I produce food. Obviously, I prefer to base my production systems on techniques that are both economically and environmentally sound. I prefer information-input (how-to-do) rather than product input (what-to-buy); not only because the former costs less but also, as I said above, because the results are more successful. But organic growers have to pursue this quest for information-input purely on their own, without outside help or encouragement—and for a very good reason.

That reason is the BUSINESS of agriculture. The business of agriculture is concerned with marketing product-inputs to the farmer. Money is made by convincing farmers they need a product and then selling it to them year after year. The business of agriculture has no interest in telling me about farm-generated systems. E.C. Large in *The Advance of the Fungi* accurately describes the pressures tending to drive farmers toward purchasing product-inputs:

> *There was nothing static about the commercial travelers; they pursued*
> *the farmers round the dairy, lay in wait for them on market days, bribed*
> *them with bread-and-cheese and beer, made demonstrations on their farms,*
> *and told the tale about the advantages…with an optimistic enthusiasm*
> *that made the angels blush for shame….The farmers sometimes paid rather*
> *dearly for this form of education…the manufacturers were not above*
> *charging the farmers as much as possible for some mythical and especial*
> *goodness in their particular preparations.*

The effective salesman is a force to be reckoned with. But more effective than the sales pitch is the result of using the products. Reliance on purchased inputs encourages growers to ignore natural components of their system that could be nurtured to accomplish the same end. Like addictive drugs, many purchased inputs come close to fulfilling the cynical economist's definition of the industrialist's ideal product, which "costs them a dime, sells for a dollar, wears out quickly, and leaves a habit behind." Economists have told us for years that the increasing cost of inputs is making chemical farming uneconomical and driving small farmers out of business. If that is true, it certainly makes little sense for organic farmers to follow the same trend.

Given the importance I have placed on information-input one might expect that the third of my categories, the SCIENCE of agriculture, has a lot to offer organic farmers. With the new recognition of organic agriculture by government agriculture departments, useful information should not be far behind. Unfortunately, with a few exceptions, the reality is quite the opposite. The craft of agriculture, that is to say, what each of us does in the field every day, is *practical.* The science of agriculture, which goes on in laboratories and test plots, is *theoretical.* As any dictionary will confirm, theoretical and practical are defined as opposites.

In my own search for organic agricultural knowledge I have become keenly aware of just how wide this gulf between theory and practice can be. Since I enthusiastically endorse the value of information-input, I pay close attention to everything published, read all I can, and keep myself well informed. Yet my conclusion after 30 years of experience is that most of the scientific research being done is not of *practical* use to me. The explanation is simple. The goals of science and my goals as a farmer are vastly different. Even when we both focus on the same problem, we are not after the same goal. The science of agriculture is concerned with understanding the mechanism; it is problem-oriented. The craft of agriculture is concerned with practical application; it is solution-oriented. In other words, science asks why, but the farmer asks how. Naturally, different questions lead to different answers. The dean of an agricultural university confirmed this fact recently when he stated that his university was "not involved with how to grow corn but rather with why corn grows."

Now, I am not uninterested in why things work. I use my understanding of the mechanisms every day to organize my farm operation. But that knowledge does not help me when I need to get my hands dirty. Understanding "why" can help me plan what needs to be done, but it can't help me do it in the most innovative and effective way. At present, the science of agriculture is providing us with too much *head* information and not enough *hand* information. All of the hand information that I value is coming from other sources.

The theoretical science of agriculture found a role in chemical farming over the past century. Many of the chemical inputs and their development and testing involve the resources of the laboratory—resources unavailable to the farmer. It may also be that the technical complexities of chemical agriculture required the services of scientists as intermediaries to interpret and explain the concepts.

But that same situation does not exist with a farming system based upon nurturing natural processes. In this case, the people who know best how to do organic farming are those who are doing it every day—the organic farmers themselves. Ironically, their experience is written off as *anecdotal evidence* and is basically inadmissible to the science of agriculture.

Research of practical use to growers was published prior to 1940. Perhaps in those years the dream of complicated chemical panaceas had not taken hold as thoroughly as it has today. Whatever the reason, many universities back then conducted farm-applicable investigations. I find that material useful, but limited. Modern organic growing is not a rehash of old practices. We are moving into new realms. I'm impressed every time I visit Holland, where the agricultural research service continues to produce practical information. Dutch growers have successfully demanded more "use-oriented" data on fine-tuning their cultural techniques. Much of this work is scale-neutral (helpful to small and large growers alike) and system-neutral (helpful to both organic and chemical growers). For example, the Dutch have developed detailed pruning instructions for the fruit trusses of greenhouse beefsteak tomatoes depending on the season of the year (see page 311). Since that sort of crop-specific technical knowledge is just what I want for my farm, I have learned to find it on my own

Finding the Information

I have two main sources of information. First is my own day-to-day experience, which increases in value the more I keep my eyes open and record what I learn. Second is the experience of other growers and agricultural investigators. It is something of a chicken-and-egg relationship, since each source grows out of the other. So let's begin with the second. I have been fortunate to visit fellow growers both in the U.S. and abroad. I learn a great deal on the visits and owe a real debt to every grower who shares information with me. I have the advantage on these trips of seeing many farms and being able to compare and analyze differences and similarities in a way that my hosts cannot, because many of them are unacquainted with each other. That overview doubles or triples the value of the individual visits. Whenever you have the opportunity to visit other growers, take it.

Those visits only scratch the surface, though. I couldn't begin to visit everyone, and, even if I could, each new idea gleaned from a visit inspires a hunger to expand or refine it. So I do most of my visiting, once a month, at my local state university library. I can gain access to everything I want to know through that service alone. If you are unacquainted with libraries, they may seem as frightening as a large foreign country, speaking an arcane language, with impenetrable local customs. I entreat you to calm your fears. Libraries provide information the way farms provide food. Like farmers, librarians are professionals and proud of their abilities. Whatever information you want to find, all you have to do is ask.

I chose my local state university library, even though it is an hour and a half away, because it has a large collection and, since it is a land-grant institution, that collection includes agriculture. When I lived nearby the best library in an adjoining state, I used that facility. University libraries are open long hours every day, so I make the most of it by arriving early and staying late. If I expect to need technical help learning a computer search system, or have lots of questions about where to find what I am looking for, I try to plan the trip for times such as school vacations or Saturday football games when most students are elsewhere.

I have nearly always found library staff polite and helpful. Since I am not a student I am usually categorized as a "guest borrower." Depending on the library that may mean I am a second-class citizen and not entitled to all the services of the library, such as computer literature searches or interlibrary loan. Sometimes the staff do things for me because, since I am older than the students, they assume I must be faculty. I have sometimes worn a coat and tie to reinforce that possibility. Other times, just looking helpless or smiling sweetly can overcome barriers. If I receive a bureaucratic "no" to my request, I will often come back after the shift changes to see if I have better luck with the next person. If all else fails, the little library in my hometown can get me almost any book or article I'm interested in, although it will usually take them a lot longer. So don't let libraries be scary places. They are filled with tons of information and people who can help you locate it.

When I was new to the library game, I started in the periodicals room and scanned the shelves for any journal or magazine about agriculture. I would skim a few issues of each to see if anything caught my eye. A lot of them were written in academic jargon beyond my comprehension. I didn't worry about understanding all the terms, but if I couldn't understand anything I moved on. I made note of the ones that were helpful, and I return to browse their new issues on each library visit. If the title of an article is interesting, I turn to it. There is usually a short summary or abstract at the start and a conclusion at the end. You can tell quickly whether there is anything practical to be gleaned. Most of the time the data will merely confirm something I have already figured out, which is reassuring if not informative.

The next step is to look further afield. The resources of the whole world are at your fingertips in the library, now more than ever before. My favorite hunting grounds are the abstract journals such as *Soils and Fertilizers* and *Horticultural Abstracts*. These journals review almost every applicable publication in the world every month and publish short summaries of each article in English along with author, title, and source. Entries are arranged by subject and can be quickly scanned. It may take a visit or two before you determine which subject headings will help narrow your search (there may be more than 1,000 abstracts each month), but you will soon become proficient. You now are in contact with the work of investigators from Egypt to Ukraine to Argentina. The research from some counties, especially the Netherlands and many eastern European nations, is much more practically oriented than ours.

If one of the abstracts sounds so specific to your interests that you would like to read the whole article, ask the librarian. Either the state library or your local branch can get you a photocopy of the original through interlibrary loan. Although many major foreign journals publish in English, the smaller ones are usually in the native language. The abstract will tell you the language of the original. But even when it is published in a language you can't read, all is not lost. The advantage of living in a world of immigrants is that somewhere in the community you can probably locate a native speaker. Ask at the university about foreign students or check out ethnic social clubs. I have always found that a basket of farm-fresh produce in trade for translation can help create smiles, loosen tongues, gain information, and make some new friends in the process.

When you do find a useful article, check out the bibliography at the end. There the author will list previous studies on the subject that were consulted. These will lead you back in time, and very often uncover older, more practical investigations or whole new approaches. More than once an older idea the author was discrediting turned out to be more practical and useful to my production system than the supposedly improved model. If, on the other hand, your starting point is an older article, there is a wonderful reference work called *The Citation Index* that allows you to search for connections towards the present. For example, if your original article appeared in 1972, looking up under the author and title in *The Citation Index* for any year following 1972 will tell you who listed that article in their bibliography and thus who is investigating that same or a related subject. A day in the library becomes a delightful game of agricultural detective work.

I have pages of handwritten notes from when I first began collecting information years ago. I remember spending long hours searching through library card catalogs. Life is easier now. Photocopy machines allow me to keep the whole article on file at home. Computerized card catalogs make it faster to locate books and also to cross-reference on specific subjects. There is an overwhelming amount of material in libraries, and it helps to focus your search as much as possible. You will soon learn to skim-read and sniff out the good stuff.

The return from all of this is more often inspiration and new possibilities rather than hard facts. But I consider that very worthwhile. On average, 20 percent of what I skim is interesting, 5 percent may be useful, and maybe 1 percent represents real gems—sort of like the one-percenters I wrote about in an earlier chapter. It makes the search both rewarding and enjoyable. Each trip to the library results in an incremental improvement in the success of my farm.

My Own Experience

I can remember the fall of 1965. I had decided to begin farming the next summer and I was reading all the books I could find on the subject. Yet every sentence seemed to create more questions in my mind. I pestered farming friends day and night and was frustrated when I couldn't seem to get my questions answered. It was a typical case of beginneritis. By the end of the next summer, after my first season of actual hands-on experience, the confusion cleared up. It wasn't that all my questions had been answered. But I now had a basis for knowing what to ask. Many questions disappeared simply because they had answered themselves. Many new ones appeared, and I could not wait to put them to a practical test the next year.

What I learn from experience in the fields on my land is the most valuable input of all. Right from the start I got in the habit of running experiments, and I continue them today. I won't claim they are always well done. I won't claim they are without possible error. It isn't easy to find time for learning when I am flat-out busy. A few times I have had mere seconds to evaluate a test plot because it happened to be growing the only mature carrots or lettuce or whatever we had run out of down at the stand. But just because I cannot publish my ragged results in a professional journal doesn't lessen their value to me. If not useful in themselves, they often provide a hint that leads to some small improvement the following year.

Increasing the Information

So these have been my teachers: the anecdotal experience of other farmers, the day-to-day experience on my own land, and ideas gleaned from books and from my monthly trips to the library. I willingly share what I have learned, because much of it came from others either directly or indirectly. Whenever growers get together and share information it multiplies exponentially, because each grower brings personal experience from a slightly different perspective. Enormous synergy is generated in the exchange of ideas. By the end no one will remember who suggested what and no one person will get the credit, nor will he or she deserve it. Ideas develop and grow through cross-fertilization. Some other farmer somewhere always has the answer to my question and vice versa. What needs to be done is to move that knowledge from our individual minds to the collective mind.

In hopes of doing just that, a friend and I organized a two-day conference in Vermont a few years ago. We invited the best organic growers from all over the Northeast—as far away as Pennsylvania and New Jersey in the south, to New York in the west, to Quebec and New Brunswick in the north. We also invited two exceptional Dutch organic growers. The stated intent of the conference was for the Dutchmen to give detailed presentations on their production practices. The ticket for admission was that each participant had to give a five-minute presentation on the best ideas on his or her farm. We set aside special sessions during the conference for those presentations. It was dynamite. In that room we had the combined knowledge of one heck of an outstanding organic grower.

In selecting the 50 or so participants at that conference, we were careful to choose those who were neither next-door neighbors nor close competitors. We hoped they might be more forthcoming if they felt they weren't giving away secrets to the person next door to them at the farmer's market. But I think our precaution was unnecessary. Once we started, everyone not only realized the benefits of this exchange, but also all participants were forthright because of their justifiable pride in their own accomplishments. I'm sure the same would be true of gatherings in other parts of the country or overseas.

Beginning with my first trip in 1974, I have traveled to Europe six times to visit organic farms. Over the years I have met and corresponded with exceptional growers from every continent. The information resource that exists on organic farms around the world is truly astounding. If some organization is looking for a program to advance the cause of organic farming, I have a suggestion. Hold a series of meetings like ours in different regions around the world. The meetings would bring together the most skilled organic growers. Instead of asking them what they can't do, ask them what they can do. The idea is to get everyone to share his or her biological or mechanical techniques, solutions, and innovations. The result would be a crop-by-crop instruction manual. I think we would be astounded how complete that manual is. The only reason this information is not presently accessible to farmers is that it has never been collected and distributed. But the fact is that it does exist.

As organic growers we must recognize the potential of farm-generated replacements for inadequate outside information, just as we have found farm-generated replacements for inadequate chemical inputs. The information for technical improvements in the craft of organic agriculture can be as much a

INFORMATION BY MAIL

Hort Ideas
460 Black Lick Road
Gravel Switch, KY 40328
If I only had one subscription, this would be it. A wonderful source of new ideas. The editors comb all the horticultural literature every month and publish abstracts and discussions of the most interesting material.

Growing for Market
P.O. Box 3747
Lawrence, KS 66046
(800) 307–8949
A great newsletter that caters to the needs of the smaller-scale grower. Lots of articles by and about people who are actually doing it.

The Grower
Nexus Media, Ltd.
Warwick House
Swanley, Kent BR8 8HY
Telephone: 441–322–660077
Even though my air-mail subscription costs me more than $100 a year for this weekly, I resubscribe every year. It keeps me informed on the latest European ideas.

Agrarian Advocate CAFF
P.O. Box 563
Davis, CA 95617
(530) 756–8518
Principally aimed at California growers. Good information from a quality publication.

Alternative Farming Systems Information Center (AFSIC)
National Agricultural Library
10301 Baltimore Boulevard
Beltsville, MD 20705
(301) 504–6559; Fax: (301) 504–5609
Helps researchers find answers to questions about sustainable agriculture, or obtain copies of an article. Lists of free information products and bibliographies are available by phoning or writing.

Appropriate Technology Transfer for Rural Areas (ATTRA)
P.O. Box 3657
Fayetteville, AR 72702
(800) 346–9140; Fax: (501) 442–9842
ATTRA, a program of the National Center for Appropriate Technology, has a staff of technical and information specialists who will provide customized research or one of about 50 sustainable agriculture information packages, summaries, and resource lists at no charge.

product of the farm itself as is the organic matter for improving soil fertility. The combined efforts of organic farmers can be their own best information service.

Resisting the Future

The history of organic farming is similar to the history of any successful idea that diverges from the orthodoxy of the moment. The orthodoxy first tries to denounce it, then tries to minimize its importance, and finally tries to co-opt it. The business and the science of agriculture are like the moneychangers and priests who have lost control of the temple. The organic idea has allowed an increasing number of agricultural heretics to escape from their grasp. Now that organic has become an obvious force, the old order is trying to regain control. But no scientific or business enterprise based on the devising and marketing of miracle products designed to replace nature is going to acknowledge that nature doesn't need to be replaced. I for one do not wish to cede my information-gathering to minds still mired in the concepts of industrial agriculture. Nor do I wish to cede my farm's biological future to the wiles of salesmen. The best inputs for organic growing are free and are a function of a whole farm system and its relationship to the surrounding environment.

The leadership of the business and the science sectors of agriculture has led chemical farming down ever more tenuous paths. I don't want to see organic farmers sold that same bill of goods. I don't want organic farming to become dependent upon its own long list of purchased "natural" inputs, which put the profits in the pockets of middlemen and put farmers on the auction block. It is easy to be co-opted by purchased nostrums, because farm-generated inputs are not running competing ads. The sales pitch for farm-generated inputs has to come from us, the organic growers, because we are the ones who understand the as yet untapped potential of biological systems.

Don't forget, the success we have achieved to date is the result of our own efforts. Sure, we have a long way to go, but there are no impossibilities here. It is a mistake to assume limits to organic growing based on what it can or cannot do today. I am using techniques now that I didn't even dream of 20 years ago. I am succeeding at things now that I failed at ten years ago. I am doing things better now than I did five years ago. These advances are a result of believing that natural biological systems can provide everything my farm needs if I keep exploring them. I didn't go out and blindly impose a vegetable farm on the landscape. I studied, and I continue to study, how to integrate my farm with nature's systems. That integration is an ongoing process.

I came to farming from an adventuring background. I was a passionate rock climber, mountaineer, and whitewater kayaker. Organic farming appealed to me because it involved searching for and discovering nature's pathways, as opposed to the formulaic approach of chemical farming. The appeal of organic farming is boundless; this mountain has no top, this river has no end. Every day I delight in the continuing adventure.

26 🦋

A FINAL QUESTION

ALTHOUGH I INTEND THIS BOOK TO BE COMPREHENSIVE, THERE IS ONE question that readers must answer for themselves. Until the answer to this question is resolved, all the best instruction in the world won't help. Let me address you directly. The final question is, "Why do you want to be a farmer?"

Why Do You Want to Farm?

I suggest sitting down with pen and paper and coming up with some answers to that question. I've found that the best way to sort out fuzzy thinking is to compose ideas in a readable form. Is it only the idealized lifestyle that you crave? A touch of "over the river and through the woods to grandmother's house we go?" Think carefully about whether a desire to farm is a positive action toward farming or a negative reaction against what you do now.

Dissatisfaction with your present career, an intolerance for city living, or a perceived lack of excitement in your life may generate that negative reaction. Future hopes are often naively focused on rural life because it fulfills the bucolic fantasies that we all share in the back of our minds. I encourage thinking long and hard about what you really want to change, where you really want to go, and why.

In a negative reaction, the would-be farmer has suddenly had enough of the city, the dead-end job, or simple boredom and jumps impulsively for the fantasy of fresh air and farm living. In contrast, a positive action stems from a long-term desire to farm, which may have been set aside for practical or economic reasons. Such an action is based on knowledge of the hard work and discipline that a career in agriculture demands. In a positive action, the move has been planned carefully, and the farmer is only waiting for the parts to fall into place and the time to be right.

Whether the motivation is understood or not, there is one option that clearly makes sense and is worth repeating—go and work on a farm. Try out the idea by laboring (and learning) with someone else. Experience the good times and the bad, the realities and the rewards. If possible, work on more than one farm. The more background and experience you can get, the better off you'll be.

289

The requirements for success in farming are like those for any small business: organizational aptitude, diligence, financial planning, the ability to work long hours, and the desire to succeed. Added to these are the need for skill at working with your hands, a sensitivity towards living creatures, a high level of health and fitness, and a love of what you are doing. Farming offers a satisfying challenge found in no other profession to those who can meet its demands, overcome its difficulties, and reap its rewards.

Groups, Schools, and Institutions

My production system is well suited to the needs of organized groups that may wish to produce some or all of their own food. I highly recommend such a course of action, but the decision should not be entered into lightly by groups any more than by individuals. Before beginning, the organizers should ask themselves some hard questions. Is this a serious commitment or just a passing fancy? Is everyone willing to share in the work, or is it going to fall on an enthusiastic few? Do we have the time and interest to carry this idea through and do a first-class job of preparing the land, planting the crops, maintaining the garden, and distributing or storing the food? For the organized group wishing to start a food-production program, this book is a reliable guide. One of the long-time exponents of institutional food production is the Mountain School in Vershire Center, Vermont. Since its founding in 1963, the Mountain School has produced the bulk of the school's food as part of its traditional academic program. Those years present a clear picture of the benefits and practical soundness of participatory food production.

Food can be produced (1) with simple, dependable, low-cost equipment; (2) by interested amateurs without expensive professional supervision; and (3) by practicing an environmentally sound cultural system that stresses selected varieties, crop rotation, green manuring, and compost. The food produced can be harvested and stored inexpensively for periods when it is not being produced by using the facilities of the average institutional kitchen and using amateur labor under in-house supervision. Money can be saved; fresher, better-tasting, and more nutritious food can be served; and the consumers can enjoy participation in the resource-efficient system by which their food is supplied.

Furthermore, organized groups, schools, and other institutions actually have many advantages over commercial operations. These advantages exist on the one hand because of the unique situation of schools and institutions and on the other through the mutual benefits that accrue from group efforts. First is land. Land for growing crops is not likely to be a limiting factor. On most institutional premises, a surprising amount of land can be found that is suitable for growing food. These underutilized acres vary from abandoned land overgrown with brush to extensive lawn areas presently requiring mowing and upkeep. If you visualize an acre as a square approximately 210 feet (70 average paces) on each side, it is easy to picture where and how gardens can fit into an existing landscape. The production from 1 acre can easily feed 40 people all their vegetables for a year, or feed a far greater number of people if, for example, only salad or fresh produce is grown. Moreover, the entire area used for food production does not have to be contiguous. Production on a number of smaller pieces is no problem and may actually be an advantage where different soil types are involved. In short, land, the first requirement, is often readily available at little or no cost other than mowing or clearing. And in the case of schools, institutions, and charitable organizations, the land they use is tax-exempt.

Next is labor. Most vegetable operations are dependent upon a supply of seasonal labor at specific times of the year. Arranging for and managing that labor is a major concern of the farmer. In a group food-production program, labor is provided by the participants as a recreational, educational, or therapeutic activity. No salaries need be paid, since the benefits received by the participants (acquisition of a skill, exercise, satisfaction, better and fresher food) are the main rewards. Any labor problems of a participatory group will lie more in using it effectively and fairly than in locating it.

Third is marketing. On average, as I have stated earlier, I think that 50 percent of the success in an agricultural operation depends on marketing skill. That includes all the operations involved in the sale and distribution of the produce. In the case of participatory food production, the difficulties of marketing are avoided entirely, since the participants provide their own market. This can result in a further advantage. Frost, hail, drought, sunscald, and minor pest problems can cause superficial damage to crops, resulting in a low price or no sale at all on the commercial market, even though in all other aspects the crop quality is high. A participatory food production program would suffer no loss, since cosmetic appearance would not affect its "market."

Despite all these benefits, food production by groups, schools, and institutions, once a widespread practice, has mostly been abandoned with the exception of a few unique operations like the Mountain School. The practice was abandoned because, within the limitations of previous agricultural concepts, it was considered necessary to hire professional horticulturists and laborers to run the professional side of the program. Their salaries made the economic side uneconomic. That need no longer be the case. The simplified equipment and production methods detailed in this manual make the doers into the professionals, whether participant, teacher, or supervisor. Food production can now be incorporated into any standard activity program at minimal cost and with maximum educational benefit. But it is more than just another activity. It is an economically productive activity, the end product of which supplies the otherwise increasingly expensive ingredients for a nutritionally sound diet.

27 ❧

L'ENVOI

The miraculous succession of modern inventions has so profoundly affected our thinking as well as our everyday life that it is difficult for us to conceive that the ingenuity of men will not be able to solve the final riddle—that of gaining a subsistence from the earth. The grand and ultimate illusion would be that man could provide a substitute for the elemental workings of nature.

—Fairfield Osborn, *Our Plundered Planet*

THERE ARE NO SIMPLE SOLUTIONS OR SHORTCUTS IN THIS WORK. NO panaceas exist. There are, however, logical answers. Viable production technologies exist that address environmental and economic realities. Some of these production technologies may require new ways of thinking, while others may appear to revive old-fashioned or outmoded ideas. On closer examination, it will be found that the "outmoded" practices were never discredited, but rather discarded during a period of agricultural illusion when science *did* seem to promise simple solutions and substitutes.

The production technologies of this biological agriculture nurture and enhance "the elemental workings of nature." They synthesize a broad range of old and new agronomic practices into an economically viable production system. These technologies are the result of a reasonable and scientifically grounded progressive development, not a return to the "old ways." This agricultural system consists of a series of interrelated plant and soil cultural practices which, when done correctly, are no more difficult (albeit possibly more thought-provoking), than chemical food-production technologies.

The information presented herein is as up-to-date as it can be. But it will change. I will modify my approach as I learn new techniques, and I will revise one practice or another. However, I have used these methods long enough to assure readers that they will not go wrong in following my recommendations. Still, each of you will want to change parts of this system. You will want to adapt it not only to fit your own particular conditions, but also to keep from getting into a rut. It is crucial to experiment, adapt, and improve. We owe a great debt to all those farmers and researchers who have gone before us, whose work has either solved problems or has left clues that will help us solve them. There are no gurus in this game—no repositories of the "correct way"—only fellow searchers. All the information for further improvement is out there waiting for us to discover it.

The skill that most benefits you as a farmer is learning how to incorporate new knowledge as a productive addition to your present system. Do not hesitate to discard present practices when experience or evidence prove them faulty. But how do you decide? By what criteria can small steps or sweeping changes be judged? In the final analysis, the only truly dependable production technologies are those that are sustainable over the long term. By that very definition, they must avoid erosion, pollution, environmental degradation, and resource waste. Any rational food-production system will emphasize the well-being of the soil-air-water biosphere, the creatures which inhabit it, and the human beings who depend upon it.

FROM ARTICHOKES
TO ZUCCHINI:
Notes on Specific Crops

OVER THE YEARS I HAVE PICKED UP LOTS OF LITTLE TIDBITS OF USEFUL information and preferred techniques. For the most part these tidbits are not the standard ABCs (which are well covered by the books listed in the Annotated Bibliography, or by other standard reference works), but rather those little refinements that are the fruits of experience and are so often left untold. The preferences described below for each crop are the best that I have arrived at. Names of specific varieties are given where I think they offer a real advantage to the organic grower.

Artichoke, Globe. Vegetatively propagated artichokes are not traditionally grown in cold climates, where the perennial plants won't survive the winter. But artichokes grown from seed offer a commercially viable new specialty crop in those areas. I have grown them in the chilly mountains of Vermont and on the cool coast of Maine. The trick is to turn the artichoke into an annual. All that's required is a little horticultural sleight of hand.

If you plant an artichoke seed, it will usually grow only leaves the first year. The following year, it will send up a stalk from which grow the artichokes—which are actually edible flower buds. If the winter is too severe (as winters in most of the northern half of the U.S. are), the first-year vegetative plants won't survive to become second-year plants. The sleight of hand involves fooling the plants to think they are two years old in the first year.

To achieve that, you need to grow the young artichoke plants first in warm then in cool temperatures. For best results I start the seeds in a warm greenhouse six weeks before the earliest date on which I can safely move them to a cold frame or unheated tunnel. I move them when I am sure the temperature inside the frame will no longer go below 25°F. (-4°C.). In Vermont I sowed on February 15 and moved the plants to the frame on April 1. I only close the cold frame to protect the plants from hard freezing. The cooler they are for the next six weeks, the better.

The change of growing temperatures from warm to cool (a practice called *vernalization* in horticulture) is what fools the plants. The first six weeks of warm growing conditions were sufficient time for the plants to complete their first "summer" season. The subsequent six weeks of cool temperatures make them think that they have experienced their first winter. Thus, although they are only 12 weeks old when I transplant them to the field, they think they are beginning their second year. The second year is when artichoke plants begin to produce the flower buds that we eat as artichokes. And so they do.

The care they receive after transplanting will determine the number and size of the artichokes. Under the best conditions, I have averaged eight to nine artichokes of medium to medium-large size per plant. The best conditions are plenty of organic matter (generously mix in compost, manure, or peat moss) and plenty of moisture (mulch with straw, and irrigate regularly).

I space the plants 24 inches apart in rows 30 inches apart. That is much closer spacing than for perennial artichokes, but these plants won't get as large. I harvest by cutting the stem beneath the bud with a sharp knife. Don't wait too long. Once the leaf bracts on the bud begin to open, the flesh gets tougher and more fibrous. In New England the production season is late July through late September—two months of a unique and delicious, fresh and flavorful specialty crop.

My favorite varieties: Almost any variety of seed-sown artichoke will work to some degree under this system. I have experience with over a dozen cultivars. Yet there is one exceptional variety that is better adapted than any other—'Imperial Star', which has been bred for annual production. 'Grand Beurre' and 'Green Globe', an old standard, are second choices.

Asparagus. This is a perennial crop and therefore is not part of the rotation. A well-cared-for planting can be productive for more than 20 years. I start asparagus from seeds rather than buying roots. Plant early, January 1 to February 1, in order to gain an extra year of growth. Cover the seeds and germinate at 72°F. (22°C.) in mini-blocks. Pot on immediately to 3-inch blocks. Grow on at 60°F. (16°C.) and transplant to the field after the last frost.

Prepare the soil with rock powders and manure. Make sure the pH is up to 7. An extra 50 tons to the acre of manure, if available, is well spent in preparing for this crop. Set asparagus out in rows 5 feet apart, with plants 12 inches apart in the row. Make a hole 8 inches deep with a posthole digger. Place one soil-block plant in each hole, and fill halfway so the greens are still above the soil. Fill the planting hole to the surface later on, once the greens have grown above ground level.

Seed a leguminous green manure—one pass with the five-row seeder—between each row of asparagus. I use a green manure rotation, starting with white clover the first year, then sweet clover, red, alsike, and back to white. As early in the spring as possible, till the surface of the bed shallowly to turn under the previous year's green manure and the asparagus fern debris.

If the seeds were started early, you can begin a light pick the year after planting. Otherwise, wait until the third season. Cut asparagus spears with a sharp knife just below the soil surface to include a bit of white stem. It keeps longer that way. Cool it immediately after harvest. Store at 32° to 36°F. (0° to 2°C.) with 95 percent humidity. When picking is over each year, sow the inter-row strip to green manure again.

My favorite variety: 'Viking', or 'Jersey Knight', one of the new all-male types.

Bean. The difficulty with beans is getting them picked economically. The mechanical bean pickers used on large-scale operations are tough price competition for the small grower who picks by hand. Given that reality, the grower can either treat beans as a loss leader (a crop that needs to be grown to keep customers happy even though it is not economical) or only grow the specialty varieties such as the extra-thin French "filet" types that sell for a sufficiently higher price to justify the picking costs. I recommend the latter, even though these gourmet varieties need to be picked every day for highest quality.

Either bush or pole varieties can be grown. The pole varieties may seem easier to pick because they are upright, but a good picker can pick faster with the bush types. Although beans are a legume, they respond well to a fertile soil. Rotted horse manure will grow better beans than any other fertilizer. I grow beans in 30-inch rows, and I aim for a plant every 4 to 6 inches in the row. Beans germinate poorly under cool, wet conditions and should not be seeded outside until the soil warms up. For the earliest crop, beans can be transplanted successfully using soil blocks. Use a 1½-inch block for single plants and a 2-inch block for multiplants (nice for pole beans). Transplant when one to two weeks old.

Beans don't need to be iced after harvest. Wilting can be prevented by high humidity. Store them at 45°F. (7°C.) and 90 to 95 percent humidity. The containers should be stacked to allow for good air circulation in storage.

My favorite variety: 'Fortex' (pole), 'E-Z Pick', or any of the French "filet" types.

Beet. This is a multiseason vegetable. Sales begin with beet greens, then move to baby beets, and on to storage roots in the fall. Different varieties are best suited to different stages. Read the variety descriptions carefully.

I plant storage beets in 18-inch rows and aim for a plant every 3 inches in the row. Early and baby beets are planted in 12-inch rows at 2-inch spacing. Beet seeds are actually fruits containing one to four seeds, and they need to be thinned. Mono-germ varieties, with only one seed, are available, but are not my favorites. The earliest crop can be transplanted in soil blocks. Plant four seeds per block. Thinning isn't necessary, since the dominant seedling in each fruit will usually prevail. Transplant at four weeks. Set out 12 inches apart in 10-inch rows.

Beets grow best with a neutral pH and an adequate supply of boron. I have found the best answer to supplementing soil boron to be a pelleted borax with a 10 percent elemental boron content. Carefully calculate the amount to be spread. Three pounds of elemental boron to the acre is usually a safe rate for beets in soil with adequate organic matter. Pelleted borax can be spread accurately with a hand-cranked, chest-mounted seeder. Beets with greens must be cooled quickly after harvest. Store at 36°F. (2°C.) with the humidity at 95 percent. Store in well-ventilated containers.

My favorite varieties: 'Red Ace', 'Merlin', and 'Winter Keeper'.

Brassicas. This heading includes broccoli, Brussels sprouts, cabbage, and cauliflower, because they all have similar growing needs. I find that all four of these crops grow vigorously and are free of root maggot damage if they are grown after a leguminous green manure. In lieu of a green manure, exceptional crops of brassicas can be grown where autumn leaves have been tilled into the soil the previous fall. When the leaves decompose in the spring, they provide a shot of nitrogen for the crop just like the legumes do. In lieu of leaves use alfalfa meal as a fertilizer.

I grow all these brassicas from transplants. These seeds should be covered when seeded in the soil block. They are set out in 30-inch rows at a 24-inch spacing. Closer in-row spacings can be used where the grower does not plan to undersow the crop. Succession plantings will spread the harvest from early summer through late fall.

Broccoli varieties with smaller central heads and better side-shoot production are ideal for the salad bar market. For a late fall harvest, choose Brussels sprout varieties with good leaf cover to protect the sprouts. Brussels sprout plants should be topped in early fall to encourage even sprout maturity for a once-over harvest. Self-blanching cauliflowers make life easier for the grower, but, even with them, a leaf should be folded over the head to provide more assured blanching conditions. Long-standing cabbage varieties give the grower some leeway in scheduling cabbage harvest.

Harvest broccoli, cabbage, and cauliflower by cutting the stem with a sharp knife. Snap Brussels sprouts off the stem with a quick side motion. To harvest sprouts for storage, remove the leaves from the plant, cut the whole stem, and store with the sprouts attached. Broccoli, Brussels sprouts, and cauliflower should be cooled quickly after harvest. All the brassicas keep best stored at 32°F. (0°C.) with a humidity of 90 to 95 percent. Excellent aeration in storage is important.

My favorite varieties: Broccoli, 'Packman', 'Arcadia'; Brussels sprouts, 'Diablo'; and Cabbage, 'Gonzales' (early), 'Ruby Perfection' (red), and 'Chieftain Savoy' (flavor).

Carrot. I have noticed over the years that consumers can readily distinguish the superior flavor of organically grown carrots more than any other vegetable. That is not surprising, since petroleum distillates are used as herbicides on conventional carrot crops, and they taste like it. Furthermore, studies have shown that carrots take up pesticide residues from the soil and concentrate them in their tissues. The quality grower can truly excel with this crop by growing succession plantings and selling fresh over as long a season as possible.

Varieties should be chosen for flavor. The earliest crop can be planted in an unheated tunnel as soon as the ground thaws. A late-planted crop can be covered with an unheated tunnel and baby carrots harvested from under a covering of straw throughout the winter. These will be the sweetest, tenderest carrots anyone has ever eaten.

Carrots are planted in 6- to 12-inch rows at a spacing of 1 to 4 inches in the row. Under tunnels, 6-inch rows with seeds at 4 inches in the row have been shown to give the earliest harvest, although I find 8 by 2 inches more productive and almost as early. I sow field carrots in 12-inch rows and aim for 1-inch spacing. Either pelleted or naked seed can be used, depending on the seeder. It is worth running your own germination test on pelleted seed before using. Germination can be disappointing. For dependable germination of carrots, it is vital to keep the soil moist from the time of seeding until they emerge. I always direct-sow carrots because I have never found a dependable system for transplanting this tap-root crop.

Don't plant carrots in a weed-infested soil. The in-row weed problems will be overwhelming. On a reasonably clean soil, one hand-weeding and careful between-row weeding with the wheel hoe will give excellent control. In the fall it is a good idea to hoe soil up over the shoulders of mature carrots to forestall greening and as extra protection against freezing prior to harvest. Carrots can be loosened in the soil by using the broadfork to make them easier to pull. When bunching carrots, cut off the upper half of the tops after tying to prevent excess moisture loss. Bunched carrots must be kept moist and cool to keep the roots from wilting.

Store carrots at 32°F. (0°C.) with a relative humidity of 95 percent. Well-grown, mature carrots will keep in excellent condition for six months. Stored carrots can turn bitter when stored with apples, pears, tomatoes, melons, or other fruits and vegetables that give off ethylene gas in storage.

My favorite varieties: 'Napoli' (winter), 'Nelson' (spring, summer), and 'Scarlet Nantes' or 'Bolero' (storage).

Celery. Celery is not a common crop on the small farm, but I believe it should be. There is a ready market for organically grown celery. The ideal conditions are a highly fertile soil with lots of organic matter and a steady supply of moisture. The grower must make sure that the soil contains adequate supplies of calcium and boron. If you are near a hatchery that has egg wastes, they are a great soil improver for celery. Irrigation is a must for successful celery crops.

Start celery in mini-blocks at 72°F. (22°C.). Mist the blocks frequently until germination occurs. Pot on to 2-inch blocks and grow at 60°F. (16°C.) or warmer. Temperatures below 55°F. (13°C.) will cause celery seedlings to bolt to seed in the first year. Transplant celery into 12-inch rows at 12-inch spacing in the row. Early outdoor transplantings must be protected with a tunnel or other heat source to keep them from bolting to seed if the weather turns damp and cool. I grow my earliest crop along the edges of the early-tomato greenhouse where the roof is not tall enough for staking tomatoes.

Store celery at 32°F. (0°C.) with a relative humidity of 95 percent. Burlap spread on the floor of the storage room and moistened with water is one way of keeping up storage-room humidity. The same advice applies to celeriac as well as celery. Celeriac, however, is slightly more forgiving about bolting and moisture requirements.

My favorite varieties: Celery, 'Tango' and 'Conquistador'; and Celeriac, 'Brilliant'.

Chard. Swiss chard is a relative of the beet and responds to similar growing conditions. I start chard in 1½-inch blocks and thin to one seedling per block. I transplant into 18-inch rows at 12 inches in the row for a cut-and-come-again harvest, or into 12-inch rows at 6-inch spacing for a one-time harvest of the whole plant. I think the eating quality is better from the latter, but a market that demands large leaves with prominent midribs will require the former. Like most leafy greens, chard does not store well. Cool it quickly after harvest, and keep the humidity as high as possible.

Corn. This crop causes a frustrating decision for the small grower. Financial return per acre from sweet corn is low, but the popularity and demand for the crop are high. What to do? If you are marketing to subscribers, you will want to grow just enough to meet your responsibilities. If you are growing a more limited list of crops, corn is not likely to be one of them unless you have extra land. If you market at a stand, sweet corn is one of the crops you can buy in from other growers.

I plant corn in 30-inch rows and aim for one plant per foot. Corn can be transplanted for the earliest crop by using soil blocks. Place the blocks in a bread tray. With the mesh bottom, air gets to all sides of the block and prevents the tap root from growing out of the block. Do not plan to hold corn seedlings more than two weeks before transplanting. Outdoor plantings are dependent on the temperature. Corn germinates poorly if the soil temperature is under 55°F. (13°C.). I have begun to experiment with pre-germinating the crop before planting in order to be able to make early seeding more dependable. All you want is to break the seed dormancy, not have a root sticking out. The idea looks promising, and I suggest that other growers may want to try their hand at it.

For a continuous supply of sweet corn, the grower should plant a number of varieties with successive harvest dates. Some experience will be necessary to determine the best varieties, since in practice varieties do not always mature as progressively as the catalog information indicates. The sugar content in corn begins to decrease after harvest, so the fresher the corn, the better the flavor. If you wish to preserve that sweet corn quality, it is most important to cool the crop quickly and keep it cool. The new supersweet corns do not lose their sweetness as quickly after harvest, but I think there is more to the flavor of corn than just sweetness. I do not believe these varieties are as nutritious, either.

Cucumber. This is a warm-weather crop, one that grows best in the most fertile soil you can provide. Greenhouse cucumber growers have always used more manure and compost for this crop than for any other. Composted sheep and horse manure have always been the favored soil amendments. Cucumber pest problems are usually a result of imbalanced fertilization—excess nitrogen from chicken manure or a lack of trace elements. Most cucumber-growing problems can be cured by amending the soil with a well-finished compost plus dried seaweed for trace elements. The results are worth the effort.

Many home gardeners grow cucumbers. Your market will be determined by excelling their quality. This is best done by growing one of the European-style, thin-skinned varieties. Most of these need to be grown in a greenhouse or tunnel. They must also be pruned to one stem and to one fruit at each leaf node.

Growing cucumbers vertically pays off in yield per square foot. Trellising the crop upwards makes the most efficient use of your highly fertile and best-protected growing areas. The plants can be trained up a mesh netting with 6-inch squares (for ease of picking) or up single strands of a strong garden twine. At the top of the support, the plants are pruned to two stems, which then descend back to the ground while continuing to produce cucumbers. Total production of the greenhouse varieties can reach 50 cukes per plant.

I start all cucumbers as transplants. Germinate them in 1½-inch blocks at 85°F. (30°C.). Pot them on to 4-inch blocks and grow at 65°F. (18°C.). Use bottom heat at 70°F. (21°C.) to keep them growing well. Transplant them to the greenhouse, tunnel, or protected outdoor bed at four weeks of age. I plant two rows of staking cucumbers in a 60-inch bed at 30-inch spacing each way. Give them plenty of water and plan to top-dress with extra compost at monthly intervals. Pick them every day to keep the quality high. Overgrown cucumbers put an extra strain on the plants and lower the yield. Store cukes at 50°F. (10°C.) with a relative humidity of 90 to 95 percent. Ethylene from apples, tomatoes, and other produce will cause accelerated ripening and cause the green color to change to yellow.

My favorite varieties: 'Diva' and 'Socrates' (a greenhouse variety).

Garlic. Fall-planted varieties are a better bet than spring-planted. The fall varieties are planted in mid-October, winter over in the soil, and mature in summer when customer interest is high. There is time for a green manure or succession crop to be established after harvest. My experience with garlic varieties is that they can be very specific to soil types. When you start out growing garlic, you should try as many different cultivars as are available and then choose the one that does the best on your soil. After that, save your own planting stock every year and select for large-sized bulbs. Garlic must be well cured and dried after harvest. It stores best at 32°F. (0°C.) and at a humidity of 65 percent.

Kale. Kale is a relative of the cabbage family, and the same soil fertility suggestions apply. I grow all kale as transplants in 1½-inch soil blocks and set them out in 18-inch rows at 12-inch spacing. Smaller plants can be grown in 12-inch rows.

I have sold kale both as bunches of leaves and as whole plants. As with chard, I recommend the latter; the eating quality of the whole young plants is better. Kale is most flavorful in the fall, after a few light frosts, and so I plant it as a succession crop. Since brassicas grow very well following a member of the onion family, kale could be the ideal crop to follow garlic. Kale can be left in the ground and harvested right up through hard frosts. Any kale still around very late in the fall makes a tasty green treat for laying hens.

My favorite field variety: 'Toscano'.

Lettuce. Lettuce, in contrast to sweet corn, has a very high dollar return per square foot of crop. On some intensive market gardens, lettuce is the major crop. That complicates crop-rotation planning. Extra compost is needed where the same crop is grown at too short an interval.

I grow all lettuce from transplants for a number of reasons. First, I want to be sure of a full crop without gaps in the rows. Since lettuce seed germinates poorly in hot, dry weather, I prefer to sow it under controlled conditions indoors. In very warm weather the seeded blocks can be germinated in two days in a cool cellar and then brought up to grow. Second, since most leaf lettuces are a 60-day seed-to-harvest crop, they can spend a third to a half of that time as seedlings before transplanting. During the three to four weeks the lettuce seedlings are in the blocks, an unrelated crop can occupy that same ground. This not only increases production but lessens crop-rotation problems. And third, lettuce is a fast-growing crop, and I want a vigorous seedling grown under ideal conditions to go into a fertile soil and grow quickly. The excellent lettuce transplants from soil blocks give me just that. Information on the timing of succession lettuce plantings is presented on pages 47 and 260.

I grow greenhouse lettuce at a 10-by-10–inch spacing and outdoor lettuce at 12 by 12 inches. The greenhouse lettuce grows on the residual fertility of the tomato crop. The outdoor lettuce receives an application of well-finished compost lightly mixed into the topsoil just before transplanting. The key to successful lettuce culture is quick growth. You want to make all the growing conditions as ideal as possible. That means not only soil preparation and irrigation, but also the quality of the transplants. Treat the lettuce transplants gently so they go into the ground without torn leaves or soil-filled hearts. When the weather conditions are too warm, you will want to harvest the lettuce at a younger age to keep up the quality and double-bag them (sell two smaller heads for the price of one).

My favorite varieties: 'Buttercrunch' (bibb), 'Rex' (greenhouse), 'Nancy' (Boston), 'Crispino' (head), 'Red Cross' (red), and 'Winter Density' (romaine).

Mâche. This crop, also known as corn salad in this country, is quickly growing in popularity, and deservedly so. It looks like a very small leaf lettuce, but it is no relation. As a salad ingredient, it complements lettuce or can be used on its own. It is very tasty. But best of all, it is extremely cold-hardy and can be harvested in midwinter.

I sow mâche in late summer to early fall with the five-row seeder. I aim for a plant every 2 inches in the row, but plant about twice that close because mâche germination is poor. I cover the plants with a field tunnel and basically pay very little attention to them except to weed and water. By December they are full-grown (about 3 inches high and wide) and usually frozen solid. Any time there is a thaw for a day or two, or when the tunnel temperature is above freezing, mâche can be harvested. It almost seems to like having been frozen and shows no damage. To harvest, cut the plant at ground level. I then wash and store them whole. They are usually served mixed in a tossed salad, with cold cooked beets, or used in one of many mâche recipes. This is the best beginner's crop for those wishing to take a first tentative step into winter salad production.

My favorite variety: 'Vit'.

Melon. Melons are another crop that requires warm weather, even more so than cucumbers. Any extra heat that can be provided through soil-warming mulches, windbreaks, or a sheltered site will pay off in a better outdoor crop. Slitted row covers over wire hoops make for excellent melon growing. The cover should be removed at pollination time. The same soil conditions apply here as for cucumbers. The more fertile the soil, the better the melon crop. A sandy soil is often preferred for melon growing, since it warms up more quickly. Extra organic matter helps a sandy soil hold water.

Muskmelons should be harvested at full slip (the stem separates easily from the fruit) for best flavor. Many of the European Charantais varieties have to be harvested before slip to be at their best. Be sure to read the catalog descriptions. Melons can be stored at 40°F. (4°C.) at high humidity for a short time after harvest.

My favorite variety: 'Gold Star'.

Onion. This is the crop that taught me the value of multiplant blocks. Since I prefer a round globe-shaped onion (as opposed to the flattened globe from sets), I grow onions from transplants. But transplanting and subsequent in-row weed control were not as efficient as I would have liked. Multiplant blocks changed all that.

With multiplant blocks, five seeds are sown in each 1½-inch block 5 to 6 weeks before the earliest outdoor transplanting date. Onions, like the brassicas, grow better seedlings if the seeds are lightly covered with potting soil. The blocks are set out in rows 12 inches apart at 12 inches in the row with the same equipment used for other block transplants at that spacing. In-row weeds are no problem, since the space between the blocks can be cultivated in both directions. The onions grow together in the clump, pushing each other aside for more room as they get bigger. At harvest, each clump is a circle of four to six onions the same size as if they had been spaced normally in the row.

Onion-family plants are greatly affected by the preceding crop in the rotation. The most favorable preceding crops are a fine grass (red-top), lettuce, or a member of the squash family. In my rotation, onions follow winter squash. I grow the onions right where the squash rows grew. I have found they do best where no green manure was sown. Carrots or some other root crop is grown in the alternate beds that did grow green manure the previous year.

I use the same multiplant technique described in the Soil Blocks chapter (Chapter 14) for scallions, but at an even higher density. Ten to 12 seeds are sown per 1½-inch block and set out 6 inches apart in 12-inch rows. At maturity, the clumps are already prebunched for harvest. The same technique works for leeks. Four seeds are planted per 1½-inch block and are planted out in deep holes made with a bulb planter. They don't get quite as large as individual leeks, but the time saving is worth it.

The onion crop is ready for harvest when the leaves begin to die down naturally. If weather conditions are good (warm and dry), pull the onions, cut the tops, and leave them to dry in the field. If conditions don't allow for field curing, remove the crop to a storage room and dry on racks at 80°F. (27°C.) with fans blowing the air around. The same bread trays used for holding soil blocks make excellent onion-drying racks. Heat can be provided with a small woodstove. Household fans provide the air movement. The complete drying procedure will take about two weeks or so, until the necks are completely dry. After drying, store at 32°F. (0°C.) with a relative humidity of 65 percent. These practices will give you the highest-quality onions for sale and storage.

My favorite varieties: 'Copra' (yellow) and 'Mars' (red).

Parsley. This is one of my favorite foods, and I snack on it while I work. I think that with some marketing effort it could be a much more important crop for the small grower than it is. The choice of flat- or curled-leaf varieties will be determined by the market.

I grow all parsley from transplants. It is started in mini-blocks at 72°F. (22°C.)

and then transplanted on to 2-inch blocks. Soil blocks are the only consistently efficient and dependable way to transplant a tap-rooted crop like parsley. I set out succession crops of parsley in any odd corner, both in the field and in the greenhouse. I harvest by cutting the whole plant and then letting it regrow new greens before the next cut. Parsley can be stored with cool temperatures and high humidity for a month or so, but I prefer to harvest and sell it fresh.

My favorite variety: 'Titan' (flat leaf).

Parsnip. Even though I enjoy eating parsnips and grow them for my own table, I do not think that the return from this crop is sufficient to justify including it in any but a guild marketing system. Parsnips need to be planted early, cultivated through the season, and ideally left in the ground to be harvested early the following spring. The cold winter temperatures turn some of the starch to sugar and make parsnips a real spring treat for those who enjoy them.

A good precision seeder like the Earthway can plant raw parsnip seed adequately, although the rows will need to be thinned. For other seeders, pelleted parsnip seed is available from some suppliers. I plant parsnips in 18-inch rows and aim for a spacing of 3 inches in the row. If a market exists, parsnips do have the advantage that they can be sold at a time of year when there is usually very little farm income. It is important to dig them just as soon as conditions permit and before they begin to sprout. Fall-harvested parsnips that can be held at a temperature of 32°F. (0°C.) for two weeks in storage can attain a sweetness close to those left over the winter in the field. The humidity level must be kept at 95 percent.

Peas. Peas have more variability than almost any other crop. There are low varieties, tall staking varieties, smooth-seeded, wrinkled-seeded, regular peas, snow peas, and sugar snaps. The problem with peas, as with beans, is getting them picked economically. For that reason, the more exotic types like sugar snaps and snow peas may be the best bet in some markets, because their prices better reflect the real costs.

I grow both the early low-growing varieties and the later staking types in order to spread out the harvest season. I plant all peas in double rows 6 inches apart. For low peas, these double rows are 30 inches from the next, and for staking peas the distance is 60 inches. With the low-growers, the two rows lean against each other to keep them more upright. With the staking peas, the rows climb either side of a 78-inch-tall, 6-inch mesh netting supported by wooden posts and crossbars.

Peas can be transplanted for an extra-early crop. Plant four seeds in each 2-inch block. Place the blocks in bread trays with mesh bottoms to get air to all sides and prevent root emergence. Transplant at two weeks of age.

Peas need to be harvested frequently (at least every other day) for highest quality. They should be rapidly cooled to 32°F. (0°C.) as soon as possible after picking. I suggest selling them the day they are picked. Old peas are bad business.

My favorite varieties: 'Strike' (early), 'Lincoln' (best flavor), and 'Sugar Snap' (hard to beat).

Pepper. This is another warm-weather crop that will repay the grower for any climate improvement he or she can provide. Floating covers, plastic mulch, and field tunnels will all aid the production of the pepper crop. I have used the spaces between greenhouses to provide a warm microclimate for a rotation of peppers, melons, and celery.

I start peppers in mini-blocks at 72°F. (22°C.). They are potted on to 2- and then 4-inch blocks in order to grow the finest early transplants. Nighttime temperature minimum is 62°F. (17°C.). I do not let fruit set on the plants before the blocks are transplanted to the soil. I get much greater production later on by reducing that early strain on the plants. It is best to avoid highly nitrogenous soil amendments like chicken manure. The extra nitrogen makes the pepper plants go more to leaf than to fruit.

After harvest, peppers should be stored at 50°F. (10°C.) at a humidity of 90 to 95 percent. Temperatures below 45°F. (7°C.) predispose these hot-weather fruits to bacterial decay.

My favorite varieties: 'Ace' or 'Red Knight' (for very short seasons).

Potato. The best return in potato growing comes not from the main crop but from extra-early harvest of baby new potatoes. That is especially true if one of the yellow-fleshed varieties like 'Charlotte', 'German Fingerling', or 'Yellow Finnish' is chosen. The gourmet market will pay handsomely for the crop, and the field is then made available for a succession planting of another vegetable or a green manure.

I plant potatoes in 30-inch rows at a spacing of 8 to 12 inches, depending upon the variety and the size desired. I pay a great deal of attention to the rotational position and soil fertility for potatoes. I do not grow them at a low pH, but I try to prevent scab by providing excellent potato-growing conditions and preceding them in the rotation with a scab-suppressing crop. The most destructive pest in my part of the world is the potato beetle (*Leptinotarsa decemlineata*). Up until 1987 it was the one pest problem I had not figured out. In that year we began specific trials to determine the stresses on potatoes and what cultural practices would help us avoid them. We found that mulching heavily with straw just after potato emergence reduced the potato beetle problem by 90 percent or more. It seems that too warm a soil and a fluctuating moisture supply are major stresses on potatoes, and both were minimized by mulching. Varied bits and pieces of published research are in agreement with that conclusion. Chisel plowing the potato field to break up any hardpan and improve soil aeration for deep root growth has also had a positive effect. I am continuing to work on perfecting the system and also on growing the mulch as a thick cover crop the fall before and planting the potatoes through the residues.

A one-row potato digger can be purchased as an attachment for walking tractors. It is a worthwhile investment if you grow many potatoes. For best storage, potatoes need a period of two weeks at 50°F. (10°C.) to heal cuts and bruises. After that, storage temperatures of 40° to 45°F. (4° to 7°C.) with 90 percent humidity will keep them in fine shape. Storage temperatures below 38°F. (3°C.) tend to make the potatoes undesirably sweet through a change of some of the starch to sugar. Potatoes that have been stored in too cool a place can be reconditioned by holding them at 70°F. (21°C.) for about two weeks before use.

My favorite variety: 'Charlotte'.

Pumpkin and Squash. I include pumpkins and squashes together, since their growing requirements are similar. Both crops thrive on a fertile soil with lots of organic matter. Both are vining crops, and both are planted in widely spaced rows. Pumpkins may only be valuable as a Halloween crop. I think the best "pumpkin" pies are actually made with winter squashes.

These are good crops to plant on weed-infested land. Since they are frost-tender and thus planted late, the field can be tilled a couple of times before planting to initiate the weed-seed germination and control process. After planting, the wide spaces between the rows and the slow early growth of the plants before they begin to vine provide further opportunities for clean cultivation. Finally, once the vines and large leaves begin to cover the ground, they do a pretty good weed-smothering job of their own.

Both pumpkins and squash can be started in 3-inch blocks and transplanted in two to three weeks. In some short-season areas, starting the plants ahead may be the only way to ensure full maturity of the fruits. I plant in rows 10 feet apart and aim to have a vigorous plant every 18 to 24 inches in the row. It is best to harvest just before frost in fall. Frost damage can inhibit the keeping qualities of the fruits. After harvest, a curing period used to be recommended, but that has been shown to be unnecessary. Store at a temperature of 50° to 55°F. (10° to13°C.)

with a relative humidity of 50 to 75 percent. Hubbard squashes are less liable to storage rot if the stems are completely removed before storage.

My favorite variety of winter squash: 'Waltham Butternut'.

Radish. A well-grown radish is a wonderful salad vegetable. In order to fulfill its potential, it must be grown quickly in a very fertile soil. Growing temperatures on the cool side will help. I like to grow radishes as a fall and spring crop in unheated field tunnels or the mobile greenhouse.

Radish rows can be spaced as close as 4 inches. The seeds should be sown about 1 inch or so apart. I plant them with the same five-row seeder used for green manures. Succession sowings every few days assure the best quality. If root maggots have been a problem, use the same autumn leaf fertilizer as for brassicas. Till leaves under in fall (up to 100 cubic yards to the acre), and till again before planting. Leaves used this way as a soil amendment release nitrogen in a form that seems to help the radishes grow right past their pests. Alfalfa meal, spread as a fertilizer for radish crops, has also given extraordinary results.

Radishes should be cooled quickly after harvest. Don't bunch them with the tops on except for immediate sale. The tops will expire moisture and cause the roots to wilt. The crisper the radish, the better the sale.

My favorite varieties: 'Tinto', 'D'Avignon'.

Rutabaga. I grow these because I like to eat them. The market is not overwhelming for this underappreciated root crop, but if served mashed half-and-half with potatoes, they will usually convert doubters to fans.

I grow rutabagas in 18-inch rows, and I aim for a plant every 4 inches in the row. The same soil-improving techniques for brassicas and radishes also apply to this related crop. I sow the rutabagas around the first of July. The best spot is where an overwintered leguminous green-manure crop has been tilled under about three weeks beforehand. The rutabagas will then grow a marvelous crop with no problems.

Spinach. The trick with spinach is not growing it in season, which should be relatively easy on a fertile soil, but growing it out of season. Spinach is a cool-weather crop, but the demand for it as a salad component and as an ingredient in many gourmet dishes extends year-round. There are a number of ways to meet that demand.

A clay soil has more body and is a better choice for growing hot-weather spinach than a sandy soil. A sandy soil can be improved with plenty of compost, additions of clay, and a good irrigation system. Under difficult conditions, spinach responds to the same feeds as celery, and so egg wastes or crab shells are also effective as a fertilizer. If a spinach crop is planted toward the end of the summer and then protected with a field tunnel, the harvest can extend through the winter months.

Spinach is not often transplanted, but it is easy enough to do. Sow four to five seeds per 1½-inch block. Transplant three-week-old seedlings every 6 inches in rows spaced at 12 inches. Instead of being transplanted, however, the early crop is usually sown the fall before and wintered over. Young spinach plants are quite hardy and will normally survive the winter with no protection if there is a covering of snow. If snow isn't dependable, a light mulch of pine branches or a floating cover will provide the extra protection. The spring crop can be speeded up by placing a field tunnel over it as soon as the ground thaws.

Spinach is usually harvested plant by plant with a knife. I saw a much more efficient and productive system in Holland. The spinach was planted in close rows using something like our five-row seeder. It grew very thick and upright. Harvesting was done by mowing carefully with a scythe equipped with a net cradle to collect the spinach. Spinach should be cooled quickly after harvest and covered with crushed ice. The relative humidity should be in the 90 to 95 percent range.

My favorite variety: 'Space'.

Tomato. When a selected tomato variety is well grown and fully ripened on the vine, there is no more appealing snack. Vine-ripened greenhouse tomatoes, along with lettuce, are the two most remunerative crops for the intensive salad grower. I most emphatically do not mean "greenhouse tomatoes" in the sense that consumers have come to regard them. These are not the tasteless, plastic-looking objects with no flavor that were picked green, ripened artificially, and sold for looks alone. I'm talking about *real* tomatoes grown in a greenhouse in order to extend the season and *improve* quality.

I recommend growing greenhouse tomatoes for a number of reasons. The tomato is a popular crop, but the outdoor season is short. Greenhouse production can greatly extend that season and bring customers to your farm. Many of the diseases of outdoor tomatoes, such as blight, are related to weather stress. Under both greenhouse and tunnel production, those stresses are lessened or nonexistent, and blight is not a problem. Much of the eating quality of a warm-season crop comes from ideal weather conditions. In the northern climates, those conditions do not usually exist. In southern climates they may not exist long enough to fully extend the tomato season. In most cases, long-season production of vine-ripened tomatoes under controlled conditions is a viable option.

I grow only *beefsteak* varieties. Seeds can be planted as early as mid-October on if you are specializing in greenhouse tomatoes. I sow my first crop in mid-January. Seeds are started in mini-blocks at 72°F. (22°C.). After eight to ten days they are potted on to 2-inch blocks and grown at 62°F. (17°C.) night temperature. After another 10 to 14 days they are potted on once more, this time to 4-inch maxi-blocks. I use a high-pressure sodium lamp for supplemental lighting. I transplant to the greenhouse when the plants are six to seven weeks old. Without supplemental light, it will take seven to ten days longer.

I grow greenhouse tomatoes in 5-foot-wide beds that are heavily amended with compost. I grow at a night temperature of 62°F. (17°C.), and I ventilate at 75°F. (24°C.). The soil temperature should be no lower than 60°F. (16°C.) for best growth. If you don't have soil heating you can warm the soil by covering the beds with clear plastic for at least two weeks before planting, and leave it on until the first compost top-dressing about six weeks later.

Grow plants in two rows 30 inches apart so as to provide 4 square feet per plant. Prune to a single stem and remove side shoots every few days. Trellis the plants to overhead supports; tie strong twine (untreated) loosely to the base of the plant and attach it to the overhead support. As the plant grows, the twine can be twisted around the stem, or the stem can be supported with special clips. According to Dutch research, for optimum production without stressing the plants, the fruit clusters should be pruned to three fruits on the first two clusters and four fruits thereafter for spring crops. (Three fruits on the first three trusses, two on the fourth and fifth, and three fruits on the sixth and thereafter for fall crops.) A top-dressing of another inch or so of compost should be added to the soil every six weeks. Irrigate regularly.

When the plants reach the overhead support (ideally, 8 feet above ground), they either can be stopped for a short production season or the plants can be lowered. In order to lower the plants (a practice known as "layering"), you will want to have left an extra length of twine at the top. Greenhouse supply companies sell special hanging bobbins for this purpose. By this stage of growth, the bottom cluster of fruit will have been harvested, and the lower stem will be bare. Untie the twine at the top and lower the plant so the bare stem approaches the soil. Do this to all the plants in the same direction along the row. At the end of the row, start training the plants around the corner and then back down the other side of the bed. Each time the plant top reaches the support, it should be lowered in this same way. As long as the top 5 feet or so of the plant is vertical it will grow normally. The bare plant stems will eventually contact the soil and send out new roots where they touch. In this way an early planting can be kept productive right through to late fall. For more detailed information consult the books on greenhouse tomato-growing in the bibliography and contact other, more experienced growers. The specialized techniques for this crop are advancing very quickly.

The first harvest (from a February 15 sowing) is around June 1 and continues until the middle of November. I pick these tomatoes only when they are vine-ripe and ready to eat. The flavor will bring customers back in a steady stream.

My favorite variety: 'Big Beef' (a productive hybrid variety with exceptional flavor and quality).

Zucchini. I will include yellow summer squash in this category as well. These are crops whose extra virtues are beginning to be appreciated. There is an eager market for fruits picked small (à la the French courgette). There is also a market for fruits picked with the blossom attached and for male blossoms. Special varieties have been developed for the blossom market.

As with other fast-growing crops, these squashes will thrive under the best growing conditions you can provide. They can be transplanted to field tunnels for an early crop. For the outdoor crop, I prefer direct seeding. The main key with zucchini and summer squash is to pick them on time. If picking small fruits, pay close attention to the plants. These squashes are only valuable when young and fresh. They are so productive that a new harvest is ready every day, and even twice a day in hot weather. Handle the fruits very carefully when harvesting. Some growers wear soft gloves to avoid scratching the tender and easily bruised skin. Don't plan to hold them for long after harvest.

My favorite varieties: 'Zucchini Elite', 'Sunray', and 'Ronde de Nice' (for the gourmet market and for beautiful, large blossoms).

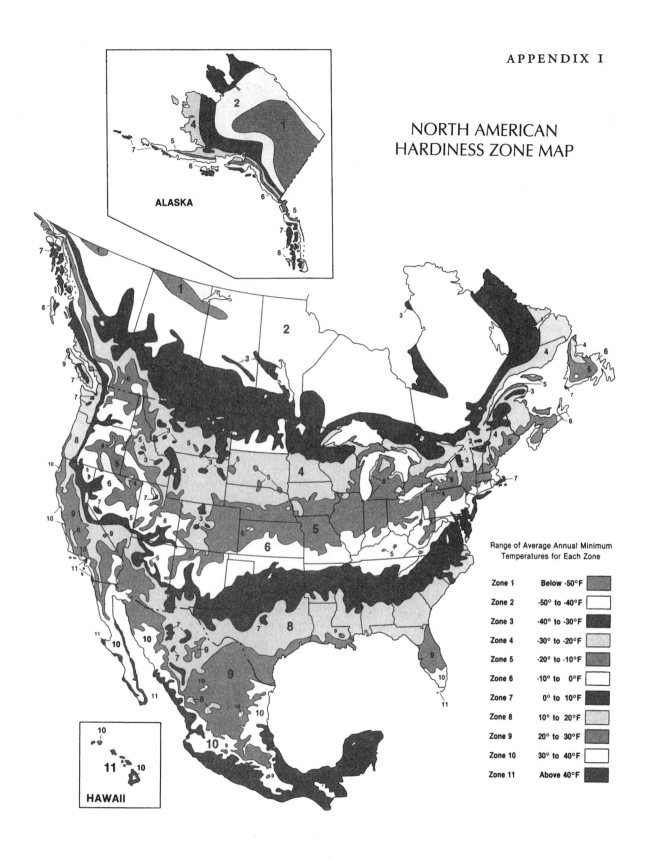

NORTH AMERICAN
HARDINESS ZONE MAP

ALASKA

HAWAII

Range of Average Annual Minimum
Temperatures for Each Zone

Zone 1	Below -50°F
Zone 2	-50° to -40°F
Zone 3	-40° to -30°F
Zone 4	-30° to -20°F
Zone 5	-20° to -10°F
Zone 6	-10° to 0°F
Zone 7	0° to 10°F
Zone 8	10° to 20°F
Zone 9	20° to 30°F
Zone 10	30° to 40°F
Zone 11	Above 40°F

A SCHEMATIC OUTLINE OF BIOLOGICAL AGRICULTURE

I originally prepared this outline as an exercise to compose my thoughts and see if everything fit together. Did it make sense on paper as well as in the field? An early grade-school teacher once told me that if the thinking behind my idea was fuzzy, I wouldn't be able to make a coherent outline.

This is pretty coherent. She would have been pleased.

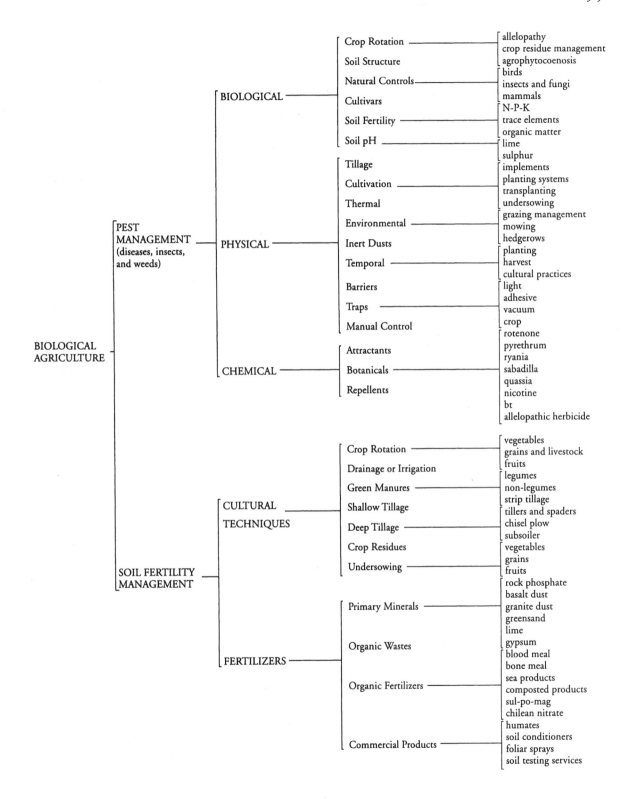

METRIC CONVERSIONS

Throughout the text of this book, U.S. units of measurement have been used; the only exception being temperatures, which are listed in degrees Fahrenheit along with their approximate equivalents in degrees Celsius.

Readers who are more familiar with the international (metric) system can use the mathematical equations that follow to convert U.S. measurements into metric units. This conversion table is not exhaustive, and is intended only as a handy reference for those units of measurements most relevant to this book and to the small-scale grower.

CONVERTING FROM U.S. TO METRIC UNITS

When You Know	Multiply By	To Determine
inches	25.4	millimeters
inches	2.54	centimeters
feet	30.48	centimeters
feet	0.3048	meters
yards	0.91	meters
square inches	6.45	square centimeters
square feet	0.0929	square meters
square yards	0.836	square meters
acres	0.4047	hectares
cubic feet	0.283	cubic meters
cubic yards	0.7646	cubic meters
fluid ounces	29.57	milliliters
cups	0.24	liters
pints	0.47	liters
quarts	0.95	liters
gallons	3.79	liters

ounces (weight)	28.35	grams
pounds	0.45	kilograms
short tons (2,000 lb.)	0.907	metric tons (1,000 kg.)

CONVERTING FROM METRIC TO U.S UNITS

When You Know	Multiply By	To Determine
millimeters	0.04	inches
centimeters	0.39	inches
meters	3.28	feet
meters	1.09	yards
square centimeters	0.16	square inches
square meters	1.2	square yards
hectares	2.47	acres
cubic meters	35.32	cubic feet
cubic meters	1.35	cubic yards
milliliters	0.03	fluid ounces
liters	4.23	cups
liters	2.12	pints
liters	1.06	quarts
liters	0.26	gallons
grams	0.035	ounces
kilograms	2.21	pounds
metric tons (1,000 kg.)	1.1	short tons (2,000 lb.)

Temperature Conversions

To convert degrees Fahrenheit to degrees Celsius, use the following equation:

$$°C. = (°F. - 32) \times 5/9$$

To convert degrees Celsius to degrees Fahrenheit, use the following equation:

$$°F. = (°C. \times 9/5) + 32$$

RECOMMENDED TOOLS
& SUPPLIERS

Tools have their own integrity;
The sneath of the scythe curves rightly to the hand,
The hammer knows its balance, knife its edge,
All tools inevitably planned,
Stout friends, with pledge
Of service; with their crochets too
That masters understand . . .

— V. Sackville-West

The following appendix contains retailer and/or manufacturer listings for the tools and supplies recommended in this book. Wherever possible, I have attempted to provide names and information on suppliers for North America, Europe, and Australia. In other regions of the world, or where no retail supplier is listed, readers are advised to contact the manufacturer directly and ask for the name of the nearest distributor to them.

Land

Fencing. The "invisible deer fence" is sold by Benner's Gardens, 1100 Schell Ln., Phoenixville, PA 19460; (800) 244-3337; www.bennersgardens.com. It is manufactured by the TENAX Corporation, 4800 Monument St., Baltimore, MD 21205; (800) 356-8495; www.tenax.com.

Soil Preparation

Colloidal Phosphate and Greensand. Your local organic fertilizer dealer should be able to supply rock phosphate or colloidal phosphate and greensand at retail, or order them for you in commercial quantities.

A wide assortment of chest-mounted spreaders are available from A.M. Leonard Inc., P.O. Box 816, Piqua, OH 45356; (800) 543-8955; www.amleo.com. Gandy spreaders can be ordered from Gandy Company, 528 Gandrud Road, Owatonna, MN 55060; phone (800) 443-2476; www.gandy.net.

Broadfork. A lightweight yet very strong model of this hand-powered subsoil loosener is sold as the "Broadfork," by Johnny's Selected Seeds, 955 Benton Ave., Winslow, ME 04901; (877) 564-6697; www.johnnyseeds.com.

A less-expensive, straight-tined model is sold as the "Soil Digger" by Gardener's Supply, 128 Intervale Road, Burlington, VT 05401; (800) 444-6417; www.gardeners.com.

An Australian-made, handcrafted broadfork is available from Gundaroo Tiller, Allsun Farm, Gundaroo, NSW 2620; phone (612) 6236 8173; www.allsun.com.au. This farm-based business makes and distributes a number of products listed in this appendix. The original hand subsoiler design, called "The Grelinette," is still manufactured in France by Olivier Grelin, 73800 Arbin-Montmellian, France; phone 04.79.84.14.53; www.grelinette.ifrance.com.

Chisel Plow. There are a number of manufacturers of small (five-shank) chisel plows that can be pulled by a 25- to 35-horsepower, four-wheel-drive tractor. Ask your local farm-equipment dealer.

Yeomans Plow Co. makes Australia's original and best non-inversion plows. Both three- and five-shank models are available from Yeomans Plow Co., 30 Demand Avenue, Arundel, QLD 4214; phone (617) 5571 6544; www.yeomansplow.com.au.

Two-Wheel Walking Tractor-Tiller. This is an excellent basic power source for the small farm. Tractor-tillers are manufactured in a wide range of sizes and working capabilities. The best models imported into the U.S. come from Italy. My favorite is a BCS 732 an 11-horsepower, gasoline-powered model distributed by BCS America, Inc., 7130 Providence Square Dr., #23, Charlotte, NC 28270; (704) 364-3244; www.bcs-america.com. It is available from many local dealers, listed on their Web site.

Reciprocating spaders for tractors are sold by Market Farm Implement, 257 Fawn Hollow Road, Friedens, PA 15541; (814) 443-1931; www.marketfarm.com.

The best models available in Australia are imported from Italy by Motorcolt, P.O. Box 115, KooWeeRup, VIC 3981; phone (03) 5997 2155; www.motorcolt.com.au. They carry both Pasquali and BCS tractors and small Tortella reciprocating spaders.

Compost. Landscape fabric for covering compost heaps (in widths from 3 feet to 12 feet and up to 250-foot lengths) is sold by A.M. Leonard, Inc., P.O. Box 816, Piqua, OH 45356; (800) 543-8955; www.amleo.com. Smaller lengths are sold by Gardener's Supply, 128 Intervale Road, Burlington, VT 05401; (800) 444-6417; www.gardeners.com.

European-style scythes for mowing compost ingredients are manufactured in Germany and Austria. In Germany they are made by Bayerische & Tiroler Sensen-Union, Franz-Huber-Str. 52, 83088 Kiefersfelden, Bayern, Germany; phone (08033) 9239-0. They are sold in the U.S. by Johnny's Selected Seeds, 955 Benton Ave., Winslow, ME 04901; (877) 564-6697; and Scythe Supply, 496 Shore Road, Perry, ME 04667;

(207) 853-4750; www.scythesupply.com. The Marugg Company (P.O. Box 1418, Tracy City, TN 37387; (931) 592-5042; www.themaruggcompany.com) sells their own complete line of European-style scythes and mowing equipment.

Seeding and Transplanting

Seeds. My favorite seed catalogs are from the following U.S. and Canadian companies:

Fedco Seeds
P.O. Box 520
Waterville, ME 04703
(207) 873-7333
www.fedcoseeds.com

The Cook's Garden
P.O. Box C5030
Warminster, PA 18974
(800) 457-9703
www.cooksgarden.com

Johnny's Selected Seeds
955 Benton Avenue
Winslow, ME 04901
(877) 564-6697
www.johnnyseeds.com

Park Seed Co.
1 Parkton Avenue
Greenwood, SC 29647
(800) 845-3369
www.parkseed.com

Stokes Seeds
Box 548
Buffalo, NY 14240
(716) 695-6980
www.stokeseeds.com
Canadian orders:
P.O. Box 10
Saint Catherines, ON L2R 6R6
(716) 695-6980

Territorial Seed Co.
P.O. Box 158
Cottage Grove, OR 97424
(800) 626-0866
www.territorialseed.com

Vesey's Seeds Ltd.
P.O. Box 9000
Calais, ME 04619-6102
(800) 363-7333
www.veseys.com
Canadian orders:
York, PEI COA 1PO
(902) 368-7333

In England, seeds of old and unusual vegetable varieties are available from Henry Doubleday Research Association, recently renamed Garden Organic, through their established Heritage Seed Programme. Subscribers to the Programme have privileged access to HDRAs seed library, along with help, information, and courses: Henry Doubleday Research Association, National Centre for Organic Gardening, Garden Organic Ryton; phone 44 (024) 7630 3517; www.gardenorganic.org.uk. Vegetable seeds for many old and new varieties, herb and flower seeds, organic fertilizers, compost, pest and weed control supplies: Chase Organics, The Organic Gardening Catalogue, Riverdene Business Park, Molesey Road, Hersham, Surrey KT12 4RG England, phone 44 (019) 3225 3666; www.chaseorganics.co.uk.

Australia's best all-round seed catalog for vegetable growers is produced by New Gippsland Seed Farm, P.O. Box 1, Silvan, VIC 3795; phone (03) 9737 9560. Bulk vegetable seed is available from Fairbanks Selected Seed Company, "Fresh Centre," 542 Footscray Road, West Melbourne, VIC 3003; phone (03) 9689 4500; www.fairbanks.com.au.

Seeders. Belt, cup, and vacuum seeders are sold in the U.S. by Market Farm Implement, 257 Fawn Hollow Road, Friedens, PA 15541; (814) 443-1931; www.marketfarm.com.

The seeder that I prefer, a plate seeder (Earthway Precision Garden Seeder, Model 1001B) is lightweight, inexpensive, and very adaptable to modification for even greater flexibility with different seed sizes or sowing distances. The manufacturer will make special seed plates on request at a reasonable charge. The Earthway seeder is made by Earthway Products, Inc., P.O. Box 547, Bristol, IN 46507; (800) 294-0671; www.earthway.com. Earthway seeders are sold in the U.S. by Johnny's Selected Seeds, Peaceful Valley, and Gardener's Supply (see above for addresses).

My five-row seeder was constructed by bolting five Earthway seeders together side-by-side, with a common front axle and a common push bar joining them at the back.*

The Saalet Seeder is manufactured by Saalet.dk, A Trading, Hagenstrupparken 103, 8860 Ulstrup, Denmark.

In Australia, the Earthway Precision Garden Seeder, Model 1001B is available from J.T. Ellis & Sons, P.O. Box 340, Kingaroy, QLD 4610; phone (800) 072 120; www.agspares.com.au. The Saalet Seeder is available from Gundaroo Tiller, Allsun Farm, Gundaroo, NSW 2620; phone (612) 6236 8173; www.allsun.com.au.

Soil Blockers. The best equipment for hand-powered soil-block production is made by Ladbrooke Ltd., The Grange, Exhall, Nr Alcester, Warwickshire, B49 6EA England; phone 44 1789 773898; www.ladbrooke.co.uk, and sold in the U.S. by Johnny's Selected Seeds, 955 Benton Ave., Winslow, ME 04901; (877) 564-6697; www.johnnyseeds.com. Another U.S. distributor is Peaceful Valley Farm Supply, P.O. Box 2209, Grass Valley, CA 95945; (888) 784-1722; www.groworganic.com. In Australia, Ladbrooke's soil blockers are available from Gundaroo Tiller, Allsun Farm, Gundaroo, NSW 2620; phone (612) 6236 8173; www.allsun.com.au.

Ladbrooke's commercial-scale models include the mini-blocker, which makes 20 cubes, 3A inch on a side; 1½- and 2-inch hand models, which make 20 blocks and 12 blocks, respectively; and a 4-inch model, which makes one maxi-block. A home-garden-scale block maker manufactured in the U.S. is sold by Gardener's Supply, 128 Intervale Road, Burlington, VT 05401, phone (800) 444-6417; www.gardeners.com.

Most of the motorized blockers are produced in Europe. In my opinion, the best designs are those from Visser Tuinbouwmaschinen, P.O. Box 5103, 3295 ZG 's-Gravendeel, The Netherlands; www.visserite.com.

*Instructions for affixing a gang of Earthway seeders to a tractor tool bar and for further modifications are given in R. B. Beverly, "A Simple Tractor Mount for a Vegetable Plot Seeder," HortScience, 22:5 (1987), p. 955.

Weed Control

Cultivators. The new-style wheel hoes equipped with stirrup hoes are made by Glaser Engineering GmbH, Im Lerchengarten 12, 4153 Reinach, Switzerland; phone 41 (0)61 713 98 84; www.glaser-swissmade.com. They are sold in the U.S. by Johnny's Selected Seeds, 955 Benton Ave., Winslow, ME 04901; (877) 564-6697; www.johnnyseeds.com. Another supplier is Peaceful Valley Farm Supply, P.O. Box 2209, Grass Valley, CA 95945; (888) 784-1722; www.groworganic.com. In Australia they are available from Gundaroo Tiller, Allsun Farm, Gundaroo, NSW 2620; phone (612) 6236 8173; www.allsun.com.au.

There are a number of different models of the lightweight, in-line cultivating hoe (also called a *collineal hoe*). In the U.S. they are carried by Johnny's Selected Seeds and Peaceful Valley Farm Supply (see addresses above). These suppliers also sell a long-handled *stirrup hoe,* which is useful if you allow the weeds to get larger than cultivating-hoe size.

In Australia an in-line cultivating hoe is sold under the name "Coleman Gung Hoe" by Gundaroo Tiller (see address above).

Flame Weeders. Some of the most innovative flame weeder designs—backpack, walk-behind, and tractor-mounted—are manufactured by Glaser Engineering GmbH, Im Lerchengarten 12, 4153 Reinach, Switzerland; phone 41 (0)61 713 98 84; www.glaser-swissmade.com. Domestically manufactured backpack models are sold in the U.S. by Peaceful Valley Farm Supply, P.O. Box 2209, Grass Valley, CA 95945; (888) 784-1722; www.groworganic.com. Small-scale models for the vegetable grower are available from Johnny's Selected Seeds and from Flame Weeders, 6263 N. County Road #29, Loveland, CO 80538; (970) 667-0809.

Pests

Plant Seed Mixtures. Good Bug Blend and Border Patrol are carried by Peaceful Valley Farm Supply, P.O. Box 2209, Grass Valley, CA 95945; (888) 784-1722; www.groworganic.com.

Bug Vacuums. Walk-behind bug vacuums used to be manufactured but are no longer available.

Walkover Sprayer. The Walkover sprayer model I use is called The Nurseryman, and it is manufactured by Hayter Limited, Spellbrook, Bishop's Stortford, Hertfordshire CM23 4BU, England, phone 01279 723444; www.hayter.co.uk.

The U.S. distributor for Walkover sprayers is Aztec Sprayers, Unit 25, Clarion Court, Clarion Close, Enterprise Park, Swansea, SA6 8RF, phone 0845 5211209; www.walkoversprayers.com.

Harvest

Knives. California-style knives are sold by Johnny's Selected Seeds, 955 Benton Ave., Winslow, ME 04901; (877) 564-6697; www.johnnyseeds.com.

Carts. My favorite utility garden cart is a traditional Vermont cart retrofitted with homemade wheelbarrow-style handles.

For those who prefer a metal crossbar handle, excellent carts are sold by Gardener's Supply, 128 Intervale Road, Burlington, VT 05401, (800) 444-6417; www.gardeners.com. They will also sell wheels separately for those who wish to make their own cart body.

Season Extension

Low Covers. The following are good sources for low covers: Johnny's Selected Seeds, 955 Benton Ave., Winslow, ME 04901; (877) 564-6697; www.johnnyseeds.com; Peaceful Valley Farm Supply, P.O. Box 2209, Grass Valley, CA 95945; (888) 784-1722; www.groworganic.com; and Gardener's Supply (see address above). Johnny's Selected Seeds also sells wire for making support hoops.

Gardener's Supply sells taller reinforced 9-gauge wire hoops that convert their row covers into 4-foot-high tunnels.

Field Tunnels and Greenhouses. Many different brands of automatic temperature-activated ventilator arms are sold by Charley's Greenhouse Supply, 17979 State Route 536, Mount Vernon, WA 98273; (800) 322-4707; www.charleysgreenhouse.com.

The hard-plastic channel and insert strip, known as Poly-Fastener, is available from Northern Greenhouse Sales, Box 42, Neche, ND 58265; (204) 327-5527; www.northerngreenhouse.com.

An excellent source for hoop tunnels and large greenhouses that are well adapted to winter greenhouse culture are Harnois Industries, Inc., Rimol Greenhouse Systems, and Four Season Tools. Harnois Industries, Inc., 1044 Rue Principale, P.O. Box 150, St-Thomas-de-Joliette, QC J0K 3L0, Canada; (888) 427-6647; www.harnois.com. Their U.S. dealer is: Greenhouse Supply, Inc., P.O. Box 97, Orono, ME 04473; (800) 696-8511. Rimol Greenhouse Systems, Northpoint Industrial Park, 40 Londonderry Turnpike, Hooksett, NH 03106; (603) 629-9004; www.rimolgreenhouses.com. Four Season Tools, 602 Westport Rd., Kansas City, MO 64111; (816) 444-7330; www.fourseasontools.com.

I purchased ball casters for the mobile greenhouses from Acme Caster Company, 68 Fairview Avenue, Poughkeepsie, NY 12601; (800) 472-2263; www.acmecaster.com.

Livestock

Electric Fence. In my experience, the best electric fence equipment is sold by Premier Sheep Supplies, 2031 300th Street, Washington, IA 52353; (319) 653-7622; www.premier1supplies.com. Greenhouse shade cloth for livestock shelters is also available from Premier.

In Australia, Electranets Masterfence and Combifence are versatile brands of electric netting fences for the control and strip grazing of all forms of livestock, from poultry to cattle. Both are available from Gundaroo Tiller, Allsun Farm, Gundaroo, NSW 2620; phone (612) 6236 8173; www.allsun.com.au.

Poultry. I've purchased day-old poultry from many different suppliers. Whenever possible it is usually best to purchase them from a nearby hatchery in order to minimize transport time. Your local agricultural extension service or other farmers will be the best sources of information for names and addresses of hatcheries.

As for day-old baby ducklings, we buy them from what we consider the best duck farm in the U.S. —Holderread Waterfowl Farm and Preservation Center, P.O. Box 492, Corvallis, OR 97339; (541) 929-5338; www.holderreadfarm.com.

Consultants

There are times when you may want someone experienced to help answer questions and evaluate your operation. Fortunately several organic agricultural consulting companies are out there that will provide such services for a fee. Two U.S. consultants whom I know to be very knowledgeable and competent are Amigo Cantisano, Organic Ag Advisors, P.O. Box 942, No. San Juan, CA 95960; (530) 292-3619; orgamigo@gmail.com and Bill Wolf, Organic Specialists, (800) 464-0417.

Caring for Tools

Keep Them Clean. Clean all tools after using them and before putting them away. Use a wooden or metal scraper to remove dirt, a wire brush for the finer material, and wipe dry with a rough rag.

Keep Them Sharp. A number of benefits accrue from keeping garden tools well sharpened. The work can be done better; the tools require less effort to use; more can be accomplished in a given time; and the worker will feel much less tired at the end of the job.

It is best to touch up the edge of a tool frequently to keep it sharp rather than waiting until it has become dull. For most horticultural tools, a flat metal file is the implement of choice for sharpening. A whetstone should be used for sickles and scythes. Knives and pruners are most effectively sharpened on an oilstone.

Keep Them Lively. Most good tools will have strong, straight-grained ash handles. These handles need to be coated occasionally with pure linseed oil to prevent the wood from drying out. Dry wood loses the valuable resiliency of a properly maintained handle and is more likely to break.

Keep Them Around. One of the neatest, best-kept, and most efficient tool rooms I have ever seen was on a small farm in Germany. There was a prominent sign over the workbench that, translated into English, read:

EVERYTHING IN ITS PLACE SAVES ANGER, TIME, AND WORDS

Hang small tools on cup hooks or a pegboard. If the location is marked by a painted outline, the tool can be easily returned to its place after use and noticed when it is missing. Another worthwhile practice is to paint a conspicuous color (red, light blue, or orange) on a nonwearing area of the metal part of the tool, so it can be seen easily if it is left lying about the fields.

A well-planned tool shed should be constructed in close proximity to the fields. It should be equipped with electricity, running water, a concrete floor, a woodstove for heat, a work bench with vises, and adequate safe-storage facilities for gas, oil, parts, and tools.

ANNOTATED BIBLIOGRAPHY

Note: Wherever possible the publisher and date are given for the earliest edition of each book listed in this bibliography.

Contemporary Sources of Information

A common characteristic of many successful organic growers is that they learned what they know without outside help. They managed to decipher the whys and wherefores of biological systems on their own plucky initiative. This prevalence of self-education is not surprising, since so little *specific* instructional material and consultation has been available. In such a situation the best teachers, after experience, are good, basic, *general* reference sources on soils, plants, and techniques. The information can be interpreted to meet the grower's specific needs. These books are not light reading, but they do offer a wealth of useful ideas and can provide the "hard data" that serve as the springboard to improved performance.

Balls, R. *Horticultural Engineering Technology.* London and New York: Macmillan, 1985. This book, along with M.F.J. Hawker and J.F. Keenlyside's *Horticultural Machinery* and John Robertson's *Mechanising Vegetable Production* (see below), are valuable both as background on how things work and as sources of ideas for home-fabricated solutions to the same tasks on a smaller scale. As a handy old Maine neighbor used to tell me, "Wal, if you can give me an idea what you want, I 'spect I can gump something up for ya." Good inspirational books for "gumpers."

Bleasdale, J.K.A. *Plant Physiology in Relation to Horticulture.* London: Macmillan, 1984. It is always nice to know what is going on behind the scenes. This book has all the "inside" information. A lot heavier going than the Bleasdale books below, but well worth the trouble for the hard facts and excellent bibliographic references.

Bleasdale, J.K.A., P.J. Salter, et al. *Know and Grow Vegetables, I and II.* London and New York: Oxford University Press, 1979 and 1982. Wonderful little books for the amateur as well as the budding professional. The authors, from the National Vegetable Research Station in England, obviously like their subject and delight in providing the reader with first-class information, both from their experience and their experiments.

Bunt, A.C., *Modern Potting Composts.* University Park: Pennsylvania State University Press, 1976. To an Englishman like Bunt, *potting composts* is the term for potting soils. This is my favorite of all the books I consulted on the subject. Everything you ever wanted to know.

Engeland, Ron L. *Growing Great Garlic.* Okanogan, WA: Filaree Productions, 1991. A highly enjoyable book about all aspects of garlic culture. Written in a down-home style by a grower for growers.

Facciola, Stephen. *Cornucopia: A Source Book of Edible Plants.* Vista, CA: Kampong Publications, 1990. This is an almost unbelievable resource. It sources every seed of every edible plant from every seed company as of the date of publication. Also features an awesome bibliography. Very well done.

Flegmann, A. W., and Raymond A. T. George. *Soils and Other Growth Media.* London and New York: Macmillan, 1979. The heaviest of the bunch, but still worth having as a reference work.

Flint, Mary Louise. *Pests of the Garden and Small Farm.* Davis: University of California, 1990. Excellent color pictures and scale drawings for identification. Practical problem-solving information.

Fordham, R., and A.G. Biggs. *Principles of Vegetable Crop Production.* London: William Collins Sons (distributed in U.S. by Sheridan House, Inc.), 1985. Very complete and not overly dry. Lots of little tidbits of useful information tucked here and there.

Grower Guides: No. 3, *Peppers and Aubergines;* **No. 7,** *Plastic Mulches for Vegetable Production;* **No. 10,** *Blocks for Transplants;* **No. 21,** *Lettuce under Glass;* **No. 26,** *Vegetables under Glass.* Parts of a continuing series published by Grower Books. Nexus Media Ltd., Nexus House, Swanley, Kent, England BR8 8HY. These are consistently informative booklets, usually under 100 pages, which do a thorough job of treating each individual subject. New titles appear frequently.

Hawker, M.F.J., and J.F. Keenlyside. *Horticultural Machinery.* New York: Longman, 1985. See my comments under R. Balls (above).

Lorenz, Oscar A., and Donald N. Maynard. *Knotts Handbook for Vegetable Growers.* New York: Wiley Interscience, 1988. An indispensable reference. All growers should have a copy. The book contains almost every fact that, sooner or later, you may need to know.

Mastalertz, John W. *The Greenhouse Environment.* New York: John Wiley & Sons, 1977. A complete factual presentation of all aspects of greenhouse growing.

Ministry of Agriculture, Fisheries and Food. *Plant Physiological Disorders,* Reference Book 223. London: Her Majesty's Stationary Office, 1985. Problems do occasionally arise, even for the best of growers. When they do, books like this — and J.B.D. Robinson's and Roorda van Eysinga and K.W. Smilde's (below), are nice "consultants" to have on hand. Clear color photos, detailed diagnoses, solid advice, and excellent references make these books a worthwhile investment.

Nelson, Paul V. *Greenhouse Operation and Management.* Reston, VA: Reston Publishing, 1978. A complete presentation of all aspects of greenhouse growing.

Parnes, Robert. *Fertile Soil.* Davis, CA: agAccess, 1990. A very informative book that is written for growers. Full of useful tables and appendices.

Robertson, John. *Mechanising Vegetable Production.* Ipswich, Suffolk, England: Farming Press, 1978. See my comments under R. Balls (above).

Robinson, D.W., and J.G.D. Lamb, eds. *Peat in Horticulture.* New York: Academic Press, 1975. Everything you ever wanted to know about peat, all its uses and horticultural qualities.

Robinson, J.B.D., ed. *Diagnosis of Mineral Disorders in Plants.* Volume I–Principles; Volume II–Vegetables; Volume III–Glasshouse Crops. London: Her Majesty's Stationary Office, 1983, 1983, and 1987.

Roorda van Eysinga, J.P.N.L., and K.W. Smilde. *Nutritional Disorders in Glasshouse Tomatoes, Cucumbers and Lettuce.* Wageningen, The Netherlands: Centre for Agricultural Publishing and Documentation, 1981.

Sarrantonio, Marianne. *Northeast Cover Crop Handbook.* Emmaus, PA: Rodale Institute, 1994. An excellent source of information and suggestions on how to assess the effects of cover crops.

Taylor's Guide to Vegetables & Herbs. Boston: Houghton Mifflin, 1987. The color photos are superb. If you don't know what a particular vegetable looks like (sorrel, arugula, orach, Malabar spinach, etc.), this book will show you.

Tite, R.L. *Growing Tomatoes: A Greenhouse Guide.* London: Her Majesty's Stationary Office, 1983. This is a British ADAS (extension) publication. A very well-done, small (32 pages) introductory booklet that will help any greenhouse tomato grower get off on the right foot.

Wittwer, S.H., and S. Honma, *Greenhouse Tomatoes, Lettuce and Cucumbers.* East Lansing: Michigan State University Press, 1979. A shade dated but still good basic information. This is the book I started with.

Classic Sources for the Organic Grower

Here is a listing of those "classic" sources that I believe most merit the attention of serious growers. Many of these are out of print, especially the classic English sources. Some of these titles have been recently reprinted. Most of the rest can be found in a good library.

As you might expect, the authors of these books do not always agree with each other. Some have written on the periphery of biological agriculture, while others were deeply involved and knowledgeable practitioners. It is important to read critically, check references, compare, and see what the other side has to say in order not to become, like so many proselytizers of a new idea, "a man of vast and varied misinformation."

Albrecht, William A. *Soil Fertility and Animal Health.* Webster City, IA: Fred Hahne, 1958. An outstanding survey of the subject by the most respected American exponent of intelligent farming. Albrecht begins with an old quote, "All flesh is grass," and proceeds to demonstrate the importance of the quality of that grass to animal health.

Aubert, Claude. *L'Agriculture Biologique.* Paris: LeCourrier du Livre, 1970. An able presentation of the case by a leading European expert. In French.

It would save much confusion if we all adopted the name "biological farming" rather than "organic farming." We should then keep the emphasis where it belongs, on the fostering of life and on biological balance, and not on just one of the techniques for achieving this, which, if narrowly interpreted, may be effective only in a certain set of circumstances.

—Lady Eve Balfour,
The Journal of the Soil Association,
January 1954

Baker, C. Alma. *The Labouring Earth.* London: Heath Cranton, 1940. A survey of agriculture from the biodynamic point of view.

Balfour, Lady Eve. *The Living Soil.* London: Faber, 1943. The important early work by a founder of the Soil Association. Lady Eve documents the evidence for biological agriculture. A fine book that should be in everyone's library. Reprinted 1975.

Billington, F. H. *Compost for Garden Plot or Thousand Acre Farm.* London: Faber, 1943. An early work giving thorough treatment to all aspects of composting. Five specific methods are described in detail. There is also a more recent edition revised and co-authored by Ben Easey.

Blake, Michael. *Concentrated Incomplete Fertilizers.* London: Crosby Lockwood, 1966. A discussion of the faults and consequent abuses of chemical fertilizers.

Bromfield, Louis. *Pleasant Valley.* New York: Harper, 1946. This is the first of Bromfield's farming books. In it, he relates how he returned to Ohio and became a farmer, and discusses the details of the early farm plans, soil conservation, and the Friends of the Land.

_____ . *Malabar Farm.* New York: Harper, 1947. Continues the story begun by *Pleasant Valley* and covers the year-round rhythm of activities at Malabar. Also focuses on Bromfield's other interests with such chapters as "Grass the Great Healer," "Malthus Was Right," and "The Organic-Chemical Fertilizer Feud."

_____ . *Out of the Earth.* New York: Harper, 1948. Stresses the need for knowledge of the many intricate, interrelated sciences involved in agriculture as a complement to the knowledge of the farm itself. Bromfield condemns the idea that "anybody can farm." Practical intelligence and dedication are necessary for success.

_____ . *From My Experience.* New York: Harper, 1955. The last of the farm books and the best of the lot. Outstanding accounts of a roadside market, farming in Brazil, building topsoils, living with the weather, and a chapter titled "A Hymn to Hawgs" make enjoyable and informative reading.

Bruce, Maye. *From Vegetable Waste to Fertile Soil.* London: Faber, 1940.

_____ . *Common-Sense Compost Making.* London: Faber, 1967. Both of Bruce's books describe composting with the aid of herbal extracts. The extracts supposedly activate the heap and produce a superior finished product. The standard work. Recently reprinted.

Burr, Fearing. *The Field and Garden Vegetables of America.* Chillicothe, IL: The American Botanist, Booksellers, 1994. A classic work, first published in 1863. Contains over 600 pages describing nearly 1,100 garden varieties grown more than 125 years ago; illustrated with woodcuts.

Cocannouer, Joseph A. *Weeds, Guardians of the Soil.* New York: Devin-Adair, 1952. Cocannouer is an enthusiastic advocate of the virtues of weeds.

_____ . *Farming with Nature.* Norman: University of Oklahoma Press, 1954. A general work with some good information. Reprinted under the title *Organic Gardening and Farming.*

Feeding quality is the most important matter of all. If a plant is healthy, and growing up to its own perfection, it must have great vitality, and it is the vitality, the living force of the plant, that heightens its food value. A vegetable can not give what it has not got; what it has, it gets from the soil. It cannot reach its "own perfection" in starved ground, still less in ground doped with chemicals.

—Maye Bruce
Common-Sense Compost Making

_____ . *Water and the Cycle of Life*. New York: Devin-Adair, 1958. A searing indictment of the mistaken farming practices that led to the Dust Bowl and their effect on the ecology of water.

Corley, Hugh. *Organic Farming*. London: Faber, 1957. "But the reason for farming well is that it is right." Corley fills this book with useful interpretations of what "farming well" is all about.

Donaldson, Frances, *Approach to Farming*. London: Faber, 1941. This book states that the "health" of the soil, of the livestock, and of the produce is the paramount consideration on any farm.

Easey, Ben, *Practical Organic Gardening*. London: Faber, 1955. An outstanding work, almost a textbook. Very thorough and well documented. Contains a lot of material found nowhere else.

Elliot, Robert H., *The Clifton Park System of Farming*. London: Faber, 1907. In his introduction, Sir George Stapledon calls this book an "agricultural classic." First published in 1898 under the title *Agricultural Changes*, it was later the work that inspired Sykes and Turner. Elliot writes of grass, pasture, and especially of his extensive seed mixture, "calculated to fill the land with vegetable matter."

Faulkner, Edward H. *Plowman's Folly*. Norman: University of Oklahoma Press, 1943. Louis Bromfield wrote that everyone including Hollywood actresses asked him about this book. It ultimately sold millions of copies. An effective condemnation of the moldboard plow.

_____ . *A Second Look*. Norman: University of Oklahoma Press, 1947. In this book Faulkner attempts to restate his case more clearly in view of the controversy stirred up by *Plowman's Folly*.

_____ . *Soil Restoration*. London: Michael Joseph, 1953. Faulkner applied his techniques to bring a worn-out farm back into production as a market garden. This is the story of that experiment.

Graham, Michael. *Soil and Sense*. London: Faber, 1941. An unpretentious but informative book about grasses, pastures, livestock, and their relationships to one another.

Hainsworth, P.H, *Agriculture: A New Approach*. London: Faber, 1954. A very reasonable and well-documented study of biological agriculture by a successful market grower. Contains a lot of new and stimulating material. One of my personal favorites.

Henderson, George. *The Farming Ladder*. London: Faber, 1944.

_____ . *Farmer's Progress*. London: Faber, 1950.

_____ . *The Farming Manual*. London: Faber, 1960. If you only read one author on farming, read Henderson. The first two books cover his entry into farming with his brother and their experience over the years. The third is a detailed guide to farm work. Henderson infuses all these books with his own love of farming and an invaluable sense of craftsmanship and pride in a job done well.

Henderson, Peter. *Gardening for Profit*. New York: Orange Judd Co., 1866. Peter Henderson was the market gardening authority of his time, and he sure knew his

As always in my experience, the destructive activity of insects came only when plants were in an abnormally weak condition. Formerly I believed that solely by virtue of the best possible soil conditions one could banish both insects and disease. I have learned better. Most diseases do seem to disappear completely as the soil improves, but insects are not so easily disposed of.
—Edward H. Faulkner,
Soil Restoration

It is the same with almost everything; we studied, compared, and observed before attempting it. Somewhere there is always someone who is doing a job a little better and there are many who are doing it a great deal worse; from either a lot can be learned.

—George Henderson
The Farming Ladder

stuff. Even after well over 100 years his advice still rings true in most particulars. Recently reprinted in a new edition by the American Botanist Booksellers of Chillicothe, IL.

Hills, Lawrence. *Russian Comfrey.* London: Faber, 1953. Comfrey is a perennial crop used for feed, mulching, and compost. This book details many useful ways of employing comfrey in the farm economy.

_____ . *Down to Earth Fruit and Vegetable Growing.* London: Faber, 1960. With typical thoroughness Lawrence Hills, founder of the Henry Doubleday Research Association, covers every aspect of the garden with straightforward, practical, and detailed instructions.

Hopkins, Cyril G. *Soil Fertility and Permanent Agriculture.* Boston: Ginn and Company, 1910. This is Hopkins' best-known work and his most thorough exposition of the concept of a "permanent agriculture."

Howard, Sir Albert. *An Agricultural Testament.* London: Oxford University Press, 1940. The most important, indeed the seminal work of biological agriculture, it inspired countless readers to try Howard's ideas. The book presents ways and means by which the fertility of the soil can be restored, maintained, and improved by natural methods.

_____ . *The Soil and Health.* New York: Devin-Adair, 1947. A continuation of the ideas of *An Agricultural Testament*, presented in a more popular form. "I have not hesitated to question the soundness of present-day agricultural teaching and research . . . due to failure to realize that the problems of the farm and garden are biological rather than chemical."

Howard, Louise. *The Earth's Green Carpet.* London: Faber, 1947. A popular recounting of the ideas of Sir Albert Howard through the eyes of his wife. Well done.

_____ . *Sir Albert Howard in India.* London: Faber, 1953. Traces the development of Howard's thought during his years as a researcher in India. A valuable record of his scientific work.

Hunter, Beatrice T. *Gardening without Poisons.* Boston: Houghton Mifflin, 1964. Undoubtedly the best-documented and most thoroughly researched work on the subject. Well-organized, with an excellent index and bibliography.

Jenks, Jorian. *The Stuff Man's Made Of.* London: Faber, 1959. The origin, the philosophy, and the scientific evidence behind biological agriculture. Jenks, for many years editor of the *Journal of the Soil Association*, has an encyclopedic grasp of the subject.

King, F.C. *The Compost Gardener.* Highgate: Titus Wilson, 1943. This small book lays down the general principles of cultivation for all the popular vegetables. Contains some unique information.

_____ . *Gardening with Compost.* London: Faber, 1944. Compost preparation and use, comments on chemical fertilizers, and sections on weeds and earthworms.

_____ . *The Weed Problem.* London: Faber, 1951. King is doubly unorthodox. He defends the control rather than elimination of weeds and he condemns turning over the soil.

By 1919 I had learnt how to grow healthy crops, practically free from diseases, without the slightest help from mycologists, entomologists, bacteriologists, agricultural chemists, statisticians, clearing-houses of information, artificial manures, spraying machines, insecticides, fungicides, germicides, and all the other expensive paraphernalia of the modern experiment station. This preliminary exploration of the ground suggested that the birthright of every crop is health.

—Sir Albert Howard, The Soil and Health

King, F.H. *Farmers of Forty Centuries.* London: Jonathan Cape, 1927. The granddaddy of them all, this classic was first published in 1911. King's trip through China, Korea, and Japan showed him how soil fertility had been preserved by returning all organic wastes to the land. Hundreds of photos and fascinating information. Recently reprinted.

Konnonova, M.M. *Soil Organic Matter.* New York: Pergamon, 1961. A technical work well worth reading for a better understanding of the processes involved in biological agriculture.

Lawrence, W.J.C. *Catch the Tide.* London: Grower Books, 1980. The horticultural adventures and investigations of W.J.C. Lawrence. Great reading.

Lawrence, W.J.C., and J. Newell. *Seed and Potting Composts.* London: Allen & Unwin, 1939. Explains much of the early work done to develop better potting mixes.

Maunsell, J.E.B. *Natural Gardening.* London: Faber, 1958. A book of unconventional gardening techniques. Maunsell is the most thorough of the no-diggers, and his use of the spading fork for "disturbing" the soil is worth noting.

Morris, Edmund. *Ten Acres Enough.* New York: The American News Co., 1864. Subtitled "How a Very Small Farm May Be Made to Keep a Very Large Family." Morris's advice is as sound today as it was then.

Northbourne, Lord. *Look to the Land.* London: Dent, 1940. One of the early inspirational works. "Mixed farming is economical farming, for only by its practice can the earth be made to yield a genuine increase." Northbourne was one of the first, if not the first, to call it "organic" farming.

O'Brien, Dalziel. *Intensive Gardening.* London: Faber, 1956. This book of original ideas describes a meticulously efficient market garden. From the layout, to the philosophy, to the composting and fertilizing procedures — even to a motion study of transplanting — everything is covered. Veganic compost (without animal manure) is used. Another favorite of mine.

Oyler, Philip. *The Generous Earth.* London: Hodder and Stoughton, 1950. Tells the story of the timeless farm life in the Dordogne Valley of France, "the land of all good things." It shows how the operation of sound farming practices will sustain fertility indefinitely.

———. *Sons of the Generous Earth.* London: Hodder and Stoughton, 1963. More on Oyler's experience in France. A valuable story from a man who values hard work, rural skills, wholesome food and drink, and a simpler way of life.

Pfeiffer, Ehrenfried. *Bio-Dynamic Farming and Gardening.* New York: Anthroposophic Press, 1938. Presents the case for nonchemical farming in general, and biodynamic farming in particular.

———. *The Earth's Face and Human Destiny.* Emmaus, PA: Rodale, 1947. A discussion of landscape characteristics and their value to the natural system.

Picton, Dr. Lionel. *Nutrition and the Soil.* New York: Devin-Adair, 1949. Mostly on nutrition, but partly about the soil. One of the earliest works on the subject and therefore of some historical interest.

We are not out to convince anyone of the truth of the discoveries we have made of the way the soil transforms itself in three years using our methods, for we are confident ourselves that time will do that for us. We put forward this method as an alternative to the orthodox gardening techniques, which to-day involve growers in heavy labour costs and outlay on stable and artificial manures, things which bite so deeply into the profits of intensive cultivation of vegetables and plants. When we describe how something should be done, we have done it that way and made a profit out of it.

—Dalziel O'Brien
Intensive Gardening

Rayner, M.C. *Problems in Tree Nutrition.* London: Faber, 1944. A report of the work done by Dr. Rayner at Wareham Heath. The use of composts in forestry to encourage the growth of seedlings in a sterile soil by stimulating the development of mycorrhizal associations.

Rodale, J.I. *Stone Mulching in the Garden.* Emmaus, PA: Rodale, 1949. An almost forgotten work and one of Rodale's best. Mulching with stones, an old and effective practice, is clearly explained in photos and text.

_____ . *Encyclopedia of Organic Gardening.* Emmaus, PA: Rodale, 1959.

_____ . *How to Grow Vegetables and Fruits by the Organic Method.* Emmaus, PA: Rodale, 1960. This and the encyclopedia above are large (1,000-page) books covering all phases of the art.

Rowe-Dutton, Patricia. *The Mulching of Vegetables.* Farnham Royal, Bucks., England: Commonwealth Agricultural Bureaux, 1957. A valuable compilation of all the research on mulching up to the date of publication.

Russell, E.J. *The World of the Soil.* London: Collins, 1957. A thorough study of the soil by a director of the Rothamsted Experimental Station in England. Reliable background information for anyone.

Seifert, Alwin. *Compost.* London: Faber, 1952. An outstanding book on the hows and whys of producing and using first-class compost.

Shewell-Cooper, W.E. *The Complete Fruit Grower.* London: Faber, 1960.

_____ . *The Complete Vegetable Grower.* London: Faber, 1968. Encyclopedic coverage of both subjects in a readable format.

Smith, Gerard. *Organic Surface Cultivation.* London: Faber, 1961. Another of the no-digging books. Deals with composts, garden planning, plus an assortment of hints and ideas.

Soil Association, The. *Journal of the Soil Association,* 1947–1972. Walnut Tree Manor, Haughley, Stowmarket, Suffolk IP14 3RS, England. A quarterly journal of invaluable reference information.

Stephenson, W.A. *Seaweed in Agriculture and Horticulture.* London: Faber, 1968. Documents the use of seaweed—especially in liquefied form—in farming, by examples of research from various parts of the world. Those interested in the subject will find some additional information in *Seaweed Utilization* by Lily Newton (London: Sampson-Low, 1951) and *Seaweeds and Their Uses* by V.J. Chapman (London: Methuen, 1970).

Sykes, Friend. *Humus and the Farmer.* London: Faber, 1946. The transformation of unpromising land into one of the showplace farms of England by methods described as humus farming. Covers renovating old pastures, making new ones, subsoiling, harvesting, and related topics.

_____ . *Food, Farming and the Future.* London: Faber, 1951. The further development of humus farming plus many peripheral subjects.

_____ . *Modern Humus Farming.* London: Faber, 1959. Discusses the danger to the soil caused by worship of "technical efficiency" and "getting more for less." Sykes puts forth his case that humus farming is as effective and productive as any other system.

I remember the time when the stable would yield,
Whatsoever was needed to fatten a field.
But chemistry now into tillage we lugs
And we drenches the earth with a parcel of drugs.
All we poisons, I hope, is the slugs.
—Punch, 1846, as quoted in *The Journal of the Soil Association,* April 1956

Turner, Newman. *Fertility Farming.* London: Faber, 1951. Turner was a practical farmer who learned conventional agriculture in college, but when he applied the teachings the results were disastrous. He then "unlearned" all his formal training and formulated his own system. Fascinating reading.

_____ . *Herdsmanship.* London: Faber, 1952. Dedicated "to the Jersey Cow, which combines beauty with efficiency." Comprehensive treatment of dairy cow selection and management from Turner's point of view. Excellent descriptions of all major dairy breeds plus sections on herbal veterinary practices.

_____ . *Fertility Pastures.* London: Faber, 1955. The value of the herbal ley (temporary pasture) is the central theme of this book. The detailed information on the character and properties of herbs and grasses for grazing is extremely interesting. Turner determined the composition of his pasture seed mixtures by "consulting the cow."

Voisin, Andre. *Grass Productivity.* London: Crosby Lockwood, 1958.

_____ . *Soil, Grass and Cancer.* London: Crosby Lockwood, 1959.

_____ . *Better Grassland Sward.* London: Crosby Lockwood, 1960. Voisin, a leading French authority of grassland management, was deeply concerned with the biological quality of produce. These works inspired the modern interest in rotational grazing.

Waksman, Selman A. *Soil Microbiology.* New York: John Wiley, 1952. An extremely valuable book. Waksman details the needs of soil microorganisms and their importance in the soil. His information is consistent with the best practices of biological agriculture.

Whyte, R.O. *Crop Production and Environment.* London: Faber, 1960. A book of plant ecology. It treats the effects on the plant of what Whyte considers to be the primary factors of aerial environment: temperature, light, and darkness.

Wickenden, Leonard. *Make Friends with Your Land.* New York: Devin-Adair, 1949. Wickenden was a professional chemist who became fascinated by organic growing. In this book he attempts to cut through some of the myths and to investigate the claims from a scientific perspective. An instructive book for the skeptical beginner.

_____ . *Gardening with Nature.* New York: Devin-Adair, 1954. An interesting book for beginner and experienced gardener alike. A practical and comprehensive treatment of all aspects of gardening.

Wrench, G.T. *Reconstruction by Way of the Soil.* London: Faber, 1946. A historical survey of soil mistreatment and its influence on civilization from earliest times. Wrench views farming as a creative art.

Wright, D. Macer. *Fruit Trees and the Soil.* London: Faber, 1960. Soil management in the orchard as the key to better-quality fruit.

The addition of large amounts of organic matter, especially fresh plant and animal residues, to the soil completely modifies the nature of its microbiological population. The same is true of changes in soil reaction which are brought about by liming or by the use of acid fertilizers, by the growth of specific crops, notably legumes, and by aeration of soil resulting from cultivation.

—Selman Waksman,
Soil Microbiology

INDEX